The Loan Officer's Practical Guide to Residential Finance

Copyright 2007

By Thomas A. Morgan

19th Printing

ISBN 0-9718205-0-3
"The Loan Officer's Practical Guide to Residential Finance"

Table of Contents

Introduction

To say this is not another real estate book would only make you think it was. But it isn't. It is the thinking loan officer's guide to understanding a business that is often arcane. It is for the Real Estate Agent who wants to know more. It is for the new Mortgage Processor, Consumer Lender, or Banker who wants to get up to speed quickly.

I started this project in 1991. I would get discouraged and depressed when I would go to a Library or even the bookstore to look at books on related subjects. There is a wealth of written material designed to help consumers understand, from their perspective, the practical applications of the real estate and mortgage finance trades. There are amortization tables, glossaries, and appendices that explain the forms, and a layman's guide to the process. What kept me going was that there is a lot of the same stuff and no hard information. You cannot read ***any other real estate book*** and learn how to "do loans." In part, this is because the business is a lot simpler than people want to think. In part, it is because you ***have to be careful about what you say - a simple "how to" tip could be construed as fraud.*** In part, it is because no one has invested the necessary amount of time to document what a loan officer does. This book teaches you that.

Loan officers are an oft-maligned group. They are charged with bringing in the business. They are the consumer's only advocates in the home loan process. They must possess that delicate balance of salesmanship and sledgehammer. They are also invariably viewed as a necessary evil - because they push the system. Loan officers are rarely accused of adhering to guidelines. There are a significant number of homeowners that would never be homeowners if their loan officer followed a set procedure.

The problem is that loan officer training is sink or swim. Handed a binder with program specifications, you are expected to be an expert immediately. Your livelihood depends on how quickly you can make an impact. This book is designed to bring the neophyte, "haven't touched a calculator since high school," non-real estate practitioner up to speed in a matter of weeks instead of months.

Introduction to the Business

A Mortgage - the paper itself - is a document recorded among permanent land records. It is the document that enforces the Note - a borrower's promise to pay - and allows a lender to take a property back from the owner if they do not keep that promise. This is why we call it the mortgage business. Sounds simple, but this is where the simplicity ends. This piece of paper forms the basis for a thriving and dynamic industry. But for all of the sophistication that has evolved over the last 50 years, the loan officer still is the primary individual performing the function of structuring residential home mortgage transactions. This book is for the new loan officer, real estate agent, homebuyer, and home seller - a practical guide to understanding the home financing transaction.

There is no substitute for practical experience. However, learning through practical experience is often a nice way of saying "learning it the hard way." The phrase "a little knowledge is very dangerous" is a description of what can happen when facts are applied without appropriate framework. Some of the descriptions herein may seem simplistic, particularly to the partially initiated. We have attempted to distill the introductory training of a loan officer in a way that gives an understanding of how, physically, things work. Knowing how and why things are done the way they are will help make sense and provide a context for all of the facts that the loan officer must commit to memory or have readily available.

The Evolution of the Mortgage Business

It is hard to imagine paying cash for a house. If it easy to imagine how difficult it would be to pay cash, you can understand why residential home lending has become so important. But it was not always so. As early as 1934, it was difficult to obtain a mortgage from a bank without at least a 50% down payment. More often, a seller might be the only source of financing for a home purchase. The terms were not customer friendly – interest-only loans with balloon features and prepayment penalties. In 1934 it was impossible to conceive of a 30-year fixed rate loan. Today, 60 years later, the 30-year fixed rate loan is the standard bearer of home financing.

Similarly, it is hard to conceive of a way to package information that takes the average person 6 months to learn. This book attempts to do that. The challenge is to determine where to start. For a seasoned professional learning about Mortgage Math - the first chapter in this book - would be ludicrous. On the other hand, it would have been impossible for the new real estate agent, loan officer or even homebuyer, to understand the conceptual framework of the Mortgage Business without a grasp of numbers and how we are expected to use them.

It is because of this challenge that we have organized this book in the way that we feel an individual would learn this information chronologically. You need to be able to explain to someone what the Principal and Interest Payment on a specific program is before you need to know how to take a complete application. The order of this book is designed to quickly provide you with a framework on a progressive basis.

The mortgage business is changing. Banks are squeezing out mid-sized institutions, computer underwriting is making it easier to get loans approved quickly, and many firms have controlled business arrangements where it is possible to get a loan through your employer without even going to a lender. Throughout this process there is always going to be the need for a person who can step in and take the time to structure a transaction for a borrower's best interests utilizing all of the options available in a widely diverse market. That is the loan officer's job - this is what I hope you will learn from this book.

Thanks

It has been a trying year. I am continually grateful for my family, our friends, and the people – some of whom we don't even know – who believe in us and keep us going.

Chapter 1
Mortgage Math

Introduction

When you were in high school math class and the teacher started to explain algebra, did you say, "I don't need to know this stuff. Why would I ever use algebra?" Mortgages are financial instruments. As a result, a grasp of the basic numerical calculations is required. Many people have an aptitude for numbers and may know some of this material. The first part of this chapter is designed to be remedial for the sufferer of "math phobia."

The second half of this chapter is devoted to use of the financial calculator. We will develop an easy method for qualifying borrowers, calculating mortgage formulas, and solving for any unknown. This will minimize the need for principal and interest factor tables, reduce computer reliance and allow the individual to perform calculations interactively.

Decimals and Fractions - Converting Decimals to Fractions

Interest rates and points are based on fractions. In the mortgage business, we talk in fractions, but write in decimals. Most numerical equations in mortgage lending are expressed verbally in fractions, but the written form is in decimals, which can be confusing for the uninitiated. For instance you might say that an interest rate of eight and one-half would carry two and one quarter points. Numerically, however, it looks like 8.5% with 2.25 points, which is exactly the same thing. Your high school math textbook would show you how to convert decimals to fractions like the following example:

To achieve the decimal equivalent of a fraction, you simply divide the numerator by the factor and the result is the decimal equivalent.

$$\frac{1}{1} = 1.0 \qquad \frac{1}{2} = 0.5 \qquad \frac{\text{Numerator}}{\text{Factor}}$$

Example: Dividing the Numerator by the Factor Results in the Decimal Equivalent

While fractions in the mortgage lending business, particularly in the secondary marketing aspect of the business, can go into the 32nds (1/32 = .03125), the smallest fraction commonly found is 1/8th. (1/8 = .125) As an aid to future conversions, following is the conversion table converting fractions to decimals:

Another way of thinking about fractions and decimals is by converting fractions to fractions that you understand. For instance, if you understand that 1/8 = .125, think about 1/2 as being 4/8ths - 4 times .125 is .500.

Converting Common Fractions to Decimals	
Fraction	**Decimal**
1/8	0.125
1/4	0.250
3/8	0.375
1/2	0.500
5/8	0.625
3/4	0.750
7/8	0.875

The Mortgage Business

The mortgage business today is the product of 70 years of evolution in process, technology and products. Despite this evolution, the roles personnel play in the process remain relatively unchanged. The loan originator, loan officer, or other advisor still is the primary interface between the customer and the company. This is true even though there are many business models that alter the way in which the customer deals with the loan officer. The functions of the loan process – processing, underwriting, and closing – have all been affected by automation, but still exist to support the completion of the loan process.

Types of Lenders/Primary Originators

The way different types of mortgage businesses operate is a function of the funding mechanism – where the money to make the loan comes from and whether the loan is subsequently sold. There are different types of lending entities. These are referred to as primary originators; small and mid-size traditional mortgage bankers and finance companies who fund loans by borrowing money on a credit line and resell the loans to investors; large, national mortgage bankers, who are generally bank owned or conglomerate subsidiaries, perform mortgage banking functions but fund loans from their own cash; mortgage brokers, who are almost exclusively small, privately owned companies, sell loans prior to closing (they are "table funded" or closed by the wholesaler) to wholesale mortgage bankers or lenders (referred to as investors) on a pre-approved basis - brokers do not lend money; smaller local banks or savings banks (known as "thrifts"); and Credit Unions, originating loans from their existing customers as their only line of mortgage business.

Entity	Description	Features
Mortgage Bankers – including banks, savings banks, credit unions	Traditional mortgage banking firms use funds borrowed on "warehouse" lines of credit to make loans. These loans are sold to investors as 1.) "whole loans" – which means that the individual loan is sold, along with the right to collect and remit payments (referred to as "servicing") or 2.) "mortgage backed securities" where a number of similar loans are "pooled" together. The securities are sold, but the mortgage banker keeps the right to collect the monthly payments ("servicing retained").	Strengths – able to control funding process and some approval issues. Can also broker loans if needed for competitive purposes. Weaknesses – on retained loans pricing is less optimal at origination.

Entity	Description	Features
Correspondent lenders	Close loans using own funds or lines of credit with the intent of selling the entire loan, including servicing rights, to a 3rd party lender, normally referred to as an investor.	Strengths – able to control funding process and deliver customer service. Able to achieve best pricing by sale of servicing
Mortgage Brokers	Mortgage brokers do not make loans. They work with other lenders – wholesale mortgage bankers and banks (sometimes referred to as "investors") – who offer their products at "wholesale pricing". The mortgage broker fulfills the origination and processing functions and submits individual loan requests to the wholesaler. The wholesaler, who is often a mortgage banker or bank, approves and closes the loan.	Strengths – able to be price competitive with small margins, able to place many different types of loans giving borrower more choices and better chance of approval. Disadvantage – no control over approval and funding.

Retail Lending

In retail lending, the lender approves, closes and funds the loan, in addition to the functions that a mortgage broker conducts – taking the application, collecting borrower documentation, preparing the file for underwriting (referred to as processing). The advantage for a borrower in working with a direct retail lender is that the lender controls the entire process, so issues with service delivery, problems with contingencies, and pricing can be dealt with directly. One potential disadvantage of working with a direct retail lender is that some lenders only offer the loan products offered by the Mortgage Company, bank, credit union, or thrift with whom the loan officer is employed. However, many direct lenders do make selected specialty products available to meet their customer's needs on a brokered basis.

Servicing (collecting payments from borrowers and forwarding the interest to the investor) can be retained on many loans. This is a long term income source fundamental to the business plan of mortgage bankers.

Reading the Rate Sheet

Decimals and fractions are part of everyday life in the mortgage business. The most pivotal numbers are expressed in this way - rates. Rates are most frequently communicated via a rate sheet or rate bulletin. This is the way mortgage pricing is discussed on an everyday basis.

Points

One point is one percent (1%) of the loan amount. Points are referred to as discount points, origination fees and broker fees. While points may be called any number of names, the essence of the point concept is any fee that offsets the costs of the loan.

Example 1 - "Par" Price

Interest Rate	8.5%	
Discount Cost (Price)	0.00	(100.00%)
Plus origination Fee	+1.00%	
Quote to Customer	0.00 + 1.00	

Example 2 - Above Par (Rebate) Price

Interest Rate	8.75%	
Discount Cost (Price)	-1.00	(101.00%)
Plus origination Fee	+1%	
Quote to Customer	0.00 + 0.00	

Example 3 - Below Par (Discount) Price

Interest Rate	8.00%	
Discount Cost (Price)	2.00	(98.00%)
Plus origination Fee	+1%	
Quote to Customer	2.00 + 1.00	

Charging points enables the lender to offer a lower interest rate on a mortgage. Points are disclosed to the general public first as origination fees and as discount points, then as broker fees. However, points are points. As a lender, the number of points quoted to the customer is the price, plus any markup required to cover the cost of originating the loan. In these examples we use a one point origination fee as the charge the lender is adding to the loan cost as the fee for taking the loan application or originating the loan.

This is a somewhat oversimplified example of pricing but is given as an illustration of the concept of the origination fee. Generally, you are given a range of pricing available at various discount fee charges. The concept of a discount fee is exactly what it sounds like - you pay a fee up front to discount the rate over time. It doesn't make any difference to the lender which price the customer selects. It is important to understand how these numbers are communicated to you. There are two manners in which rates and pricing are communicated: the **"Fee/Rebate"** format and the **"Purchase Price"** format.

The Mortgage Broker Business

Mortgage brokers are individuals or companies that do not underwrite, approve or fund loans. Mortgage brokers contract with wholesale lenders who approve, fund and prepare closing documentation. Mortgage brokers usually work with at least several, but often hundreds of different wholesalers. This business model allows the loan officer of a mortgage broker to seek out the best rates and terms – and can pass the most competitive rate on to the borrower. In addition, the mortgage broker has the ability to seek through the hundreds of products available to find specialty products that help borrowers with unusual circumstances or special needs. A borrower working with a broker may find a competitive advantage if the broker passes these benefits through to the consumer. The broker will select a lender and then work with the borrower to obtain all the necessary documentation to consummate the loan – referred to as processing.

Since the broker doesn't actually approve loans, prepare closing documentation, or provide funding, a potential disadvantage facing a borrower is that the wholesaler's service may not be as responsive as a direct lender's. Since the broker is the intermediary between the wholesale lender and the public, the public may never learn the identity of the final lender until closing. Since the wholesaler is insulated from the public in this way, the borrower has no recourse for service with that wholesaler. In addition, until the loan is funded, the wholesaler may continue to add loan contingencies creating delays.

Broker Pricing Model Based on 1.5 Point Margin

Rate	Wholesale Cost	Broker's Margin	Net Price	Borrower Cost
6.750	102.00	1.50	100.500	-0.500
6.625	101.50	1.50	100.000	0.000
6.500	101.00	1.50	99.500	0.500
6.375	100.50	1.50	99.000	1.000
6.250	100.00	1.50	98.500	1.500
6.125	99.50	1.50	98.000	2.000
6.000	99.00	1.50	97.500	2.500

Brokers earn money by adding fees to the wholesale cost of loans. The net cost to a borrower would be competitive with the price of a retail lender, depending on the margin that the broker is trying to achieve.

What is a Basis Point?

A basis point is 1/100th of a point. Normally this description is used when discussing yields or rates in the secondary market, because this is the smallest possible fraction. However, the term is often applied colloquially. It sounds so much more professional to say, for example, "275 basis points" or "275 "bips"" instead of "two and three-quarters" - even though it means the same thing.

The "Fee/Rebate" Format

This format identifies the cost, in points, required for certain rates. This is the way most retail rate sheets are distributed to real estate agents. An example:

In this example, the lender is simply showing that they will charge 2 percent of the loan amount (or 2 points) for a mortgage with a rate of 7.75%. At the same time they will pay (or rebate) 2 percent of the loan amount (or 2 points) for a mortgage with a rate of 8.75%.

Interest Rate	Fee/Rebate
7.50%	3.00
7.75%	2.00
8.00%	1.00
8.25%	0.00
8.50%	-1.00
8.75%	-2.00

Common Wholesale Pricing Formats

Interest Rate	Pricing Shown in Fee/Rebate Format	Pricing in Purchase Price Format	"Mix and Match" Pricing
8.500%	-2.000	102.000	-2.000
8.375%	-1.500	101.500	-1.500
8.250%	-1.000	101.000	-1.000
8.125%	-0.500	100.500	-0.500
8.000%	0.000	100.000	100.000
7.875%	0.500	99.500	99.500
7.750%	1.000	99.000	99.000

The "Purchase Price" format

This format is more likely to be found among inter- or intra-lender communications, like a corporate mortgage bank communicating to its branch or a wholesaler. The idea is that the lender will purchase a loan at a certain percentage of its face value, thereby determining the price.

Interest Rate	Price
7.50%	97.00
7.75%	98.00
8.00%	99.00
8.25%	100.00
8.50%	101.00
8.75%	102.00

Again the concept is that the lender will purchase a loan at a certain percentage of its face amount. The difference between the face amount and the price determines how many discount points must be charged. For example a $100,000 loan at

```
  100,000
x      98%
   98,000  = Amount Funded/Purchase Price
 -100,000 = Actual Loan Amount
    2,000 = Discount Cost, or 2%
```

7.75% in the above example would be sold at 98% of its face value.

You will notice that the pricing is exactly the same under both formats, but communicated differently.

The Origination Fee/Discount Points

"What do I have to charge?" is the loan officer's question. Above, pricing is shown, as it is most likely to be distributed. Pricing with -0- discount is referred to as "par." Pricing "below par" connotes that the rate must be discounted, while "above par" means that the lender/investor will pay a premium/or rebate money to the originator. If, as a loan officer, your company requires that you charge the borrower one-point origination fee, what must you tell the customer the price is? At par (0 discount) the quote would be 0 (discount) plus 1-point origination fee. In the above example that would mean the rate would be 8.25% 0 plus 1, to the customer. If the rate were 7.75 and required 2 discount points, the loan officer would quote 7.75%, 2 discount plus 1 origination. In an "above par" situation the cost of the origination fee would be received from the lender/investor. So if the rate were 8.5% with a price of -1.00 or 101.00, the quote to the customer would be 8.5%, 0 discount and 0 origination.

Understanding Lock Terms

While the actual price format may change between the "Fee/Rebate" format and the "Purchase Price" format, the basic cost of the loan remains the same. What does change the pricing of the loan is the length of time that the loan is "locked-in." Lenders provide a guaranteed rate for a certain period of time which is known as a "lock-in." Borrowers have the option of guaranteeing their interest rate by reserving an interest rate, or "locking-in," or they may defer the decision to reserve an interest rate, which is referred to as "floating" or "floating at market."

Because interest rates change from moment to moment (most lenders price on a daily basis with intra-day price changes dues to substantial fluctuations in the market), the longer that an interest rate is guaranteed, the more risk of unfavorable rate change a lender is exposed to. As a result, locking in for 15 days costs less than locking in for 60 days. When the borrower's lock in expires, standard

Expired Lock-in Rule
Market Rate
OR
Original Lock-in
Whichever is <u>HIGHER</u>

industry practice is to give the borrower the market interest rate or the original lock-in rate, WHICHEVER IS HIGHER. This is an extremely important concept for loan officers and borrowers to understand. The loan officer must choose a lock period that meets the borrower's need for closing time frame. A lock-in that is valid for 30 days does not help a borrower who is closing in 60 days.

Regulators and state licensing authorities report that the largest percentage of complaints about mortgage lenders derive from the issue of rate disputes between borrowers and lenders. These complaints happen most frequently when interest rates rise and borrowers are unable to meet their expected closing date. The lock-in the borrower originally received is no longer valid, and he or she believes that the lender should honor the original lock-in. Technically, the lender is under no obligation to honor the original lock-in if the expiration occurred due to situations beyond the lender's control. However, most regulators also believe that the lender has a professional responsibility to anticipate delays based on a borrower's circumstances. If it is obvious that the lender delayed the closing in order to avoid funding a loan when market conditions deteriorate, the state regulator often will force the lender to honor the original lock-in terms. When this is the case, the loan officer can easily see how important it is to provide the borrower with a lock period that is appropriate for their needs.

Reading the Pricing Sheet

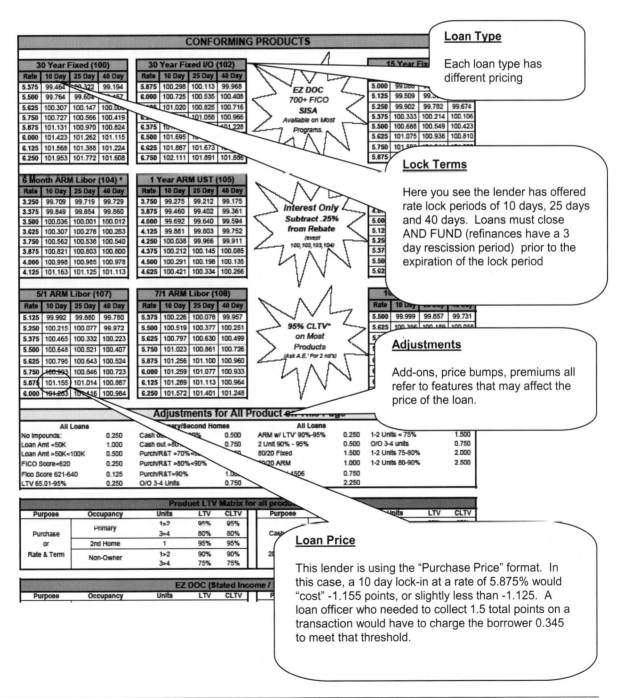

Principal And Interest or Interest Only - Amortization

When someone talks about a loan term being 30 years or 15 years, and how that affects the monthly principal and interest payment, they are referring to the fact that the loan payments are designed to leave the loan balance at -0- at the last scheduled payment. When a scheduled payment is devoted partially to principal on a fixed term loan, the intent is to steadily reduce the balance to zero. This process is referred to as amortization. It works on the concept that on a mortgage, interest accrues on the balance outstanding. At the end of a period, the interest is due. An additional amount is applied to the balance. As a result of the payment to the loan balance each subsequent payment is devoted less to interest because the remaining amount is slightly smaller. The process accelerates through the life of the loan so that the last payment consists almost entirely of principal.

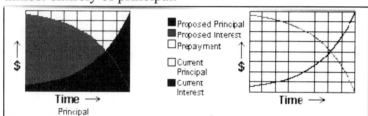

Simple Interest Calculation	
Loan Amount	$150,000.00
Multiply by Rate	7%
Equals Annual Interest	$10,500.00
Divide by 12	12
Equals Monthly Interest	$875.00

Solving for X - Mortgage Math and the Financial Calculator

Learning to use a financial calculator will save you hours of time and will increase the accuracy of your calculations. As an additional benefit each component of an equation can be substituted with another component to modify the result. Because subsequent entries change the result you can "fine-tune" results to solve for subsequent unknowns. But the first step is always learning how to compute Principal and Interest Payments (P&I).

Keystrokes to Compute Payment

1.) Enter Present Value (Loan Amount)
2.) Enter Interest Rate (per period)
3.) Enter Loan Term (number of years)
4.) Compute Payment (principal & interest)

Once you have learned to use the financial calculator to calculate monthly payments for principal and interest, you know the keystrokes required to manually calculate an amortization schedule, solve for a maximum loan amount, interest rate, or payment - you can even determine APR. The benefit of a calculator is that it allows you to make adjustments to formulas with information you have already entered, without having to start from scratch. Particularly in qualifying, this process is known as solving for the unknown - an algebraic equation called solving for "x."

Algebra uses the process of isolating unknown quantities within an equation by substituting known numbers. This is also known as "solving for x", an algebraic process by which the known quantities are moved to the left of the equals sign to solve for the unknown "x."

For instance
1.) $(2 * x) + 4 = 8$
2.) $(2 * x) = 8 - 4$
3.) $(2 * x) = 4$
4.) $4/(2) = x$
5.) $2 = x$

To solve for x, you need to make a complete formula, or move x to the other side of the equal sign. This is exactly the process utilized for qualification calculations: taking the information that is known and trying to find acceptable solutions. The financial calculator allows you to plug in what you don't know and insert what you do know - in effect, solve for x. As pointed out above, there are four components of the qualification equation, each one can be used to solve for any variable.

The samples in the following pages describe the financial calculations most commonly needed to compute basic mortgage equations. Think of each of the entry keys on the financial calculator as one of the variables of the pre-qualification equation. In any scenario where you are trying to achieve an answer, some of the variables are known. In some cases, you will need a range of results and can generate those results by modifying one element of the equation.

Components and Keystrokes of the Qualification Formula
Payment = (PMT)
Loan Amount = (PV)
# of Payments = (N)
Interest Rate = (i%)

Choosing a Financial Calculator

The BA35 is the most affordable, reliable and versatile calculator you can choose. It is sufficiently complex so that the average borrower or real estate agent will be impressed by your knowledge.

It suffers the stigma among lenders of not having much prestige by virtue of its clamshell sort of appeal.
We recommend it because:
- It is inexpensive to replace if lost or stolen ($19).
- It allows the easy functionality of changing data in a string of calculations without having to conduct a string of store and recall commands.
- It is solar and never runs out of batteries
- The keypad replicates a personal calculator which makes it easy to use as an adding machine too.

N=Number of payments
%I = interest rate (must be divided by 12)
PV = Loan Amount
PMT = Payment
FV = future value - almost always "0"
Keystrokes are entered in any order

HP combats its legacy of calculator tools that are difficult to use and expensive with the 10 B ($35)

In addition to being able to compute all standard financial calculations, it has features that allow the loan officer to scroll forward in the amortization schedule, and change settings. In addition, the keystrokes for simple mathematical equations are more similar to traditional calculators, making it a better basic calculator.

N=Number of payments
%I = interest rate (must be divided by 12)
PV = Loan Amount
PMT = Payment
FV = future value - almost always "0"
Keystrokes are entered in any order

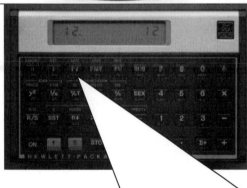

The HP12C was one of the first "modern" calculators and continues to be popular even though the technology is nearly 40 years old. It sells well even as a premium priced product ($85) because it has unique looks, is heavier and has become accepted as a symbol of success the way a Mont Blanc pen has.

The calculator is based on RPN entry – Reverse Polish Numeration – which means that you key the value that you wish to utilize, then enter it into the system

N= number of payments - use the g key to convert years to months
i= interest rate - use the g key to convert annual rate to monthly rate
PV=loan amount
PMT=payment

The Pocket Real Estate Master ($30) by Calculated Industries is a mortgage or real estate specific calculator that performs all the basic functions required of a financial calculator. In addition, the calculator has the added simplicity of its interface, which is designed to reflect the terminology used in the business. For example "Loan Amount", instead of "PV" for Present Value, which represents the loan amount in the calculation.

Calculated Industries offers many other calculators, performing many of the same functions, with more elaborate keys. These can range upwards of $129, but this model is more than sufficient for the loan officer.

On a financial calculator each of the components of the qualification formula relates to one of the input numbers. The loan amount, the number of payments, the interest rate and payment are the components that are moved around to generate each answer. As you learn how to make these keystrokes, practice with the numbers seeing how the changes impact the outcome. There are only a few calculations you use daily. With experience and practice you will manipulate the results to provide customers with the information they need to make an informed decision.

Palm/PDA Shareware Financial Calculators

With the migration to mobile computing, many PALM/PDA handheld computers offer an opportunity to combine the need for a financial calculator with a planner and telephone. Before purchasing a separate handheld financial calculator, investigate whether one can be combined into your PDA.

"What is the Payment?"

A customer wants to know what the monthly payment for a $100,000 mortgage is. Enter the known information and solve for the unknown payment. This is one way of avoiding giving mortgage interest rate quotes by giving an array of payments for different rates. Or try a different loan term to determine the monthly payment. See what the difference is with a slightly larger mortgage or a smaller mortgage.

How to Calculate the Monthly Payment (Principal and Interest)		
Enter Loan Amount	100,000.00	(PV)
Enter Interest Rate	8.75	(i%)
Enter the Number of Payments	360	(N)
Press Compute	(CPT)	(PMT)
Record Result	-786.70	

Do NOT Clear the Calculator Memory

Rather than clearing the numbers from the calculator now, try manipulating the calculations. Change the interest rate, the term of the loan and loan amount to fine-tune computations. The key is to leave the data you have computed stored in the calculator to re-use. REMEMBER THAT YOUR CALCULATOR MAY GIVE A NEGATIVE NUMBER AS A PAYMENT RESULT. This is because a mortgage is a "reverse annuity". IF YOUR CALCULATOR DOES THIS, YOU MUST ALWAYS ENTER THE PAYMENT AS A NEGATIVE NUMBER BY USING THE CHANGE SIGN (CHS, +/-) KEY.

What is the Balance Over Time?

Amortization is the process by which monthly payments are applied first to interest then to principal to pay off the loan in a specific period of time. To determine the balance of the loan at any given time, repeat the payment calculation, and then enter the months

Enter Loan Amount	$ 100,000.00	(PV)
Enter Interest Rate	8.75	(i%)
Enter the Number of Payments	360	(N)
Press Compute	(CPT)	(PMT)
Record Result	$786.70	
Enter remaining # of Payments	300	(N)
Press Compute	(CPT)	(PV)
Record Result	$ 95,688.92	

remaining on the loan at the time that you wish to calculate. (In this example we are using 5 years or 360 months - 60 months = 300 months.) Then, compute the loan amount. With a variable rate or changing payment mortgages the term of the loan does not change, so the amortization/balance calculation stays the same. This is a way the Loan Officer can show the borrower the financial planning aspect of a mortgage. This is also a critical calculation to show the effect of prepayment.

What is the Maximum Loan Amount I Qualify For?

Using the Pre-Qualification worksheet, calculate the total monthly income, monthly debts and determine the maximum P&I payment for a sample borrower. In this example, our borrower has an annual income of $48,000/year or $4,000 per month. Assume that he has no other debts.

Monthly Income	$4,000.00	
Multiply by Ratio	28%	
Equals Maximum PITI	$1,120.00	
Subtract Tax & Insurance	$ 170.00	
Enter Result (P&I) as Payment	$ 950.00	(PMT)
Enter a term	360	(N)
Enter a rate	8.75	(i%)
Compute Loan Amount	(CPT)	(PV)
Record Result	$120,758	

In this case we can record a series of results by changing one factor - the interest rate. Take this one step further and divide the loan amount by the approximate down payment percentage and see what the maximum sales price is. For instance, if the borrower is looking for a 5% down payment loan, you would divide the result (120,758) by the LTV required (95%) to achieve the maximum sales price.

"I Know How Much I Need to Borrow. What is the Maximum Rate?"

Using the above borrower whose maximum payment is $950, imagine he needs to borrow more than what we have shown he can afford above. He wants to know what rate would qualify him for the loan he needs. In this case a rate of 6.5% would qualify the borrower for the loan requested.

Maximum Payment	-$950.00	(PMT)
Loan Needed	$ 150,000.00	(PV)
Loan Term	360	(N)
Compute Maximum Rate	(CPT)	(i%)
Record Result	6.52%	

This formula is used to determine whether a reduced payment program will help the borrower afford the loan being requested. It also helps to determine which type of payment or interest rate reduction product is suited to the customer's needs.

How Much Income is Required for a Certain House?

Someone who does not want to volunteer financial information may want to know how much income is required to finance a specific property. Once again, fill in the information that you know to learn the information that you don't

Sales Price (200,000) x 90%	$ 200,000.00	
x LTV Ratio and Enter as Loan Amount	$ 180,000.00	(PV)
Enter Interest Rate	8.75%	(i%)
Enter Loan Term	360	(N)
Compute Payment	(CPT)	(PMT)
Result	$ 1,416.06	
Add Tax and Insurance	$ 250.00	
Total	$ 1,666.06	
Divide by Qualifying Ratio	28%	
Monthly Income Required	$ 5,950.22	

know. In this case assume a Property Sales price of $200,000 with a 10% Down Payment.

By using the financial calculator you can confirm the borrower's income based on what they are trying to achieve. This is also the same basic calculation the loan officer would perform to pre-qualify a house - advise the buying public of the financing options and income requirements for a specific property. This is also known as an open house financing option spreadsheet.

What is the Maximum Loan Term with a Specific Payment?

We have put each of the variables of the pre-qualification computation at the end of the equation to compute the result. One of the most frequent customer requests is how many months will my loan be if I make a specific prepayment. In this example a customer has a payment of $665.30, but he wants to make a $900

Loan Amount	$ 100,000.00	(PV)
Rate	7%	(I/Y)
Loan Term	360	(N)
Compute	CPT	(PMT)
Payment	-$665.30	
Enter Payment w/ Prepayment	-$900.00	(PMT)
Compute Number of Months	(CPT)	(N)
Record Result	179.59	

payment – how does this affect his loan term? We see that the loan term goes from 360 months (30 years) to 179.59 months (less than 15 years).

Throughout this book there will be other opportunities for you to expand the number of calculations you can use to manually calculate various results. For instance, in Chapter 2 - Loan Types, you learn about prepayment and the value of points; in Chapter 8 - Property Types, there is an Investment Property pre-qualification model. In Chapter 9 - Refinancing, many of these computations are made again under various scenarios. Obviously in Income Qualification there are many opportunities to use these calculations. While you may rely on computers for more detailed computations, it is important to be quick with the hand-held calculator. It will allow you to quickly gauge the viability of a potential borrower.

Understanding Ratios – Loan to Value - LTV

A Ratio is simply one number as compared to another. Ratios are an objective way to express guidelines. For instance, if you were buying a home and you were putting 5% down, the Loan to Value ratio would be 0.95:1.00 (a fraction again - 95/100 converted to decimals is 0.95 or 95%) This is the Loan to Value Ratio (referred

$$\frac{\text{Loan Amount}}{\text{Sales Price}} = \text{Loan to Value Ratio}$$

to by the acronym LTV). If there is more than one mortgage, then the 1st and 2nd Mortgage together divided by the sales price would result in the Combined Loan to Value (CLTV).

Understanding Ratios – Qualifying Ratios

The other important ratio guidelines are the **Housing Expense Ratio**, also known as the "Front" or "Top" ratio, and the **Total Debt Ratio**, also known as the "Back," "Bottom" or "DTI" (debt to income) Ratio. The Front Ratio measures the percentage of a borrower's monthly income that can be devoted to housing expense (Principal & Interest, Taxes, Insurance and HOA Fees, also known as PITI). The Back Ratio measures the total obligations; the housing expense (front ratio) PLUS all liabilities such as car payments, credit cards, student loans and any other recurring required payment.

Different investors have different guidelines - For example, if the housing expense ratio is 28% and a borrower makes $1,000 per month, the most the borrower can afford to pay for housing is $280 per month ($1,000 x 28% = $280).   The chart shows how the amount the borrower qualifies for increases simply by increasing the qualifying ratio.

Illustrating Change in Qualification using Different Programs

Interest Rate 7%
Borrower Income $ 5,000
Real Estate Taxes/Ins/HOA $ 200

Program	FNMA/ FHLMC	FHA	VA	Jumbo	ALT A - Choice
Housing Expense or "Front" or Top Ratio	28%	31%	41%	33%	45%
Total Debt, Back or "DTI"	36%	43%	41%	38%	50%
Maximum Housing Expense	$1,400	$1,550	$2,050	$1,650	$2,250
Total Debt (Including Housing)	$1,800	$2,150	$2,050	$1,900	$2,500
Maximum Loan Amount	$180,369	$202,915	$278,069	$217,946	$308,131
Maximum Debts	$400	$600	$0	$250	$250

The Effect of Computer Automation on Qualifying Practices

With the popularity of computer based underwriting models, many companies and loan officers have de-emphasized the importance of pre-qualifying a borrower in the analysis process. The loan officer simply applies the borrower's information against the model and reports the result back. This is an unfortunate development for both the loan officer and the borrower.

The qualifying process is a sales system for the loan officer. Without qualification, the borrower must actually apply for a mortgage to receive any information – and many borrowers are not ready to supply a social security number initially. The loan officer's only other opportunity to build rapport is through personal conversations or by committing interest rates or programs that the borrower may not be eligible for.

The qualifying process is educational for the borrower. Having an understanding of the basic limits of what he or she can afford – from the perspective of the percentage of income most people devote to a housing expense – can temper how much that borrower tries to borrow. Today programs can be structured which allow almost any borrower to obtain a mortgage approval. This does not mean that the borrower SHOULD obtain that financing or that it is appropriate for their circumstance. The loan officer's detailed analysis will allow the borrower to choose the option that best suits them.   Completing the pre-qualification or qualification process is a natural lead in to the further discussion that helps the loan officer solidify the relationship with the borrower – which product?

"Pre" and "Re" Qualifying - Doing the Math

There is no substitute for practice in learning how to qualify a borrower. In fact, qualification *calculations* themselves are simple. It is not until you learn more about the business that you realize that the information being used to determine qualification is far more important than just determining the ratios.

QUALIFICATION WORKSHEET

1. PROPOSED MONTHLY PAYMENTS		2. TOTAL MONTHLY OBLIGATIONS	
First Mortgage P & I	$	Housing Payment (#1)	$
Second Mortgage P & I	$	Other Mortgages (Rent Income-	
Mo. Hazard Insurance	$	Payments = Negative)	$
Mo. Real Estate Taxes	$	Auto Loans	$
Condo/Association Fees	$	Other Installment Loans	$
Mortgage Insurance(PMI)	$	Charge Card (5% of Balance)	$
TOTAL HOUSING PAYMENT	$	Other Monthly Payments	$
		TOTAL MONTHLY OBLIGATIONS	$

3. FRONT RATIO CALCULATION		4. BACK RATIO CALCULATION	
(#1) Total Housing Payment divided by(#5) Total Income	%	(#2) Total monthly obligation divided by (#5) total income	%

5. MONTHLY INCOME			6. DOWN PAYMENT	
	Borrower	Co-Borrower	Down Payment	$
Base Income	$	$	Closing Costs	$
Other Income	$	$	Less Seller Contribution	$
Total Income	$	$	Total Cash Required	$

TO DETERMINE MAXIMUM LOAN AMOUNT: Working backwards from income to determine maximum loan amount requires examining whether the front or back ratio is the limiting qualifying factor. To determine this

1.) Multiply Total Monthly Income (#5) by 28%. Enter Result as Total Housing Payment. Deduct real estate taxes and hazard insurance (#1)
2.) Multiply Gross Monthly Income (#5) by 36%. Enter Result as Total Monthly Obligations (#2). Deduct all debts. Enter Result as Total Housing Payment.
3.) The smaller of these two numbers is the maximum PITI. Subtract all components (real estate taxes, insurance, etc.) from the smaller number. Result is Maximum P&I. Divide this number by the factor from the table (appendix page iii) and multiply by $1,000 to arrive at maximum loan amount.

Example 1:				Example 2:			
Step 1:	Monthly Income	$	4,000.00	Step 1:	Monthly Income	$	4,000.00
	Housing Ratio		28%		Housing Ratio		28%
	Maximum PITI	$	1,120.00		Maximum PITI	$	1,120.00
Step 2:	Monthly Income	$	4,000.00	Step 2:	Monthly Income	$	4,000.00
	Max. Total Debt		36%		Max. Total Debt		36%
		$	1,440.00			$	1,440.00
	Less Debts	$	(100.00)		Less Debts	$	(400.00)
	Maximum PITI	$	1,340.00		Maximum PITI	$	1,040.00
Step 3:	Smaller of 1 & 2	$	1,120.00	Step 3:	Smaller of 1 & 2	$	1,040.00
	This is Maximum PITI				**This is Maximum PITI**		

These examples show that borrower #1's qualifying is limited by housing expense. Borrower #2's qualifying is limited by the amount of total debt. The borrower qualifies using the **lower** of the two results.

The "Qualifying Worksheet" walks you through determining the ratios for a specific transaction. In other words, what are the ratios? When pre-qualifying, instead of starting with a sales price and determining ratios, you work backwards from income, using pre-determined ratios. When "Pre-Qualifying," you are determining how much a borrower can afford ***before*** they buy. This is one of the most valuable services we as lenders provide. Often we must re-check this information or "Re-Qualify" the borrower. Borrowers may resist being re-qualified, but this questioning process may uncover real needs or deficiencies. It is useful and critical to keep a written record of each qualification the loan officer performs. At a minimum, the qualification should address the income, debts and asset qualification of the borrower and assure that the computations are within guidelines.

Qualifying and Pre-Qualification – Two Different Things

The pre-qualification is an important step in the home buying process. This is when the borrower gets an idea of how much they can afford BEFORE they start shopping for, or contract to buy, a property. It also allows the loan officer to avoid focusing on interest rates and on what the borrower is trying to achieve from a needs analysis perspective. When a borrower has already got the property they are trying to finance, then the loan officer must qualify them for a loan for that property - hence the "pre" means qualifying before the borrower has a property.

Reverse the Ratio to Achieve the Result

When you have a ratio in an equation, you are normally expected to multiply it against a number to achieve the measure. You can reverse this by dividing a result by a ratio. For instance, if you know the payment is $1,000, and the ratio is 28%, you can divide the numbers to determine the monthly income ($3571 in this case). The same can be applied to LTV's.

Advanced Concepts - The Concept of Leverage

Leverage applies to financing in that it is utilized to maximize the return of an investment. Thinking of a home as an investment can assist a purchaser in rationalizing the cash investment against bank investments. A simple example: If you put $10,000 in the bank at 10% it will yield $1,000 yearly. If you purchase a $100,000 home with a $10,000 investment, and the property appreciates at a rate of 2.5%, it will yield $2,500 yearly. The leverage of financing allows a smaller amount of cash to purchase a larger investment. Even though the yield of the larger asset is lower, the

Without Leverage	
Certificate of Deposit	$10,000
Yield	7.5%
Annual Return	$ 750
Using Leverage	
Home Price	$ 100,000
Cash	$ 10,000
Leverage	$ 90,000
Appreciation	2.5%
Annual Return	$ 2,500

leverage creates a higher overall yield. Obviously, there is a carrying cost for the leverage - or the mortgage, in this case. The idea of leverage in this context is that, whether you rented your residence or owned it, you would still be paying for shelter.

The Concept of Taxable Equivalency

When dealing with the exchange of dollars there is always the issue of taxation and how it impacts the actual cash flow. Tax implications affect theoretical cash flows in the following situations: 1.) Determining the comparable rent payment to the mortgage payment after the mortgage interest and real estate tax deductions; 2.) Determining the

How much is a Non-Taxable Dollar Worth?	
Bracket	Non-Taxable $ is Worth
28%	$1.389
33%	$1.493

increased impact for qualifying purposes of income that is not taxed. It is important to note that these calculations are prospective. Prospective income, while not actually utilized to qualify a borrower, can be a compensating factor. Increasing the amount of non-taxable income used for qualifying purposes is referred to as "grossing up" non-taxable income. Not every lender allows the use of "grossed-up" non-taxable income.

Method 1 - Rental Equivalency Illustration

Mortgage interest and real estate taxes are deductions that can be itemized on Federal 1040 tax form Schedule A. As a result, to compare a rental payment to a mortgage payment, the impact of these deductions must be factored in. This answers the question "I am paying a certain amount in rent. What does that work out to in Mortgage Dollars if I own instead?" It is the same method as determining the degree to which non-taxable income can be increased for qualifying purposes. Here we have illustrated that a $1,707 mortgage payment is the same, on a tax basis, as paying $1,278 in rent.

There are two methods for determining rental equivalency and taxable equivalency. The first method is illustrative and makes assumptions that ignore the borrowers other tax implications. This should only be used as an approximation. The idea is that home mortgage interest and real property taxes are deductible expenses and the borrower will itemize these at tax time and have a lower taxable income. Because this calculation does not take into consideration the borrower's actual income - except to the extent that we know their tax bracket - it is inaccurate.

Illustrative Method - Savings from Owning		
Principal & Interest	$	1,467.52
Real Estate Tax	$	200.00
Homeowner's Ins.	$	40.00
Total "A"	$	1,707.52
Deductible Portion		
Interest	$	1,333.33
Real Estate Tax	$	200.00
Total Tax Deductible	$	1,533.33
Multiply By Tax Rate		28%
Tax "Savings"	$	(429.24)
Subtract from "A" to determine "After Tax/Rental Equivalent"	$	1,278.28

Method 2 – Actual Withholding Table Computation

The second method examines the borrower's monthly income tax withholding status and takes the actual tax withholding tables comparing the current situation to the withholding adjustments that would be accurate after the transaction is complete. Theoretically, a borrower could legitimately adjust withholding allowances with their employers based on this computation. This method is suggested only because there is no way of knowing precisely how much to withhold for Federal

Income Taxes. It is important not to under- withhold because there are severe penalties for under-estimating taxes by more than 10%.

In this example you can see how the impact on regular withholding allowances moves the borrower to a level where there is a higher take home pay because of lower monthly withholding.

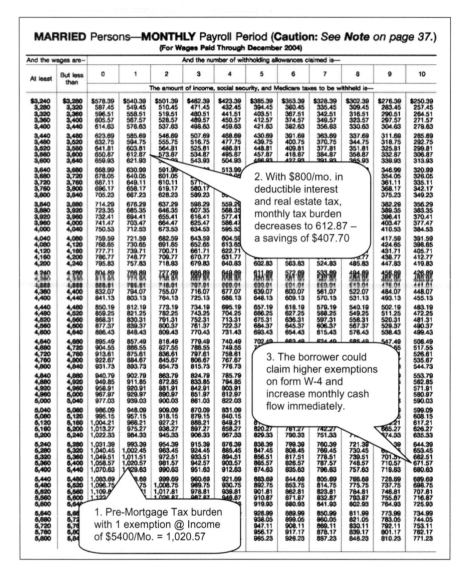

In these cases what we are trying to achieve is an understanding of what the borrower's current situation is, and consider the tax consequences of the new situation. If a borrower currently rents their home, they are not receiving the tax benefits of the mortgage deduction, and they are also losing:

- The inflation hedge provided by real estate because today's dollars will be worth less than tomorrow's in an inflationary environment.
- Any appreciation they might gain by the property value increase.

But they also expend the costs of closing, and realize the loss of the use of the funds they apply as a down payment.

We Are Not Tax Advisors

These calculations are ways to help a borrower understand the tax implications of the home financing process. A person's tax situation is only minimally impacted by the mortgage interest deduction. Second homes and investment properties involve different criteria.

What these calculations allow is a "relative basis" computation - comparative with another individual or the current situation.

SuperQual™ Worksheet

Step 2: Information Gathering

It is very important in this part of the process to make sure we are using accurate information to go forward. With that in mind, would you please authorize a credit check right now? This will allow us to continue to discuss your needs while we retrieve the credit history. I will fax/mail you an authorization (see reverse), but do I have your authorization to do this now? Y/N.

If yes, mother's maiden name: _____

Borrower Prospect Name		Social Sec. #
Coborrower		Social Sec. #
Property/Mailing Address		
Single Family/TH/Condo	Phone (Home)	
Current/Requested Loan Amount	Phone (Work)	
Value or Sales Price	LTV	

1. PROPOSED MONTHLY PAYMENTS		2. TOTAL MONTHLY OBLIGATIONS	
a.) First Mortgage P & I	$	a.) Housing Payment (#1g)	$
b.) Second Mortgage P & I	$	b.) Other Mortgages (Rent Income-	
c.) Mo. Hazard Insurance	$	Payments = Negative)	$
d.) Mo. Real Estate Taxes	$	c.) Auto Loans	$
e.) Condo/Association Fees	$	d.) Other Installment Loans	$
f.) Mortgage Insurance(PMI)	$	e.) Charge Card (5% of Balance)	$
g.) TOTAL HOUSING PAYMENT	$	f.) Other Monthly Payments	$
		g.) TOTAL MONTHLY OBLIGATIONS	$

3. FRONT RATIO CALCULATION		4. BACK RATIO CALCULATION	
(#1) Total Housing Payment		(#2) Total monthly obligation divided by	
divided by(#5) Total Income	%	(#5) total income	%

5. MONTHLY INCOME			6. DOWN PAYMENT	
	Borrower	Co-Borrower	a.) Down Payment	$
Base Income	$	$	b.) Closing Costs	$
Other Income	$	$	c.) Less Seller Contribution	$
Total Income	$	$	d.) Total Cash Required	$

Step 1
Suggested Needs Analysis Questions

Thank you for taking the time to speak with me.

- Have you been pre-qualified for this mortgage?
- Do you have a minute to do this now?
- Are you purchasing or refinancing?

PURCHASE
- How much are you putting down?
- How many points is the seller paying?
- Any closing cost contributions?
- What is the settlement date?
- Are you currently renting/or owning?
- If you own, what kind of loan do you have now?
- Will you sell your current home first?
- What is your current payment?
- How long do you think you will be in this property?

REFINANCE
- What is the amount of your current mortgage?
- Is there a second mortgage/home equity line? What are the payments? Are you planning to pay off your home equity line?
- Would you like to take cash out with this transaction? What will you pay off?
- What are your current payments?
- Does this include taxes and insurance?
- Are you more interested in lowering your payments or paying the loan off faster?

Have a Worksheet

The use of a worksheet will help the new loan officer guide any of the customer conversations and keeps the calculations reviewed in this chapter on hand.

Available with the purchase of The Loan Officer's Practical Guide to Marketing.

Monthly Payment (P&I)			Blended Rate Comparison				What is the Interest Rate		
Loan Amount		(PV)	a.) 1st Trust Rate	8.25%	(I%)		Payment		(PMT)
Interest Rate		(i%)	b.) 1st Trust Amount	$200,000	(PV)		Loan Needed		(PV)
# Payments		(N)	c.) 1st Trust Payment	$1,502.53	CPT		Loan Term		(N)
Compute	(CPT)	(PMT)	d.) 2nd Trust Rate	9.50%			Compute	(CPT)	(i%)
Max Loan for Income			e.) 2nd Trust Amount	$25,000			Record Result		
Income from #5		(#1g)	f.) 2nd Trust Payment	$210.21			**Amortized Balance**		
x DI Ratio		(#4)	Combined Loan (b+e)	$225,000	(PV)		Loan Amount		(PV)
Subtract Expenses		(#2b-f &1b-f)	Combined Pmt. (c+f)	$1,712.75	(PMT)		Interest Rate		(I%)
Available for P&I			Compute Rate	(CPT)	(I%)		Loan Term		(N)
Enter a term		(N)	Record Result				Compute	(CPT)	PMT
Enter a rate		(i%)					Remaining Mos.		(N)
Compute	(CPT)	(PV)					Balance	(CPT)	(PV)

FHA Loan Amount Calculation

Loan to Value Formula				
Sales Price x LTV				
Low Cost States		High Cost States		
x 98.75% < $50,000				
x 97.65% < $125,000		x 98.75% if <$50,000		
x 97.15% above		x 97.75% if >$50,000		

Up Front MIP		>95%	90-95%	<90%
1.50%	30 Years	.50% Life of Loan	.50% 12 Years	.50% - 7 Years
	15 Years	.25% - 8 Years	.25% - 4 Years	None

VA Loan Amount Calculation

Sales Price	
x75%	
Plus Entitlement	
Max Base Loan	
x Funding Fee	
Total Loan	
Funding Fee	
< 5% Down	2.00%
< 5% Restored	3.00%
<10% Down	1.50%
>10% Down	1.25%
Streamline	0.50%

Mortgage Insurance Premium Plans

PLAN TYPE	Standard Coverages		1st Year/Initial Premium Rate			Renewal Premium Rate Years 2-10		
	Coverage	LTV	30Fix	ARM	ARMI	30Fix	ARM	ARMI
Traditional Plan where a lump sum premium is paid to cover year 1. Subsequent Renewals are at a lower rate	30%	95%	1.5	1.55	1.75	0.49	0.54	0.54
	25%	90%	0.65	0.65	0.75	0.34	0.44	0.44
	12%	85%	0.29	0.3	0.34	0.29	0.3	0.34
Monthly Plan where each month is paid as it is accrued. True pay as you go. Ensures lower escrow and closing costs.	35%	97%	1.04	N/A	N/A	1.04	N/A	N/A
	30%	95%	0.78	0.85	0.89	0.78	0.85	0.89
	25%	90%	0.52	0.58	0.62	0.52	0.58	0.62
	12%	85%	0.29	0.3	0.34	0.29	0.3	0.34
One Time Premium - may be paid in cash or financed on top of loan amount if LTV's are not exceeded.	Coverage	LTV	One Time Premiums - Cash			Financed One Time Premiums		
	25%	90%	2.5	2.85	3.15	2.85	3.25	3.6
	12%	85%	1.5	1.6	1.65	2.15	2.35	2.5
Lender Paid Mortgage Insurance - Increased interest rate pays for PMI instead of borrower.	LTV		30 Year Fixed		15 Year Fixed		ARMs	
	95%		0.875%		0.625%		1.250%	
	90%		0.625%		0.375%		0.750%	
	85%		0.375%		0.250%		0.500%	

Notes: These premiums are representative of current plans available. Terms may vary from state to state. Lower premiums are available for shorter term loans such as 25 or 15 Year Loans. Where applicable, all premiums shown are Non-Refundable. Refundable premiums may be available but are generally at a higher rate.

Review – Self Test

Calculate the Payment

Enter Loan Amount	(PV)	$ 100,000	$ 175,000	$ 220,000	$ 485,000	$ 290,000	$ 66,000
Enter Interest Rate	(i%)	8.750%	6.000%	5.125%	6.750%	7.000%	7.500%
Enter the Number of Payments	(N)	360	180	240	300	360	120
Press Compute	(PMT)	(CPT)	(CPT)	(CPT)	(CPT)	(CPT)	(CPT)
Record Result							

Pre-Qualification - What is the Borrower's Maximum Loan Amount and Sales Price?

Assume Interest Rate is	7%	Loan Term	360	
Income	$64,500	38,125	44,150	98,000
Monthly Debts	$490	164	550	900
Down Payment	10%	3%	0%	10%
Housing Expense Ratio	28%	29%	41%	33%
Total Debt Ratio	36%	41%	41%	38%
Maximum Loan Amount				
Maximum Sales Price				

Chapter 2
Major Loan Types

Introduction

Before 1938 and the inception of the Federal Housing Administration (FHA) Mortgage Insurance program there was no fixed rate, regularly amortizing mortgage. (Amortization is the process of applying a portion of a payment towards interest and principal as well, thereby paying a loan off over its term.) Loans were generally interest only, may have had a short term - such as five years, and may have had a "call" provision - where the lender could require that the loan be repaid on short notice at the lender's sole discretion. With the FHA Insurance program, and the subsequent Veteran's Administration (VA) Loan Guaranty programs, long-term fixed rate, regularly amortized loans became prevalent, if not ubiquitous. With the long period of low interest rates that followed World War II, there was no reason to take a mortgage other than a 15- or 30-year fixed rate loan when buying a house. However, in late 1968, interest rates began to rise, and when fixed rate mortgages started carrying double digit interest rates, lenders and borrowers alike needed a wider variety of loan programs in order to afford housing and protect against future interest rate increases or decreases.

Today we have the genesis of 60 years of mortgage evolution. Every conceivable way in which money can be lent and paid back in conjunction with a mortgage has been packaged into a loan program. The programs offered often reflect the current market conditions as to interest rates, but most importantly, it is now easier than ever for the professional loan officer to interview a prospective applicant and find a loan program that specifically suits a borrower's needs.

Choosing a Fixed Rate Mortgage

Fixed rate mortgages are the most popular financing instruments because they combine the safety of fixed payments with an affordable amortization schedule for a given period of time. The interest rate cannot change and, because of their wide availability, rates offered by various lenders are extremely comparable and competitive.

How are fixed rate mortgages different from each other?

Term/Amortization: Fixed rate mortgages can vary by the length of time over which the payments are due.

<u>30 YEARS:</u> This term maximizes the affordability of the loan in monthly payments while maintaining a large proportion of the initial payments towards interest, thus enhancing the home mortgage interest deduction.

<u>15 YEARS:</u> The 15-year term features a major savings over the life of the loan because there are 180 payments instead of 360. The savings are achieved at the cost of higher monthly payments. Because there is so much interest savings, tax savings are quickly diminished. The rate available may be lower, generally, than the same 30-year mortgage.

You can also customize the loan term of many fixed/regularly-amortizing loans to the needs of the borrower. For instance, 25-, 20- and 10-year loans are available too. You can even make a 12-year or 27-year loan. While some lenders place restrictions on the terms offered, these loans are sold into the secondary market just like most loans (See Chapter 10 – The Secondary Market). A restriction is that the interest rate for the loan is usually determined by the next longest loan term. For instance a 25-year loan has the same rate as a 30-year loan and a 10-year loan may have the same rate as a 15-year loan. Depending on market pricing, more favorable terms may be available for loans with shorter terms. Currently Federal National Mortgage Association (FNMA) will purchase 10- & 20-year loans with 10- & 20-year pricing.

Interest-Only

"Interest-Only" or "Simple Interest" refers to a repayment schedule that is not amortized. Traditionally, interest only financing was only available for adjustable rate loans. In 2001 FNMA made this program available on a fixed rate basis. The principal balance is multiplied by the annual interest rate and divided by the number of payments in the year. The benefit of interest only financing is that the minimum payment is lower owing to the fact that there is no

Determining the Interest Only Payment	
Loan Amount	$100,000
Times Interest Rate	x 7.5%
Annual Interest	$7,500
Divided by Months	12
Monthly Payment	$625.00

principal being applied. The interest only loan may have a balloon payment at the end of the term, or may be turned into a 15- or 20- year amortized loan at the end of 15 or 10 years for a total term of 30 years.

Prepayment

One of the most popular features of a fixed rate loan is the ability to "prepay," or reduce the principal balance of the mortgage, without any penalty. While prepayment is generally available without penalty, the benefit of prepaying a fixed rate loan is that subsequent payments are devoted more to principal and less towards interest, paying down the loan balance prior to scheduled maturity. A prepayment strategy looks at ways of paying off a loan as quickly as possible while still keeping the proportionately lowest payment to save the maximum amount of interest.

Effect of Monthly Prepayment on Loan Term

Loan Amount	$ 100,000.00
Interest Rate	7.50%
Amortized Term	30
Principal and Interest	$ 699.21

Extra Monthly Prepayment Amount	Total Payment with Prepayment	Loan Term in Months After Extra Payment	Loan Term In Years After Extra Payment	Total of Payments as Scheduled	Interest Savings
$0	$ 699.21	360	30.00	$ 251,717.22	$ -
$20	$ 719.21	326	27.19	$ 234,628.57	$ 17,088.66
$50	$ 769.21	269	22.39	$ 206,677.98	$ 45,039.24
$75	$ 844.21	216	18.03	$ 182,696.81	$ 69,020.41
$100	$ 944.21	174	14.51	$ 164,350.06	$ 87,367.16
$150	$ 1,094.21	136	11.33	$ 148,703.80	$ 103,013.42
$200	$ 1,294.21	106	8.82	$ 137,003.18	$ 114,714.05

Other Prepayment Strategies - The Bi-Weekly Mortgage

Monthly prepayment is not the only strategy to achieve interest savings. The same effect can be achieved by making an "extra" mortgage payment each year. This reduces the loan term between 5 years and 15 years, depending on interest rates. This concept - making an extra payment every year - forms the basis of the bi-weekly mortgage. Making a payment every two weeks is tantamount to making an extra mortgage payment every year because there are 26 bi-weekly periods in a year (13 months). The Bi-Weekly Mortgage is a fixed rate or adjustable rate loan with a payment plan that allows borrowers to make a payment every two weeks instead of once a month. This theoretically helps people who are paid every two weeks manage their cash flow. However, it may be more practical to utilize an independent prepayment strategy as opposed to taking out a bi-weekly mortgage because: 1.) There is a greater potential for the incidence of late payments (twice as many payments); and 2.) The rates for the bi-weekly loan are not as competitive as those for standard monthly plans.

Bi-Weekly Mortgage Comparison

Loan Amount	$ 200,000
Interest Rate	7.50%
Loan Term	30

		Number of Payments year	Total Payments	Loan Term in Months	Effective Loan Term in Years
Monthly Payment	$ 1,398.43	12	$ 16,781.15	360	30
Bi-Weekly Payment	$ 699.21	26	$ 18,179.58	279.839	23.31991
Results in Annual Prepayment of			$ 1,398.43		
Effective Monthly Payment			$ 1,514.96		

Other "Fixed Rate" Mortgages

A fixed rate loan is pretty simple to understand. What you see is what you get. But there are many borrowers whose needs are not met by a fixed rate loan. It is for these customers that there may be a creative "hybrid" fixed rate loan that provides a solution.

Keystrokes to Compute Balance of Balloon Payment		
Enter Loan Amount	$ 100,000.00	PV
Enter Interest Rate	7.75%	%int
Enter Amortization Term	360	N
Compute Payment	CPT	PMT
Enter # months remaining at Balloon Date	300	N
Compute Loan Balance	CPT	PV

Balloon Mortgages

The term balloon illustrates the feature of this loan plan. The payments are fixed for a certain period, and then there is one large payment - or a "balloon" payment. This feature may also be referred to as a "call," a "demand" or a "bullet." The loan is generally based on a long amortization term such as 30

Conditional Refinance Provisions
1. Must live in property (owner-occupied)
2. No second mortgages/liens
3. Must be current/no late payments in past 12 months
4. Rate cannot be more than 5% over note
5. Pay fees/sign documents

years, with a balloon in 5, 7, 10 or even 15 years. There may be a feature for converting the loan to a fixed rate loan after the balloon. This is referred to as a conditional refinance. It is important for customers to understand that a balloon is not an ARM - that a conditional offer to refinance at maturity does not guarantee financing. This feature is the same as provisions contained in ARMs with a "conversion option" – the ability to convert to a fixed rate.

The Two-Step ARM

Like a balloon this loan offers a fixed period at a rate that is lower than prevailing 30-year loans. However, there is no balloon feature. There is a single rate adjustment at the end of the term, which is what makes this an ARM. The terms of the adjustment may vary, but are generally 2.5% (margin) over the then prevailing 10-year Treasury Bill averaged to a constant maturity (index) with a maximum change of 6% (cap).

The Balloon and the Two Step ARM may seem similar, but the Two Step is a 30-year loan while the Balloon only exists until the call date. There is no consumer protection on the Balloon, so the lender is not exposed to future interest rate changes as with the ARM. As a result the Balloon may offer much lower interest rates than the ARM. It is important that borrowers understand the reason for the distinction in price between the two.

Growing Equity Mortgages

Also referred to as a "GEM" or "EQUAL" loan, this program has a Fixed Rate feature with a 15-, 20- or 30-year amortization. The initial payments under these plans are not sufficient to amortize the loan, so there are scheduled payment increases in which the payments "catch up" to what is required to amortize the loan. This is an ideal program for a borrower who wants a 15-year mortgage but cannot qualify for the 15-year mortgage payments. In this example we have used a 15-year loan. Because so much of the 15-year loan's monthly payment is devoted to principal, even

Growing Equity/Graduated Payment Mortgage			
Interest Rate		7.50%	
Loan Term/months		180	
Loan Amount		100000	
Level Principal & Interest		$921.25	
Initial Rate		2.50%	
Year	**Payment Increase**	**Payment**	**Ending Balance**
1	n/a	$ 665.40	$ 99,515.16
2	7.50%	$ 715.31	$ 98,395.10
3	7.50%	$ 768.96	$ 96,547.26
4	7.50%	$ 826.63	$ 93,868.77
5	7.50%	$ 888.63	$ 90,245.43
6	7.50%	$ 955.27	$ 85,550.57
7	7.50%	$ 1,026.92	$ 79,643.85
8-15	7.01%	$ 1,098.90	$ -

In this example a loan is paid off in 15 years with a much lower initial payment and increasing monthly payments until the loan fully amortizes.

with a payment that is 5% below the note rate, the payment is enough to cover the interest that is due.

The same is not true of the 30-year version of this program. It is not as effective because in order to achieve a significant reduction of the initial payment rate, the lender has to structure a Temporary Buydown to avoid scheduled negative amortization.

The interest rate on this loan does not change. It is the payment that is reduced to the point where the required payment simply covers the interest due on the loan. The payments gradually increase to the point where the loan is amortized. In addition, the program governs the amount that the payment can change at 7.5%. With the most popular version of this program - the EQUAL - the loan officer could reduce the interest rate on a fixed rate loan on a sliding scale to as low as 5% and predict how the payments would change for the entire life of the loan. This loan is a good program for borrowers who want to build equity and who cannot currently afford higher payments, but who can predict that their income will gradually increase.

Graduated Payment Mortgage

The Graduated Payment Mortgage (GPM) is similar to the Growing Equity Mortgage in that the interest rate is fixed and the initial payments are reduced. However, this program takes the reduced payment concept one step further. Not only are the initial payments not sufficient to amortize the loan, they are not sufficient to cover the interest due on the loan. The result of this is that the interest that is not paid over the course of the monthly payments is simply added to the initial principal amount of the loan in a process known as "negative amortization." The payments then increase not only to curtail the process of negative amortization but also to amortize the loan as necessary. GPM's are offered by FHLMC and are eligible for FHA Mortgage Insurance and VA Loan Guaranty provided there is a GNMA security into which they may be sold.

Buydowns - The Low Down on Interest Rate Reduction

A Buydown is not really a loan program. In fact, the underlying mortgage can be any fixed rate or adjustable rate program. A Buydown is exactly what it sounds like - paying fees (or buying) to reduce (down) the payments on a mortgage. The beauty is that there is no fixed or required temporary Buydown arrangement - each one is a work of art and subject the to needs of the transaction.

A Buydown may permanently or temporarily reduce the payments on a mortgage. A permanent Buydown is also known as a rate discount - paying discount points to permanently reduce the rate of the mortgage. For example, a lender may offer a rate of 10.5 % with no points, or 9.75 with 3 points. 9.75% in this example is a "discounted" rate. This is quite different from a temporary Buydown. Permanent Buydowns can be achieved by viewing a rate sheet and seeing how low the permanent rate will be by paying discount points. "Points," then, become closing costs, which are covered in a later chapter.

Temporary Buydowns

A temporary Buydown is created when funds are placed in escrow - outside the control of the borrower or then lender - to offset the monthly payment required by the terms of the note. The funds in escrow reduce the effective payment rate but not the note rate. To illustrate this, take an example where a typical 30-Year Fixed Rate mortgage at 10% interest can carry an effective payment of 8% in the first year, 9% in the second year and revert to the note rate in the third year.

Buydown Cost Calculator

Use this worksheet to determine the actual buydown cost.

Loan Amount	$ 300,000	Loan Term	30 Years	
Note Rate	7.25%	Loan Type	30 Year Fixed	

Payment Rate Reduction	Payment Rate	Buydown Payment	# Mos	Note Payment	Monthly Cost	Annual Cost
2.000%	5.250%	$ 1,656.61	12	$ 2,046.53	$ 389.92	$ 4,679.01
1.000%	6.250%	$ 1,847.15	12	$2,046.53	$ 199.38	$ 2,392.53
0.000%	7.250%	$ 2,046.53	336	$2,046.53	$ -	

Total Cost	$ 7,071.54	
Point Cost	2.357%	

The Buydown cost may be borne by a seller or a borrower. In some cases the Buydown funds may be paid by the lender in what is known as a "lender subsidized" Buydown where the note rate of the loan is increased to reduce the up front cost of the subsidy. This is a "reverse" discount. The example above might be 8.5-9.5-10.5 % with one point and no Buydown cost.

You can "tailor" a program to meet very specific needs, but the concept remains the same. There are as many variations of a Buydown as you can create in your imagination. These are not limited to buydowns on fixed rate mortgages either - you may, depending on guidelines, elect to utilize a permanent

Qualify for a Larger Loan Using a Buydown		
Monthly Income		$4,000
Multiplied by Housing Expense %		x 28 %
Equals Maximum Housing Expense		$1,120
Reducing the Interest Rate Temporarily Increases the Mortgage Amount		
Interest Rate	10%	8% (Using 2-1 Buydown)
Monthly Payment	$1,120	$1,120
Maximum Mortgage	$127,600	$152,600
Difference In Mortgage Qualification		$25,000

Buydown on an Adjustable Rate Mortgage. Get creative!! Mix and match the concept and even try a Buydown on an ARM. Some variations include:

"1.50-.50 Buydown": Reduces the payment in increments of less than 1% per year. The objective is to achieve a specific qualifying rate without increasing the Buydown cost any more than necessary. (Not every lender allows qualification at the lowest rate.)

"Compressed Buydown": Changes payments every 6 months instead of every year. The classic example is a 3-2-1 Buydown where the buyer qualifies at the second year rate, but also has the benefits of lower payments.

"1-1-1 Buydown": The payments are reduced a smaller amount for a longer time period.

Full Principal and Interest Subsidy/Buydown is also known as the "Live Free" Buydown. The effect is to completely reduce the principal and interest payment in total for as long as the subsidy account will allow. With a Live Free Buydown, the borrower makes only the Tax and Insurance portion of the monthly payment. This is used to advertise those "move in and make no payments for 6 months," new home builder specials.

Why Use A Buydown?

The primary reason for utilizing a Buydown is to qualify for a larger loan. Obviously, if your monthly payment is lower, you can afford a larger mortgage as the example illustrates.

The temporary Buydown can also offer a psychological benefit by allowing a borrower to ease into a higher housing expense. If a borrower is accustomed to paying $1,000 a month, but wants to purchase a more expensive home, a larger mortgage is required and the monthly payment will be higher. A Temporary Buydown can offset the difference between the desired payment and the required payment. In fact, the Buydown can be customized to meet the exact payment requirement of the borrower.

A popular application of the Temporary Buydown utilized frequently among the homebuilding community is to advertise dramatic temporary interest rate buydowns as an enticement to purchase a new home. If interest rates are in the 10% range, a Buydown can allow you to offer a fixed rate mortgage as low as 7%. Alternately, a full principal and interest Buydown can mean that the builder can advertise "no payments for six months."

It is important to remember that the subsidy rate is not the real interest rate of the mortgage. The money for the reduction in interest rate has to come from somewhere and can increase the cost of a transaction dramatically. So temporary buydowns should only be used when deemed necessary, as there are no real interest rate savings involved. Another facet that should always be considered is that temporary Buydown funds, once committed to the Buydown escrow account, are not refundable - even if the loan is paid off early.

The Bottom Line On "Points"

If a Temporary Buydown achieves a short-term payment reduction, a "Permanent Buydown" can be achieved by "discounting" the interest rate – or paying points. All loan types offer a range of rate and point options. The ability to compare the short term and long-term costs are an important component of helping the borrower select an appropriate loan type.

Often, the first question a prospective borrower asks when they begin shopping for a mortgage is how many "points" they must pay. A point is 1% of the mortgage amount. For example, a lender offers a rate of 6.75% with 3 points or 7.5% with 0 points. Which scenario is better for the borrower? The answer lies in the borrower's motivation - how long will you be in the property? The loan officer must perform the "Breaking Even on the Point Investment" calculation.

In this example, a borrower would invest $3,000 in points to save $50.62 per month, showing that it would be 59.27 months before the cash investment at closing would begin to be worthwhile. This means that if the loan were in effect for less than 5 years the borrower would lose money.

Breaking Even on the Point Investment			
Loan Amount	$ 100,000.00		
Interest Rate	7.50%	6.75%	
Points	0.00%	3.00%	
Point Cost	$ -	$ 3,000.00	$ 3,000.00
Payments	$ 699.21	$ 648.60	$ 50.62
Cost Divided by Savings equals number of			
months to break even			59.27

Measuring Annual Percentage Rate (APR), or loan fees, against monthly payments, determines the actual cost of your credit. The following example shows the APR of loans with points and without. Consider, though, that this also impacts on a prepayment strategy. If a borrower buys a new home without selling a previous home there is the potential for a large gain in the future. When that home is sold and the proceeds are used to prepay the new mortgage, this can impact the value of having paid points. Those points are suddenly inflated in relation to a paid down mortgage.

Computing the effect of Point on APR based on Time

Term	Loan with 3 Points				Loan With No Points			
	Rate	Point Cost	Aggregate Cost	APR	Rate	Point Cost	APR	Aggregate Cost
360	6.75	$ 3,000.00	$ 236,495.31	7.050%	7.5	$ -	7.500%	$ 251,715.60
300	6.75	$ 3,000.00	$ 197,579.43	7.086%	7.5	$ -	7.500%	$ 209,763.00
240	6.75	$ 3,000.00	$ 158,663.54	7.143%	7.5	$ -	7.500%	$ 167,810.40
180	6.75	$ 3,000.00	$ 119,747.66	7.240%	7.5	$ -	7.500%	$ 125,857.80
120	6.75	$ 3,000.00	$ 80,831.77	7.437%	7.5	$ -	7.500%	$ 83,905.20
60	6.75	$ 3,000.00	$ 41,915.89	8.033%	7.5	$ -	7.500%	$ 41,952.60
36	6.75	$ 3,000.00	$ 26,349.53	8.816%	7.5	$ -	7.500%	$ 25,171.56
24	6.75	$ 3,000.00	$ 18,566.35	9.774%	7.5	$ -	7.500%	$ 16,781.04
12	6.75	$ 3,000.00	$ 10,783.18	12.503%	7.5	$ -	7.500%	$ 8,390.52
6	6.75	$ 3,000.00	$ 6,891.59	17.387%	7.5	$ -	7.500%	$ 4,195.26

ADJUSTABLE RATE MORTGAGES

Understanding a fixed rate loan is fairly easy, even with some of the features that can be added with buydowns and other variations. Another category of loan types features changing interest rates - known as Adjustable Rate Mortgages (ARMs). Fixed rates are different from ARMs in that an ARM interest rate can change - ARMs are different from each other in how the interest rate can change.

ARMs have been unfairly characterized as very risky financing alternatives. This is the genesis of what were at one time extremely risky programs, born of a time when fixed interest rates were very high. From 1979 to 1985 fixed interest rates were in the 12 - 18% range. As a result, no one could afford to buy a home or take out a mortgage. The banks, too, were unwilling to lend on a fixed rate basis. This was due to another phenomenon - the first Savings and Loan (S&L) crisis. S&L's were the primary source for home loans until the 1970's. They lent billions of dollars to homebuyers on a fixed rate basis at 1960's rates - 5% to 8%. When rates began to rise, S&L's had to increase the rates they paid on deposits. They were making between 5-8% on their mortgages and paying out 8-14% to get deposits. It nearly destroyed the industry.

What the adjustable rate loan allowed lenders to do was to offer a rate below the current market to attract borrowers and allow future interest rate risk (up or down) to be shared with the borrowers. These programs drew rapid acceptance among borrowers, but there were some dramatic pitfalls as well. Initially, many ARMs offered did not offer any protection against interest rate changes. "Payment Shock" became the watchword of these loans. These pitfalls changed the way the preponderance of ARMs now offered work. Caps (maximums) on rate changes in lieu of payment caps, maximum life interest rates, and a number of qualification guidelines addressed these risks, making today's ARM, in general, a more reasonable risk.

ARM Components - The Basic Four

ARMs are different from fixed rates in that the interest rate changes. How the interest rate can change is how ARMs differ from each other. There are four major components - frequency of changes, Index, Margin, and Caps.

Frequency of Changes

How often can the rate change? The frequency of rate change often is how a program is named. For instance, a 1-Year ARM with annual rate changes is called (not surprisingly) a 1-Year ARM. However, the rate may be fixed for 3 years, turning into a 1-year ARM - known as a 3/1 ARM. It would be impossible for us to catalog each type of ARM ever devised. A Federal Home Loan Mortgage Corporation (FHLMC) negotiated commitment representative once said that FHLMC had purchased over 10,000 different types of ARMs from institutions throughout the country. In fact, this is a beauty of ARMs - they can truly be tailored to customer's desires and needs. ARMs are now available with fixed periods for up to 10 years, turning into 1-year ARMs. The other end of the spectrum is the monthly ARM, such as certain Savings and Loan ARMs (COFI – Cost of Funds Index) and the most popular financing instruments available today - the Home Equity Line of Credit and credit cards, all of which adjust monthly. These are loans that are generally based on the Prime Rate and can change in rate at any time. Is a 1-Year ARM riskier than that?

It is generally considered that the frequency of adjustments determines the amount of risk associated with an ARM. An unfortunate phenomenon is that as one moves out longer along the maturity curve (the longer the loan is fixed), the higher the initial rate. The Comparative Rates and Maturities follow the yield curve that measures the market's perception of future interest rate risk. There is also a diminishing return for accepting an intermediate term fixed period as compared to a fixed rate or longer term ARM.

Comparative Rates and Maturities (Yield Curve)	
6 month ARM	2.750%
1 year ARM	3.750%
3 year ARM	4.125%
5/1 year ARM	4.750%
7/1 year ARM	5.125%
10/1 year ARM	5.500%

The shorter the adjustment term, the lower the initial rate (unless other factors such as very low caps or margins apply). Because ARMs with longer adjustment periods begin to replicate fixed rate products in terms of the lender's risk, the initial "teaser" rate factor begins to diminish.

Frequency of rate changes can be used to tailor the plan to the borrower's risk tolerance, the length of time that the loan will be in place and the borrower's view of future interest rate movements. If a borrower wishes to accept absolutely no risk, in order to accept an ARM, they must have an absolute time frame in which they will be using the loan. Then, the frequency of adjustments in conjunction with the maximum rate changes can be an aspect that most customers focus on in deciding whether to use an ARM. This is referred to as the worst-case scenario and is an unsophisticated, but risk-free approach.

Index Name	Description
Treasury Bill Constant Maturity (TCM)	The Treasury Bills are the most common index. They have a large array of maturities (90 days, 6 mo, 1 Yr., 2 Yr., 3 Yr, 5Yr, 7Yr and 10 Years, among others). The securities themselves are traded from minute to minute, so it is a dynamic index. The Constant Maturity is a yield computation that takes the volatility out of the fact that the securities themselves are issued daily so they do not all mature on the same date.
LIBOR (London Inter Bank Offered Rate)	This is the rate at which different money center banks in London loan each other money.
COFI (Cost of Funds Index) – Also known as COSI (Cost of Savings) or CODI (Cost of Deposits)	Associated with the 11th Federal Home Loan Bank Board, (California) this number is derived monthly and reflects the aggregate rate at which California Savings and Loans pay on deposits.
Certificate of Deposits (CDs)	This is an index recently derived by FNMA which is the median rates paid by banks for six-month certificates of deposit.
Prime	The Prime Rate published in *The Wall Street Journal* is the rate at which money center banks lend to their best customers. It is important to note that *The Wall Street Journal* publishes a compiled number. Each bank, however, can charge whatever it likes for prime.
FNMA 60-Day Mandatory Delivery	This is an index for loans that will convert to fixed-rate loans for the remaining term at a future date, such as Balloons or Convertible ARMs. It is based upon FNMA's actual required net yield for 30-Year fixed rate mortgages that must be delivered within 60 days.

The Index

Frequencies of payment/rate adjustments dictate how often the rate can change. How the interest rate can change is a function of the index added to the margin. The index of an ARM is the basis of future interest rate changes. From the borrower's point of view the Index should:

1.) *Be regularly published in a source accessible to the public.*
2.) *Be beyond the lender's control. If the index is linked to the lender's performance, or risk experience, theoretically they could increase the index whenever they needed to make more money.*

As there are many adjustment periods, there are many indices to which ARMs are linked. The characteristics of these indices can impact other features of the loan.

The variables of each index are a factor in analyzing the future performance of an adjustable rate mortgage. For instance, if the index is stable, future interest rate increases may not be dramatic, but there is less likelihood that there would be an improvement in the event of future interest rate decreases.

The Margin

The margin is set by the lender and is the amount above the index that the interest rate can adjust at the time of adjustment. The result of the index plus margin formula is the new interest rate.

> **INDEX + MARGIN = NEW RATE**

This is the "real" or "true" interest rate of the ARM. It is important to consider this real cost because most ARMs - particularly short term ARMs - are "discounted." A discounted rate indicates that the points paid in conjunction with the loan artificially reduce the initial interest rate to attract borrowers. The result of the Index plus Margin Equation is also referred to as the **Fully Indexed Accrual Rate** (FIAR).

Each loan may offer a different Margin. This is a critical part of analyzing the ARM. In this example all things are equal, except the margin. The Margin is higher on loan 2, which means that the FIAR, or the true rate of the loan is higher on the second loan. This means that, regardless of what happens with interest rates the customer who chooses loan 2 will pay a higher interest rate over the life of the loan. This is true of any ARM.

The ARM with the Lowest Margin Offers the Lowest Cost		
	Loan 1	Loan 2
Initial Rate	5.5	5.5
Index	4.875	4.875
Margin	2.5	3.75
New Rate	**7.375**	8.625

Another fact to note is that the APR will vary on adjustable rate mortgages, but that the payment schedule provided to the borrower is always based on the current FIAR, taking into consideration any rate caps.

Interest Rate Caps & Payment Caps

The above example shows the actual mechanics of how ARM rates can change. This illustrates how, if indices rise as they did in the late 70's and early 80's, people could experience huge increases in their monthly payments. As a borrower contemplates accepting a loan program that entails interest rate changes as opposed to a fixed rate, they focus on risk - "What is the worst case?" Obviously, if interest rates could change unimpeded, there would be great risk to the borrower. In order to make ARMs more appealing to borrowers, and to provide some consumer protection, most of today's ARMs offer maximums, or "caps," on the amount that rates can change.

Rate Adjustment Caps:	This is the maximum - up or down - that the interest can change per period above the previous period.
Life of Loan Caps:	The maximum that the interest rate can change over the initial rate over the life of the loan.

The caps modify the ARM interest rate change formula from Index plus Margin to Index plus Margin or Rate Plus Cap, **WHICHEVER RESULTS IN A SMALLER CHANGE.** This facet of the ARM changes the analysis process. Instead

INDEX + MARGIN
or
RATE + CAP
whichever is a smaller change

of comparing only the fully indexed rate, the borrower now must compare the impact of caps too. The caps are most frequently utilized in an unsophisticated analysis referred to as the "worst case scenario." The Worst Case Scenario basically assumes that the worst possible event will occur and then send the ARM rate through the ceiling. This only examines the caps, allowing the borrower to examine the absolute risk.

Initial Adjustment Cap

Particularly in programs where the initial interest rate is set for a longer period of time, the transitional cap - when the first rate change occurs - may be different from the caps addressed as the loan adjusts annually thereafter. The rate may be allowed to increase to the lifetime caps, and subsequent adjustments may be based upon that new rate. This must be investigated because due to borrower concerns about frequency of changes, the change caps may be overlooked as an unimportant factor.

The Adjustment Cap Limits the Rate Change Per Adjustment

	Loan 1	Loan 2
Initial Rate	5.5	5.5
Margin	2.75	3.25
Index	5.375	5.375
Year 2 Rate	7.5	7.5
Year 3 Rate	8.125	8.625

Payment Caps

This is a feature that affects not the interest rate, but the rate at which the borrower must make payments. The inimical aspect of payment capped ARMs is that interest rates may increase dramatically and almost immediately from the initial offered rate. The borrower may not be aware that, while the required payment hasn't changed or can only change a certain amount, the payment may not be sufficient to pay all of the interest (or even principal) due. When this occurs, it is referred to as negative amortization. Negative amortization means that the shortfall in monthly payments is added to the principal balance of the loan. Most loan programs (with the exception of GEMs, GPMs and interest only loans) are positive-amortizing, meaning that the portion of the balance is retired with each payment. Negative amortization is the reverse - instead of paying the loan down, the balance increases.

An additional risk is that, when limiting his payments to the minimum in a rising rate environment, the borrower must redraw the loan documents when the original balance exceeds 120% of the original balance. This is unlike the GEM or GPM where the borrower knows there is the potential for negative amortization and the loan payments are scheduled to increase enough to create positive amortization. The cycle can then start again, and be recast until the loan matures. Some positive features of this loan are that the borrower may have up to 3 options making payments that will: 1.) Positively amortize the loan, 2.) Cover only the interest due, or 3.) Meet the minimum required payment. The borrower can maintain some control over personal cash flow as well as mitigating interest rate shock. However, before choosing such a loan, all components must be analyzed and compared.

The "Option" ARM

We have all seen the rate sheets and advertisements shouting about great low rate Adjustable Rate Mortgages, but when the numbers start to seem too good to be true, a closer look at the loan program is warranted. The recent rise in popularity of "interest only" and low "teaser" rate ARMs are examples of this.

In theory, there is nothing wrong with a "teaser" rate. A borrower may be able to use the low introductory rate for specific benefit. For instance, using the period when the interest rate is low to pay additional amounts towards the loan principal is a time tested strategy, particularly when the borrower also is able to identify a finite period of time that the loan will be in place. The difficulty is that many Loan Officers do not understand the basic functions of an ARM, and so are not very good at explaining loan mechanics to borrowers. As a consequence any borrowers enter into loan contracts they do not understand.

As an example, a loan officer offering a 1 Year ARM helps the borrower understand that the interest rate will change every year. The borrower then hears of an incredible 1% 1 Year ARM. Because the public has been taught that lower interest rates are better, the borrower is compelled to request the low rate product. How different could the terms be?

In this case, the terms are quite different. A 1 Year ARM offers an interest rate that is fixed for one year. The 1% 1 Year ARM offers PAYMENTS that are fixed at the 1% level, but that do not reflect that the underlying interest rate is changing. The introductory rate and subsequent payment rate changes are based on the payment rate NOT THE INTEREST RATE. The deficit between the payment rate and the actual interest rate carrying cost on the loan can result in principal being added back to the loan – a process known as negative amortization.

Payment Caps = Negative Amortization

In the illustration shown here, the borrower's loan balance increases far more dramatically with deferred interest than it decreases with amortization. This is because negative amortization is compounded interest – interest on interest. While this isn't horrific in itself, this illustration only shows what

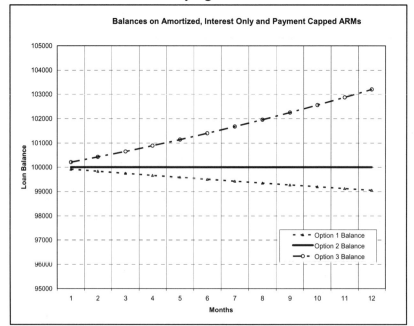

happens when interest rates increase moderately – at the rate of 1% per year. In today's rising short term interest rate environment, rates are likely to rise much more rapidly, adding more to the loan balance.

Is This a Bad Option for Borrowers?

There are many loan officers who advocate the use of the teaser rate ARM to bridge a particular situation:

- An investor purchasing a property to sell in a short period of time (flip)
- A borrower who is purchasing a home and who has to make two mortgage payments (old home and new home) for a defined period of time
- A borrower who believes their home will appreciate faster than the loan balance accrues and so borrows from appreciation to offset deferred interest
- A borrower who is using the option ARM as a modified version of a reverse equity loan

These are all rational justifications for accepting this type of loan. A sophisticated borrower will appreciate that he or she has multiple options – amortized, interest only, or deferred interest - for making payments. They will be aware and capable of handling the consequences of each choice. An uneducated borrower may choose this product for the visceral appeal of that very low payment. This type of loan doesn't suit that borrower, as the pace of negative amortization will soon sweep the equity away from the property, even at a high rate of appreciation. **A senior citizen should never choose this option.** Select a reverse mortgage instead.

Comparison of Payments and Loan Balances for Option Arms

Rate Formula	Initial Loan	100000										
	Term	360										
	Intro Rate	1.750%										
	1	2	3	4	5	6	7	8	9	10	11	12
Index	3.97	4.12	4.24	4.39	4.48	4.6	4.72	4.8	4.91	5.02	5.13	5.24
Margin	2.75	2.75	2.75	2.75	2.75	2.75	2.75	2.75	2.75	2.75	2.75	2.75
New Rate	6.72	6.87	6.99	7.14	7.23	7.35	7.47	7.55	7.66	7.77	7.88	7.99
Option 1 Fully Amortized	$ 646.61	$ 657.13	$ 665.14	$ 675.18	$ 681.23	$ 689.30	$ 697.41	$ 702.82	$ 710.28	$ 717.76	$ 725.26	$ 732.77
Option 1 Balance	$ 99,913.39	$ 99,828.26	$ 99,744.63	$ 99,662.93	$ 99,582.17	$ 99,502.81	$ 99,424.80	$ 99,347.53	$ 99,271.41	$ 99,196.43	$ 99,122.57	$ 99,049.79
Option 2 Interest Only	$ 560.00	$ 572.50	$ 582.50	$ 595.00	$ 602.50	$ 612.50	$ 622.50	$ 629.17	$ 638.33	$ 647.50	$ 656.67	$ 665.83
Option 2 Balance	$100,000.00	$100,000.00	$100,000.00	$100,000.00	$100,000.00	$100,000.00	$100,000.00	$100,000.00	$100,000.00	$100,000.00	$100,000.00	$100,000.00
Option 3 Payment Rate	$ 357.24	$ 357.24	$ 357.24	$ 357.24	$ 357.24	$ 357.24	$ 357.24	$ 357.24	$ 357.24	$ 357.24	$ 357.24	$ 357.24
Option 3 Balance	$100,202.76	$100,419.17	$100,646.87	$100,888.48	$101,139.09	$101,401.32	$101,675.30	$101,957.76	$102,251.35	$102,556.19	$102,872.39	$103,200.11
	13	14	15	16	17	18	19	20	21	22	23	24
Index	5.35	5.46	5.57	5.68	5.79	5.9	6.01	6.12	6.23	6.34	6.45	6.56
Margin	2.75	2.75	2.75	2.75	2.75	2.75	2.75	2.75	2.75	2.75	2.75	2.75
New Rate	8.1	8.21	8.32	8.43	8.54	8.65	8.76	8.87	8.98	9.09	9.2	9.31
Option 1 Fully Amortized	$ 740.30	$ 747.85	$ 755.41	$ 762.99	$ 770.59	$ 778.20	$ 785.82	$ 793.46	$ 801.12	$ 808.79	$ 816.47	$ 824.17
Option 1 Balance	$ 98,978.08	$ 98,907.41	$ 98,837.75	$ 98,769.10	$ 98,701.42	$ 98,634.70	$ 98,568.90	$ 98,504.03	$ 98,440.05	$ 98,376.94	$ 98,314.69	$ 98,253.27
Option 2 Interest Only	$ 675.00	$ 684.17	$ 693.33	$ 702.50	$ 711.67	$ 720.83	$ 730.00	$ 739.17	$ 748.33	$ 757.50	$ 766.67	$ 775.83
Option 2 Balance	$100,000.00	$100,000.00	$100,000.00	$100,000.00	$100,000.00	$100,000.00	$100,000.00	$100,000.00	$100,000.00	$100,000.00	$100,000.00	$100,000.00
Option 3 Payment Rate	$ 384.04	$ 384.04	$ 384.04	$ 384.04	$ 384.04	$ 384.04	$ 384.04	$ 384.04	$ 384.04	$ 384.04	$ 384.04	$ 384.04
Option 3 Balance	$103,512.67	$103,836.84	$104,172.73	$104,520.51	$104,880.31	$105,252.29	$105,636.59	$106,033.39	$106,442.83	$106,865.10	$107,300.36	$107,748.80

The Option ARM – with three payment options – suits particular borrower situations.

- A borrower with variable income who receives most of his or her income at more sporadic intervals than monthly, such as an attorney receiving annual or quarterly distributions.
- A seasonal business owner or worker, such as a landscape or pool contractor, might benefit from the low cash flow requirement in the winter months.

Drawbacks of Potential Negative Loan Balances

Prepayment Penalties: Option ARMs normally have a prepayment penalty to prevent the borrower from refinancing within the first 2 or 3 years. Being saddled with negative equity, and being unable to refinance to more favorable loan terms, tend to exacerbate the impact a loan that grows to be unaffordable.

Negative Amortization Cap: The loan balance can grow as deferred interest gets added to the principal balance. This cannot proceed unabated, and the lender normally caps the negative amortization to 110% – 125% of the original principal balance. Once this cap is reached, the monthly payments are re-cast (new monthly payments established) as a fully amortizing loan. Even if the negative equity balance is not attained, many loan documents require that the loan be re-cast every five years.

Effect of Negative Amortization on 2nd Mortgage Lendable Equity	
Property Value	$ 200,000.00
Lendable Equity %	80%
a. Gross Lendable Equity	$ 160,000.00
Original Loan Amount	$ 100,000.00
Max Negative Balance	125%
b. Max Potential Loan	$ 125,000.00
Net Lendable Equity a - b	$ 35,000.00

Subordinate Liens: Many second trust lenders are unwilling to accept 2nd lien position behind a loan that will potentially erode the equity in the house. At best, the lender will determine if there is any "lendable equity" if the loan reaches is full potential negative amortization, and base their loan amount calculations on this amount.

Homeowners and Title Insurance: Title Insurance policies must offset potential negative amortization and will include a rider that protects the loan up to its full potential balance.

Benefits of Monthly ARMs and Potential Negative Amortization

Ultimately, if the loan offers a favorable margin, it may still be competitive with an intermediate term adjustable rate mortgage. Compare the terms of other interest only ARM products available, such as the 3/1 or 5/1 ARM.

One of the risks lenders assume is the danger of rising or falling interest rates affecting the value of the lender's investments. In the case of the Option ARM, the lender is taking virtually no interest rate risk. Because of the mitigated interest rate risk, the lender is able to absorb more credit risk, on an actuary basis. As a result, these loans may offer more expanded criteria than other investment grade loans.

Comparing ARMS

The stigma of ARMs as risky can be offset by a careful analysis of the loan terms. Depending on 1.) the amount of time the mortgage is needed and 2.) the borrower's view of future interest rates, an ARM may be a suitable alternative to a fixed rate loan. Most borrowers can understand how a fixed rate loan works. To help the borrower understand the adjustable rate mortgage you can compare it to a fixed rate loan on the basis of what is referred to as the "worst-case scenario." The "worst case scenario" is what would occur if the interest rate on the mortgage went up as high as the terms allowed – to the cap at each adjustment.

The "worst-case comparison" is performed by comparing the fixed interest rate to the **_average_** interest rate on the adjustable rate mortgage to. To achieve the "average interest rate" for a period, add the interest rate amount and divide by the number of years.

Various Scenarios Indicate that ARM Performance Changes Based on the Index (Market)

Performance of 1 Year ARM 2/6 Caps & 2.75 Margin	Index Rate	Initial Rate	2nd Year	3rd Year	4th Year	4 Year Average	30 Yr Fixed
Index Rates Stay at Today's Rate	5.3	5.5	7.5	8.125	8.125	7.31	8
Index Rates Go up 2% (Somewhat)	7.29	5.5	7.5	9.5	10.125	8.15	8
Index Rates Go up Significantly	14.9	5.5	7.5	9.5	11.5	8.5	8

In the above example, in a current or even somewhat increasing interest rate environment, an ARM may be more favorable than a fixed rate loan. This is because short-term rates are lower and, depending on the term of the adjustment, the borrower may gain an interest rate benefit that, when averaged over time, provides a lower overall interest cost. This comparison is then tailored to the amount of time that the borrower intends to be in the property.

In the following example use the worst-case scenario average to conclusively prove that 1.) a 1-year ARM has an average interest rate advantage over a fixed rate loan for the first 3 years (not just the first year) and 2.) that a 5/1 ARM has an average interest rate advantage for the first 7 years (not just the first 5). This scenario assumes the worst case and so can be used to help borrowers who are extremely risk averse and perceive ARMs as risky.

Worst Case Scenario Comparison - Fixed vs. ARM

		Year 1	Year 2	Year 3	Year 4	Year 5	Year 6	Year 7	Year 8
30-Year Fixed	Worst Case Rate	6.5	6.5	6.5	6.5	6.5	6.5	6.5	6.5
	Average Rate	6.5	6.5	6.5	6.5	6.5	6.5	6.5	6.5
1-Year ARM 2/6 Caps	Worst Case Rate	3.75	5.75	7.75	9.75	9.75	9.75	9.75	9.75
	Average Rate	3.75	4.75	5.75	6.75	7.35	7.75	8.03571	8.25
5/1 ARM 2/6 Caps	Worst Case Rate	5.125	5.125	5.125	5.125	5.125	7.125	9.125	11.125
	Average Rate	5.125	5.125	5.125	5.125	5.125	5.45833	5.98214	6.625

Conversion Options

A Conversion Option (Convertibility) is a feature that provides the borrower with the ability to convert to a fixed rate at a specified point or time frame during the life of the loan. It is easy to misunderstand the option, believing that this offers the ability to convert to a rate based upon the initial ARM rate. Unfortunately, this is not the case. The conversion option is basically a conditional refinance. This means the current market determines the interest rate. There may be a cap on the conversion option, but the terms for conversion are similar to those of the Balloon (see Balloon, this chapter). The benefits of the conditional refinance, or conversion, are:

1. Borrowers may take advantage of dips in interest rates to fix their mortgage rate without the cost of refinancing or the risk of re-qualifying.
2. An appraisal may not be required - alleviating concerns over property values.

Disadvantages

1. The conversion interest rate equation is a margin plus index equation. The conversion formula is based on current rates for 30-year mortgages, plus a margin - a borrower may almost always obtain a better rate for a fixed rate loan by shopping for a refinance.
2. Because fixed rates are always higher than ARM rates, the rate on the ARM may be lower than the conversion rate.

Hybrid ARMs

In the "what will they think of next" category, it's always fun to see what kind of new programs are being made available. From time to time, an idea can catch on and become really popular, changing the way we think about loans. Here are some recent additions.

The Component ARM is actually two loans with one loan document. It is 50/50 ARM and fixed rate. This is truly a program for the person who cannot make up his mind. This loan is not currently accepted in the secondary market and, as a result, is not really attractively priced.

The Stable ARM was devised by FNMA and sold as a program that mitigated the ARMs risk of dramatic future interest rate increases. The concept is to take 25% of the index value instead of the entire index. For instance, if the one-year treasury were 5.5% at the time of the adjustment, the lender would use 25% of that number or 1.125% as the basis for the change. The problem is that, to attract investors, the margin is so high (6%) as to diminish the benefit of stability as opposed to a fixed rate.

The Life Cap ARM offers the benefit of an initial interest rate that is also the life cap. Priced right, it competes with a 30 year fixed. At each adjustment the interest rate is the market rate or the cap. Choosing this product allows the borrower to have the security of a fixed rate (worst case scenario) or lower.

Second Mortgages

The term "Second Mortgage" simply refers to the timing of the recording of security instruments such as a mortgage or deed of trust. "Second" alludes to the fact that there is another mortgage recorded prior in a first lien position, or before any other second mortgage is recorded. This means that during a forced sale the second lien holder receives proceeds after the first mortgage lender's claim has been satisfied. Second priority also means that foreclosure proceedings cannot be initiated without the consent of the first mortgage lender. As a result second mortgage loans are considered riskier investments for lenders than first mortgages.

Second Mortgages come in two basic varieties. The fixed rate or term loan offers repayment terms similar to first mortgages. Fixed term loans normally have all of the loan proceeds disbursed at closing. The advantage of a fixed term loan is that it allows payments to be scheduled and the rate may be fixed. Home Equity Lines of Credit are open-ended loans that act like a credit card. The balance may be drawn up or paid down and interest is due on the balance owed. These loans are like ARMs, in that the interest can change regularly. The benefit of the line of credit is that you don't pay interest for money that you don't need to borrow. There is more flexibility in borrowing and repaying because if there is a significant over-payment, that money may be accessed right back.

A whole class of financing has initiated from this practice. Ordinarily the basis for approval of a second mortgage is the equity, or down payment, in a property - hence it is also known as equity lending. In the terminology of the current residential first mortgage lending, second mortgages connote "creative financing." Home equity lenders, banks, conduits and private individuals (a home seller who accepts a loan against the subject property in lieu of part of the down payment is a lender too) are all second mortgage sources. While they may be riskier for lenders, they are useful tools to do things that cannot be achieved with a first mortgage alone. A Home Equity Line of credit, for instance, is a second mortgage that allows a borrower to advance and repay a credit line to manage their cash flow. Many banks now offer car loans secured by homes so that the interest is tax deductible.

The Tandem - When Two Mortgages are Better Than One

It may be possible to structure a lower rate package by using secondary financing. The most inexpensive mortgages available have loan amounts below those set by FNMA and FHLMC ($359,650 as of 12/01/04), however, many people have a need for larger (jumbo/non-conforming) loans. These Jumbo or Larger loans generally carry a higher rate. A rate reduction may be achieved by using the "Tandem" strategy.

1st & 2nd Mortgage Comparison				
Sales Price	$ 250,000.00	Loan Term in Years		30
Down Payment	10%	Interest Rate		8.75%
Standard Transaction		**1st & 2nd Mortgage**		
1st Trust Amount	$ 225,000.00	1st Trust Amount	$	200,000.00
1st Trust Payment	$ 1,770.08	1st Trust Payment	$	1,573.40
1st Trust PMI	$ 97.50	1st Trust PMI	$	-
		2nd Trust Rate		9.50%
		2nd Trust Amount	$	25,000.00
		2nd Trust Payment	$	210.21
Standard Payment	$ 1,867.58	**Combined Payment**	$	1,783.61
Monthly Savings				$83.97

The Tandem may also be referred to as a "piggyback," "combo" or "blend." This example shows there is a significant saving in monthly payments ($83.97/mo.) utilizing the Tandem 1st & second Mortgage Combination. This is due to the cash flow savings from avoiding Private Mortgage Insurance. PMI, unlike mortgage interest, is not tax deductible. Even if there were no dollar for dollar monthly payment savings, more of the payment is tax deductible, hence there is a benefit.

Computing the Blended Rate

One powerful tool to help customers understand the relative rate impact of the first and second mortgage strategy is to show the effective, or "blended," rate of the two loans together. Comparing this to the first mortgage with PMI can enlighten a customer as to the

Computing the "Blended Rate"		
1. Add the payments for both loans	$1573 + $210	=
2. Enter the total as the Payment	$ 1,783	PMT
3. Add the two loan amounts	$200000+$25000	=
4. Enter the total as the Loan Amount	$225,000	PV
5. Enter the Term	360	N
6. Compute Interest Rate	CPT	I%
7. Record Result	8.830%	

real comparison and can be a tremendous selling tool. This formula is just like computing the maximum interest rate for a given payment and loan amount.

Bridge Loans and Reverse Bridge Loans - 2 Strategies

A bridge loan is a second mortgage on a property that is pending sale. There are reasons that bridge loans are risky. A lender is freeing up the equity in a current home to allow a buyer to purchase a new home. This works badly for a number of reasons. The home may not sell, even if it is under contract. Often, the costs of a bridge loan, because of the perceived risk, are much higher than traditional financing. Bridge loans normally come due within 90-270 days, which could put undue pressure on a home seller to dispose of the property at a loss.

A Bridge Loan is a Poor Solution
- A transaction in another area of the country beyond your control
- A second closing with more opportunities for errors
- More closing costs

One solution is not to rush to try and sell the previous home. Leverage the proposed transaction as much as possible using a Piggyback first and second mortgage. Then, when the previous home does sell, pay down or pay off the second mortgage and be left with the original mortgage that was intended. This is a "reverse bridge loan." Similarly, if there is the likelihood of significant prepayments in the early years of a loan, a first & second mortgage combination can be a good way to plan to have a lower payment in later years.

Often a borrower is making a substantial down payment towards a new home. While the result is a low loan to value transaction that is easy to approve, you can increase the borrower's access to their down payment by placing a Home Equity Line of Credit at the time of the purchase closing. This can assure that there is the ability to access the down payment equity in an emergency. Imagine – the borrower could even pay the first mortgage with the second mortgage.

Seller held Mortgages, Assumptions and Wraps

Sellers can become lenders when they agree to an installment sale. This practice was more widely used when interest rates were higher. A seller may entertain financing a property to a new purchaser if there is significant equity in the property. Occasionally a seller may need to get out from under a mortgage and so will allow the borrower to assume an existing loan. There are two classifications of assumptions. One is that the borrower assumes an underlying mortgage and is approved by the lender to take over the payments. This is normally done only if the terms on the existing mortgage is very attractive, which may be the case when rates are high.

A wrap has been through many permutations. The concept is the same as a land installment sale, a deferred purchase money loan, or more recently it has been known as a contract for deed. The seller's old loan remains in place and the payments continue to be made by the seller. The buyer pays the seller a negotiated amount until such time as they can obtain financing. The seller may hold part of the financing, or may just take the difference of cash at closing. The reason it is called a wrap is that all financing is wrapped into one payment that the buyer makes to the seller. There are numerous problems with settlements that occur under these terms, but they generally serve the purpose of disposing of a piece of difficult-to-sell property.

Using Software to Compare Programs

There are many software programs in the marketplace that can create the "Side-by-Side" comparison that loan officers can use to provide this type of analysis for their customers.

Learning to work with spreadsheets like these can help you achieve a wider proficiency in assisting your customers in determining which product is most appropriate for them. The benefit of using these spreadsheets instead of a program is that the cost is minimal – if you already have a spreadsheet program. There are many financial calculation software packages available in the marketplace. You can visit www.quick-start.net for recommendations.

A significant financial and time savings can be realized with the purchase of pre-formatted spreadsheets like this one, contained in the Loan Officer's Practical Guide to Marketing – available for sale at www.quick-start.net/lomarketingguide.htm.

Reverse Mortgages for Seniors

The most popular reverse mortgage is the federally-insured reverse mortgage, called the FHA Home Equity Conversion Mortgage Program (HECM). The other major product is the Home Keeper reverse mortgage, developed by FNMA. One "jumbo" private reverse mortgage product is offered by Financial Freedom Senior Funding Corp., of Irvine, CA. This is the Cash Account Plan. The HECM and Home Keeper products are available in every state, while Financial Freedom's product is offered in 21 states and the District of Columbia.

A reverse mortgage is a payment plan. The underlying mortgage is either a monthly or 1 Year ARM. The FHA annual ARM has 1/5 caps. Instead of making payments, the borrower receives equity from the property in 1 of 5 ways. The loan has no repayment for as long as the borrower lives in the property they own.

While there are nuances, all Reverse Mortgages follow the FHA template. The FHA insured HECM reverse mortgage can be used by senior homeowners age 62 and older to convert the equity in their home into monthly streams of income and/or a line of credit to be repaid when they no longer occupy the home. The loan is funded by a lending institution and insured by FHA. FHA charges a 2% initial premium and .5% annually based on the balance of the loan. The HUD reverse mortgage does not require repayment as long as the home is the borrower's principal residence. Lenders recover their principal, plus interest, when the home is sold. The remaining value of the home goes to the homeowner or to his or her survivors. The heirs have the choice of refinancing the property to payoff the balance of the reverse mortgage, paying it off from any other assets, or selling the property. The borrower can never owe more than the home's value. In the event that the sale of the home doesn't satisfy the outstanding mortgage HUD insurance pays the lender the difference.

Homeowners 62 and older, currently living in their home with a large equity position are eligible to participate in HUD's reverse mortgage program. The only other borrower requirement is participation in a consumer information session given by an FHA approved counselor. The program allows homeowners to borrow against the equity in their homes using one of five plans:

5 Payment Plans offered under FHA's Reverse Mortgage Program

Tenure	equal monthly payments as long as at least one borrower lives and continues to occupy the property as a principal residence
Term	equal monthly payments for a fixed period of months selected
Line of Credit	unscheduled payments or in installments, at times and in amount of borrower's choosing until the line of credit is exhausted
Modified Tenure	combination of line of credit with monthly payments for as long as the borrower remains in the home
Modified Term	combination of line of credit with monthly payments for a fixed period of months selected by the borrower

The mortgage amount cannot exceed current FHA insurance limits, and is based on the age of the youngest borrower and actuarial tables, so older borrowers will receive larger payments. The current interest rate and the actual closing costs affect the amount of the loan.

Sample Loan Amounts based on 9% Interest

Home Value $ 300,000.00

Borrower's Age		Loan Amount
65	$	66,000.00
75	$	123,000.00
85	$	174,000.00

Chapter 3
Loan Plan Specifications

PROGRAM SPECIFICATIONS - UNDERSTANDING GUIDELINES

The types of loans offered - the products - each offer a specified return on financial investments for lenders. They represent a way for investors to lend money, secured by real estate, where they can obtain a reasonable return. These instruments offer a risk as well as a return. The risk of default – also known as credit risk - may preclude an investor from being repaid and is the first concern of lenders. One way to lessen the risk is to establish standard guidelines that allow lenders to easily determine what an "investment quality" loan is. These types of guidelines establish what investors deem as a prudent risk, and constitute the basis for the majority of mortgages provided today. These guidelines are also known as loan plan specifications.

For the Loan Officer, learning loan plan specifications is the first step in establishing a conceptual understanding of the products that are offered. Specifications are the first step in underwriting because they represent the basic absolutes that the eventual purchaser or guarantor of a mortgage will accept. Think of the loan specifications as a sieve - the first grid through which a borrower must pass in the process of obtaining a loan.

Loans are made based on risk – the amount of risk the lender is willing to accept comes from experience with areas of a borrower's profile that lenders have identified as having an impact on risk. The guidelines are used to limit exposure to higher risk aspects of a profile. While every program guideline has a nuance, they all address these basic elements. The loan officer must understand what these mean.

Criteria	Definition/Explanation
LTV/Occupancy	Owner occupancy (O/O) is the primary driver of risk. If the borrower lives in the property he has more incentive to make the payment than someone who rents the property. Likewise, if the borrower makes substantial cash investment, he or she is less likely to walk away from the property. Program guidelines are more restrictive as to LTV when owner occupancy is not present. 2nd Homes are vacation properties where no rent is used in qualifying the borrower – so may be treated more leniently. Investment property (NOO) is the riskiest Occupancy.

Criteria	Definition/Explanation
Transaction	Purchase Transaction – Risk + - when a borrower is making a cash investment in a purchase transaction, there is a positive risk aspect. In addition, when a property is being purchased, valuation is based on the truest indication of property value – what someone is willing to pay for a property – purchases are less risky.
	Rate/Term R/T (No Cash Out /NCO) Refinance – Risk = - when a borrower refinances to reduce the rate or term of a loan, the new loan is obviously more beneficial to the borrower and, hence, less risky. However, the borrower is likely extracting equity from the property to pay for the refinance, and that tempers the benefit of improved terms. In addition, valuation is based on an appraiser's estimate, so value is subjective. Rate/Term Refinances are risk neutral.
	Cash Out – or Equity Recapture – When a borrower refinances to take equity out of the property, this erodes the equity position and increases the risk. This is compounded by the valuation issue.
Eligible Properties	Property Types affect the risk of the loan. Condos and 2-4 Family (Income) properties are riskier than Single Family Detached (SFD) properties.
Multiple Properties	Many investors limit the number of properties they will finance for one borrower.
Mortgage Insurance	PMI or other mortgage insurance is required for loans with higher LTVs. Investors will specify the limits of coverage required which may be higher for riskier loans.
Assumability	Assumability is a feature that allows a buyer to take over payments on a loan with the lender's permission. Most lenders do not allow this.
Programs Offered	The type of loan programs – fixed, ARM, Balloon, and repayment plans such as Interest Only, buydowns – affect the risk of the loan.
Documentation Types	Full Documentation – Direct Verification of Income/Assets Alternative Documentation – Using Borrower's documentation i.e.; W-2's, Pay stubs, Bank Statements Reduced/Stated/NIV – Borrower States Income – Doesn't verify, Verifies Assets No Documentation – Borrower States Income/Assets Doesn't Verify No Ratio – Borrower Doesn't State Income/Assets – Doesn't Verify
Qualifying Ratios	The Debt Ratios used to qualify borrowers. Ordinarily, debt ratios will not be as important when Automated Underwriting is used.
Employment History	Normally, lenders want a 2 year history to verify stability as well as income.
Trailing Spouse	When a borrower is being relocated by his or her company, the non-relocating borrower is referred to as a "trailing spouse". In some cases this borrower's income can be used to help qualify.
Non-Resident Aliens	Citizenship may be required on certain loan programs, but many lenders now allow non-permanent resident aliens if they have a 2 year work and credit history.
Non-Occupant Co-Borrowers	A co-borrower is a non-occupant if they are buying a property, but will not live in the property. Even though the transaction is considered owner occupied from an occupancy perspective, the borrower who lives in the unit is perceived to be the one who will really be making the payments. They must have to have enough income to support the request individually.
Seller Contributions	The amount that the seller gives to the buyer to help pay for closing costs. Can substantially reduce borrower cash requirements. Excessive contributions can indicate value concessions so are limited by lenders
Cash Reserves	Borrowers cannot divest all their cash for closing and down payment. Lenders require that there are some post closing reserves as a contingency. Normally measured as a number of months of PITI.

Criteria	Definition/Explanation
Gift Letters	Bona-fide gifts that don't have to be repaid are a major source of funds. Verifying that the gift is not expected to be repaid normally means identifying the relationship between the donor and recipient, verifying the source of funds and making sure that the funds actually comes from the source listed and that those funds are deposited into the borrowers account. The risk of a gift is that it must be repaid and the repayments are not counted in the overall debt analysis.
Secondary Financing	2nd mortgages must not cause potential problems for the borrower such as a short balloon, negative amortization.
Borrowed Funds	If they are allowed, they must be counted towards borrower's debts
Credit Scores	FICO credit scores are an indication of a borrower's statistical likelihood of default on unsecured obligations. Because scores are based on statistical models, lenders use scores as another indication of a borrower's desire
Mortgage History	More than overall history, the mortgage payment history is a reflection of the borrower's commitment to maintain residence payments. A borrower who has been unable to do this is a questionable risk for the lender.
Major Derogatory Credit	Judgments, Tax Liens, Major Collection actions, Charge Offs, and Credit Counseling are all indications of current issues that could impair the borrower's ability to make future payments.

Conventional Loans - What is Conforming?

Any loan that is not related to a government agency is considered a conventional loan. Sources of conventional loans can be banks, savings and loans, credit unions, life insurance companies, private lenders, and mortgage bankers. These loans may be held in the institution's portfolio or sold into the secondary market in pools of Mortgage Backed Securities (MBS), Collateralized Mortgage Obligations (CMOs) or Real Estate Mortgage Investment Conduits (REMICs). These conduits have familiar names such as RFC, Ryland, Sears, General Electric, and Prudential, to name a few. Where the loan ends up dictates the guidelines to which it is underwritten and approved.

In 1938, the federal government chartered the **Federal National Mortgage Association (FNMA - known as Fannie Mae)** whose job was to create a secondary market to buy mortgages secured by homes. This action was in response to the banking crisis that brought on the Great Depression. Being able to sell mortgages to FNMA created for banks and would, hopefully, alleviate another crisis. Originally FNMA purchased FHA-insured and VA-guaranteed loans as well as conventional loans. Today, however, the majority of loans FNMA purchases are conventional. FNMA was taken public as a private sector stock corporation in 1968 in tandem with the creation of the **Government National Mortgage Association (GNMA - known as Ginnie Mae).** GNMA took over FNMA's job of being the principal buyer of FHA and VA Loans. The savings and loan crisis of the late 60's and 70's precipitated the need for a secondary market for seasoned loans – a place for struggling thrift institutions to sell their home loan portfolios and gain liquidity. FNMA was not meeting this need prompting congress to charter a competing secondary market corporation - the **Federal Home Loan Mortgage Corporation (FHLMC - known as Freddie Mac)** - to purchase conventional loans. These are private corporations owned by stockholders. Their government charter restricts which loans they may purchase, most notably the maximum loan size. FHLMC and FNMA are regulated by a recently established oversight agency – the **Office of Federal Housing Enterprise Oversight (OFHEO).**

FNMA is the nation's single largest purchaser of mortgages. It stands to reason that FNMA guidelines for loans they will purchase would be the model for all guidelines for all purchasers of mortgages, since theoretically any loan could be resold to FNMA. FHLMC's guidelines, with some exceptions, mirror FNMA's. Today they are referred to generically as "conforming" or "Fannie-Freddie" guidelines.

A loan is referred to as conforming if it meets either FNMA or FHLMC guidelines.

A non-conforming loan can be a loan that is over congresses sanctioned maximum loan amount ($417,000 for 1 unit as of December 1, 2006). This is referred to as a Jumbo Loan. A "Non-conforming" loan doesn't meet specific eligibility criteria for (or conform to) FNMA or FHLMC guidelines. This is not the only criteria that makes a loan non-conforming – any aspect of a borrower's profile that does not meet FNMA's specifications make it ineligible for sale to FNMA. Borrowers should strive to meet "conforming" guidelines because the rates and terms of these loans tend to be the most attractive.

Loan program highlights, guidelines or specifications can vary from company to company so that even a "conforming loan" can have different attributes from lender to lender. FNMA and FHLMC are "quasi-governmental agencies" referred to as government sponsored entities (GSEs). They publish standard guidelines. These guidelines have become a blueprint for underwriting investment quality mortgages that are intended for sale into the secondary market. As a result many specifications for other loan programs intended for sale in the secondary market simply state "Follow FHLMC and FNMA guidelines," and note exceptions. Because of this, FNMA and FHLMC are good places to start understanding guidelines.

Lenders can negotiate special commitments with secondary market investors like FNMA and FHLMC. These commitments can override standard specifications. This is referred to as a "niche." Locating these exceptions and utilizing them can help borrowers who fall outside standard guidelines. FHLMC and FNMA offer specialized programs that address the needs of borrowers with above or below average credit and risk profiles.

	Above Average	Exceptions Allowed	Below Average	Exceptions Allowed
FNMA	"FLEX"	• 90% No Ratio • 90% LTV Investor • 90% LTV Cash Out	Expanded Approval EA I, II, III	• Descending Grade • Late mortgage • Lower scores
FHLMC	"A Plus"	• 100% LTV Purchase • Reduced Documentation	"A Minus"	• One grade • Pricing affected by LTV

Risk is assessed by the use of **automated underwriting (A.U.)** models. While relying on published guidelines, these models define standard acceptable risk and which loans are eligible for purchase. FNMA's model is known as **Desktop Underwriter or "D.U."** FHLMC's A.U. model is based on its Gold Measure manual risk assessment system and is called **Loan Prospector or "L.P."** Because of these advancements it is possible to receive an underwriting approval electronically for a loan application that does not appear to meet standard underwriting guidelines.

Investor	**FNMA/FHLMC - "Generic" Conforming**						
LTV Matrix							
LTV/Occupancy	Owner Occupied		2nd Home	Investor	Property Type	Loan Amount	(AK, HI)
Transaction	LTV	CLTV	LTV	LTV			
Purchase or Rate and Term Refinance	95%	90%	90%	70%	Single Family, Condo	$ 417,000	$ 625,500
	90%	90%	N/A	70%	2 Unit	$ 533,850	$ 800,775
	80%	80%	N/A	70%	3 Unit	$ 645,300	$ 967,950
	80%	80%	N/A	70%	4 Unit	$ 801,950	$ 1,202,925
Cash Out	75%	75%	70%	65%	Single Family, Condo	$ 417,000	$ 625,500
Refinancing	Streamline or Limited Qualifying to 95% LTV if current loan is FNMA Serviced – Over 90% cannot Include Closing Costs or Prepaid Items. Existing 2nd Mortgages must be "seasoned" for 12 Months or payoff is considered "cash out". Limited Cash Out < $2,000 or 2% back to borrower.						
Eligible Properties	Single Family Detached (SFD), Single Family Attached (SFA), 2-4 Unit Residential, Planned Unit Developments (PUDs), Condominium - New PUDs, all condos have eligibility criteria - see *Chapter 8 - Property Types* for Eligibility						
Multiple Properties	Owner Occupied No Limit Investment/2nd - no more than 4 financed						
Mortgage Insurance	Conventional Private Mortgage Insurance required for all owner-occupied properties and second homes with loan to values greater than 80%. In some cases required for investor loans over 70% and, when allowable, 80-10-10 secondary financing.						
Assumability	Conventional loans all have a due-on-transfer clause - this precludes assumption						
Programs Offered	95%	All Occupancy Types		30, 20, 15, 10 Year Fixed			
	95%	Owner/2nd Only		7 & 5 Yr 2 Step, 2-1 Buydown, Interest Only, 3/1, 5/1, 7/1 ARM			
	90%	Owner/2nd Only		1 Year ARM, 7/23 & 5/25,3-2-1 Buydown			
Documentation Types	Full/Alternative - Income Verification may be waived by DU/LP						
Income/Borrower Restrictions							
Qualifying Ratios	95% LTV – 28/36 or DU/LP 75% LTV – 33/38 or DU/LP			ARMs Qualify at 2nd Year Rate Buydowns Qualify at Start Rate			
Employment History	Minimum 2 Years History, 2 Years in same business for Self-Employed						
Trailing Spouse	Corporate Sponsored Relocation Only. 80% LTV Max, 6 Months Reserves, 25-50% of spouse's income may be used if it can be documented that former employment is available in new location.						
Non-Resident Aliens	No restrictions - must have 24-month work, asset and credit history.						
Non-Occupant Co-Borrowers	Max LTV for using non-occupant co-borrower's income for qualifying is 90% LTV. Occupant borrower must still have 38/45 ratios and have 5% of own funds invested.						
Asset Restrictions							
Seller Contributions	95% LTV - 3% 90% LTV - 6% 75% LTV - 8%			Investor - 2%			
Cash Reserves	95% LTV - 3 Months PITI 90% or Less - 2 Months			2 months – May be waived under affordable gold, community homebuyer			
Gift Letters	80.01 - 95% LTV borrower must have 5% of own funds invested into transaction. < 80% LTV - No limit. Source, transfer and receipt must be documented. Donor must be "family" member.						
Secondary Financing	Maximum LTV for 1st Mortgage is 75% (i.e. 75-15-10 is o.k.) 2nd mortgage maturity must be at least 5 years; payments must cover minimum interest. 2nd may not be ARM if 1st is ARM. 1st Mortgage may not be a balloon.						
Borrowed Funds	Must be secured/counted for qualifying						
Credit Restrictions							
Credit Scores	Bureau Scores are applied. With two scores take the average, with three scores take the middle. Scoring regimen is not absolute but follows the following guideline.			Eligible for Enhanced Criteria Cautious Not Eligible for Max Financing		Over 700 660 - 620 below 620	
Mortgage History	0 x 30 days late for last 12 Months						
Major Derogatory Credit	Must have 2 years RE-ESTABLISHED history. Time elapsed since resolution Bankruptcy - Chapter 7 - 4 Years; Chapter 13 - 2 Years; Foreclosure 4 years.						

Investor   **Jumbo - Generic Non-Conforming**

LTV Matrix					
Transaction	LTV	CLTV	Property Type	Maximum Loan	Maximum Financing
Owner Occupied Purchase Rate/Term Refinance	95%	90%	1 Family, Condo	$ 300,000	$ 650,000
	90%	90%	1-2 Family, Condo	$ 400,000	$ 650,000
	80%	90%	1-4 Family, Condo	$ 650,000	$ 650,000
	70%	90%	1 Family, Condo	$ 750,000	$ 750,000
	60%	90%	1 Family, Condo	$ 1,000,000	$ 1,000,000
Owner Occupied Cash Out	75%	75%	1-2 Family, Condo	$ 650,000	$ 650,000
2nd Home Purchase Rate/Term Refinance	90%	90%	1 Family, Condo	$ 300,000	$ 500,000
	80%	90%	1 Family, Condo	$ 400,000	$ 500,000
	75%	90%	1 Family, Condo	$ 500,000	$ 500,000
2nd Home Cash Out Refinance	70%	70%	1 Family, Condo	$ 300,000	$ 300,000
Investor Purchase Rate/Term Refinance	70%	70%	1-4 Family, Condo	$ 300,000	$ 300,000
Programs Offered	30- and 15- Year Fixed Rate				
Buydowns	Allowed. 2-1 and 1-1.				
Eligible Properties	SFD, SFA, PUDs, Condos must meet FNMA Guidelines - Max 4 stories				
Secondary Financing	Maximum LTV for 1st mortgage is 80% (i.e 80-10-10 is o.k.) 2nd mortgage maturity must be at least 5 years; payments must cover minimum interest.				
Refinancing	Up to 95% LTV Over 90% cannot include closing costs or prepaid Items. Existing 2nd mortgages must be "seasoned" for 12 months or payoff is considered "cash out". Amount of cash out is limited. To 75% LTV - Max cash is $50,000; 70% - $100,000; 60% - $200,000				
Private Mortgage Insurance	Required for > 80% LTV. 35% Coverage for 95% LTV; 22% for 90%; 12% for 85%.				
Assumability	No - Conventional loans all have a due on transfer clause.				
Income Restrictions					
Qualifying Ratios	90.01 - 95.00% LTV - 28/36 < 90% - 33/38 Buydowns qualify at start rate				
Documentation Types	Full, Alternative and Reduced Documentation				
	Reduced Documentation LTVs				
	LTV	CLTV	Property Type	Maximum Loan	Maximum Financing
	70%	90%	1 Family, Condo	$ 300,000	$ 650,000
	65%	90%	1 Family, Condo	$ 400,000	$ 650,000
	60%	90%	1 Family, Condo	$ 650,000	$ 650,000
Non-Occupant Co-Borrowers	Max LTV for using non-occupant co-borrower's income for qualifying is 90% LTV. Occupant Borrower must still have 38/45 Ratios and have 5% of own funds invested.				
Self-Employment	Minimum 2 Years - Self-Employed/Commissioned				
Trailing Spouse	Not Allowed				
Asset Restrictions					
Seller Contributions	95% LTV - 3% 90% LTV - 6%		Investor - 2%		
Cash Reserves	95% LTV - 3 months PITI 90% or less - 2 months				
Borrowed Funds	Must be secured. Secured loans must be counted in ratios.				
Gifts	80.01 - 95% LTV borrower must have 5% of own funds invested into transaction. < 80% LTV - no limit. Source, transfer and receipt must be documented. Donor must be "family" member.				
Credit/Borrower Restrictions					
Credit Scores	680 Minimum				
Multiple Properties	Borrower may have no more than 4 properties financed.				
Non-Resident Aliens	Not allowed				
Derogatory Credit	0 x 30 last 24 Months on Mortgage. NO bankruptices, foreclosures or major derogatory credit allowed				

Automated Underwriting – Electronic Decision Engines

	Approved	**Suspended**	**Declined**
Desktop Underwriter – "D.U." – FNMA Conventional Loans, some Jumbo Loans	**Approve – Eligible**: The loan is approved and a live underwriter must simply review required conditions or exhibits.	**Approve – Ineligible**: The loan meets guidelines and receives an approval recommendation, but due to one or more characteristics, a human underwriter must approve it.	**Ineligible**: The loan does not meet A.U. parameters and must be underwritten and approved by a human underwriter.
Loan Prospector – "L.P." – FHLMC Conventional Loans, some Jumbo Loans, FHA and VA Loans	**Accept**: The loan is approved and a live underwriter must simply review required conditions or exhibits.	**Refer**: The loan meets guidelines and receives an approval recommendation, but due to one or more characteristics, a human underwriter must approve it.	**Decline**: The loan is ineligible for sale to FHLMC; must be underwritten to other guidelines by a human.

There are several results you can expect from Desktop Underwriting or Loan Prospector. Besides these two major decision engines, most major lenders have adopted some sort of credit decision engine and have a private label for it. The important issue to note is that if a file does not meet the decision engine's credit guidelines, the loan is then underwritten to more rigorous "manual" underwriting guidelines as set forth in these pages.

Simple Troubleshooting Strategies

A common error made by new loan officers is to rely on the initial approval from the engine as a "firm" approval. The approval really is still subject to underwriter review of the underlying documentation. Ordering a full appraisal instead of a limited appraisal prior to receiving findings can result in adverse underwriting of the appraisal. Appraisals may be waived by the engines, and getting a full appraisal can cause additional conditions and potentially a declination.

Variance Tolerance

An unexpected problem in the underwriting submission flip-flop occurs when the underwriter validates data. If there are significant changes in the information between what was used to derive the initial approval – initially submitted data – and the final verified information, the loan findings can change because of

Post Submission Variance Tolerance in D.U.	
	Tolerance
Debt Ratio Increase	< 2%
Income Decrease	< 5%

increased risk ratings. DU is sensitive to undisclosed or improperly disclosed information. There is a stated tolerance for changes, and care should be taken in loan submission to insure that debts are not understated and income is not overstated.

When an adverse decision is received from one of the engines, the common approach is to re-submit the request to another approval engine hoping for a more favorable outcome. For example a loan officer may submit to Desktop Underwriter and receive a decline. To attempt to solve the problem, the loan is submitted to Loan Prospector in order to reverse the decision. To avoid additional charges enter the LP Key number for each subsequent submission ($20 each). LP allows credit reports from any source – even DU, or a third party. Prior to simply submitting it to an alternative engine, analyze the findings first. Evaluate whether the initial information input to the system was correct, and resubmit before seeking alternative approvals.

DU or LP?

Guideline	DU or LP	Description
Condominium Warranty	LP	Less restrictive guidelines
Condominium Documentation	DU	Condo limited review option can generate new business (high investor condo projects).
Non-Occupant Co-Borrower	LP	Allow occupant borrower more flexibility
Multiple Properties	LP	No maximum number for owner occupied/stated debts for A Plus
Low Credit Score, Good Trades	DU	DU evaluates balanced debts to evaluate risk. Slow accounts a problem.
High Credit Score, Poor Trades	LP	LP evaluates FICO score to assess risk. Slow accounts may be acceptable.
Expanded Approval - A-	DU	More aggressive A- offering through DU - EA 1, 2, 3
Bankruptcy	DU	Bankruptcy & Foreclosure guidelines allow loans to be originated 24 months from the file date (lower LTV and strong reserves could generate approvals).
High Reserves	DU	Adding at least 2 mos. PITI reserves can positively impact risk analysis. Investor - need 2 mos PITI on 1 Unit (6 Mo. DU 2 - 4 Unit, LP 1-4 Unit)
Low Reserves	LP	Use cash out funds as reserves. DU Lack of reserves (cash out refinances) can result in adverse findings
Debt Ratios to 65%	DU	Enter all liquid assets, including 401k, retirement accounts - 70% of balance.
Debt Ratios over 65%	LP	Lower LTV's - very high total expense ratios.
High Debts	LP	AcceptPlus - no leases or tax returns. Use stated debts.
Multiple Investment Properties	DU	Qualify "new" borrowers purchasing or refinancing investment property with the total PIT1 (subject net cash flow);with approve eligible this overrides the 2 yr. management, history rule and avoids rent/loss insurance.
Second Homes Multiple Propertie	LP	No limit on number of financed properties on second home.
Cash Out used for Reserves	LP	Enter the cash out amount as reserves in LP - reduced risk.
Unseasoned Lot Value	LP	Permanent or Construction Permanent
Elderly Parent/Disabled Child	DU	Children purchasing a home for elderly parents or parents purchasing a home for a disabled child.
Seller Contributions	LP	On 1st & 2nd Combo DU uses CLTV; L.P. still uses LTV.
Self-employed	DU	Self-employed - one year history with 6 months of income on filed tax returns. LP - if self-employed borrower receives Accept Plus, period of self employment not considered.
Commissioned/Variable	LP	Contractor w < 25% ownership of business NOT considered self employed.
Commissioned/Variable	DU	Contractors, Commissioned - < 2 Year History may only need 6 months of income on filed tax returns. Bonus & Overtime average by 12 mos, not 24
Source of Funds	DU	Use FLEX guidelines allowing unsecured loans from acceptable sources when a gift is not an option.
Boarder Income - Community	DU	Rental income from boarders is allowed on CHP loans.
HELOC/2nds	DU	Re-subordinate - use current balance, not max line, to compute LTV
Reduced Doc		$1 of income with strong borrowers; accept plus allows stated income/debt approvals
Shorter Term Loans	LP	25 or 20 year Term Lower Risk. DU does not consider.

Common Problems with AU (Automated Underwriting)

Most often a loan is declined or referred by A.U. due to input error; name and address mistakes, incorrect calculation of total debts; underwriting discrepancies, un-reconciled liabilities between credit report and submission, mortgages/HELOC's incorrectly coded, "stale" mortgages not omitted, HELOC's not "paid at closing", student loans without a payment (use 1% if deferred), active debts without a payment amount, collections and 30 day accounts without paid in full balance, "closed" accounts with an active balance not included, duplicate debts, auto lease payments excluded, undisclosed debts from the 1003 like alimony/child support, or private mortgages, amounts entered for liens, mortgage balances and debts to be paid off do not match the credit report, "free and clear" property without taxes/insurance.

"Generic Jumbo" Non-Conforming

There is a wide array of non-conforming loans - also referred to as "Jumbo." The basic Jumbo program guideline (shown here as "Generic Non-Conforming") is similar to conforming, but the loan limits are higher. These guidelines will vary from lender to lender. These "generic" guidelines are the most prevalent because every lender can sell loans that meet them into any collateralized mortgage obligation (CMO).

Other First Time Homebuyer Programs

The impetus for large financial institutions to participate in first time homebuyer programs has been huge. In this litigious society no bank, savings and loan, Mortgage Company, or other financial institution wants to have a record of discriminating against lower-income borrowers. Penalties for discrimination are quite severe, and may cause difficulty in regulatory approval for future consolidations or mergers. As a result, there has been a proliferation of first time homebuyer/affordable housing programs offered by the secondary market, mortgage insurers and private institutions. While some may offer below market rates, most of these programs offer

Institution	Program Enhancements/Incentives Offered Above Standard Guidelines
FNMA Community Homebuyer Program	Down Payment Options • Based on targeted SMSA • 3/2 Option allows 3% down payment and 2% gift, grant or loan from a non-profit institution. Limited to households within central cities or those which fall within 100% of median family income (SMSA) • 5% down with family income within 115% of median income in SMSA. • 97% LTV/3% down payment. • 100% LTV/0% down payment • Reserves may be waived. • 33/38 qualifying ratios.
FHLMC Affordable Gold	Same as FNMA Community Homebuyer except • 40/40 Qualifying ratios • 97% LTV with lower PMI Coverage • 100% LTV with lower PMI Coverage
Community Lending Guidelines	Under FSLIC/FDIC/FIRREA Guidelines, certain savings banks can make "community" loans on non-discounted (non-teaser rate) loans: • 95-5-0 (no money down) transactions with 5% coming from unsecured, or borrowed funds • 5% down transactions with 5% seller contribution • Limited down payment

relaxed guidelines for first time homebuyers instead of rate or other incentives.

FNMA's introduction of so-called "FLEX" guidelines, which offer lower down payments, reduced qualifying criteria, and reduced PMI costs, have eroded the excitement that these "Community Homebuyer" programs created. However, for the loan officer, the ability to offer the first time homebuyer training program as a value added service for referral sources, while still meeting the requirements of the community homebuyer loan program, can increase the borrower's choices.

Private Mortgage Insurance (PMI)

Private Mortgage Insurance protects lenders against actual losses in the event of default and is required when the proposed down payment is lower than allowed by guideline. Borrowers pay for the mortgage insurance as an inducement for a lender to approve a loan with a smaller down payment. A number of private mortgage insurance companies (MI's) entered the market to insure loans in the early 70's as a cost effective alternative to the Government's mortgage insurance program administered by FHA. Before PMI it was difficult to induce conventional lenders to make loans in excess of 80% loan to value. It has made this country's real estate market much more dynamic.

Until the early 80's obtaining mortgage insurance was a "rubber stamp" formality. But the prevailing dire economic conditions - hyperinflation, the oil belt's demise, and the end of rampant real estate speculation - caused the insurers to lose money. High interest rates, negative amortization and uncapped ARMs took their toll on portfolios and default rates skyrocketed. Insurers had relied on lenders to make prudent underwriting decisions and had issued insurance certificates more or less in concurrence with the lenders approval. Since it is the MI who pays the preponderance of the loss in the event of default, their only recourse was to begin to diligently review and approve each submission independent of lender review. The result is that there is a second "matrix" of guidelines that a Non-Government insured loan must meet before it can be fully approved.

Meet the Insurers

Each geographic area has its dominant PMI companies. Most people are only aware of 5 or 6 Mortgage Insurance Companies (MI). There are many MI companies and this contributes to the complexity of matching a loan to the appropriate MI for the underwriting. It adds to diversity and the ability to place loans with different MIs for different reasons.

> **Top Private Mortage Insurance Companies**
>
> Genworth (Formerly GE)
> United Guaranty Insurance Company (UGI)
> Mortgage Guaranty Insurance Corp. (MGIC)
> Radian Guaranty
> Republic Mortgage Insurance Company (RMIC)
> Triad Guaranty Insurance
> CMG Insurance Group (Credit Union)

Mortgage Insurance Coverage Requirements

It is a common belief that PMI covers the amount of the mortgage above 80% loan to value because that is the level over which PMI is generally required. This is not the case. Depending on the risk, a lender may require "deeper" coverage. For instance FNMA requires basic coverage which reduces its exposure (the

Calculating Mortgage Insurance Coverage Requirements		
Sales Price	$	100,000
Down Payment	5% $	5,000
a.) LTV/Loan Amount	95% $	95,000
b.) Exposure Allowed	75% $	75,000
c.) % of Loan Insured/Coverage (c/b)	0.21 $	20,000

amount of the loan that the lender is liable for in a loss) to 70% LTV. Coverage requirements vary substantially. The best source of information is a PMI representative. While lenders traditionally are responsible for obtaining mortgage insurance coverage, brokers should be aware of the guidelines and may also direct the placement of PMI.

Mortgage Insurance Premium Plans

Mortgage Insurance Premium Plans

PLAN TYPE	Standard Coverages		1st Year Rate			Renewal Rate Years 2-10		
Traditional Plan where a lump sum premium is paid to cover year 1. Subsequent Renewals are at a lower rate	Coverage	LTV	30Fix	ARM	ARMI	30Fix	ARM	ARMI
	30%	95%	1.5	1.55	1.75	0.49	0.54	0.54
	25%	90%	0.65	0.65	0.75	0.34	0.44	0.44
	12%	85%	0.29	0.3	0.34	0.29	0.3	0.34
Monthly Plan where each month is paid as it is accrued. True pay as you go. Ensures lower escrow and closing costs.	35%	97%	1.04	N/A	N/A	1.04	N/A	N/A
	30%	95%	0.78	0.85	0.89	0.78	0.85	0.89
	25%	90%	0.52	0.58	0.62	0.52	0.58	0.62
	12%	85%	0.29	0.3	0.34	0.29	0.3	0.34
One Time Premium - may be paid in cash or financed on top of loan amount if LTV's are not exceeded.	Coverage	LTV	One Time Premiums - Cash			Financed One Time Premiums		
	25%	90%	2.5	2.85	3.15	2.85	3.25	3.6
	12%	85%	1.5	1.6	1.65	2.15	2.35	2.5
Lender Paid Mortgage Insurance - Increased interest rate pays for PMI instead of borrower.	LTV		30 Year Fixed		15 Year Fixed		ARMs	
	95%		0.875%		0.625%		1.250%	
	90%		0.625%		0.375%		0.750%	
	85%		0.375%		0.250%		0.500%	

Notes: These premiums are representative of current plans available. Terms may vary from state to state. Lower premiums are available for shorter term loans such as 25- or 15-Year Loans. Where applicable, all premiums shown are non-refundable. Refundable premiums may be available, but are generally at a higher rate.

Mortgage insurers, just like other insurance companies, are regulated by individual states for consumer protection purposes. Premiums charged cannot change without the insurer filing for a rate change within a state. In addition, premiums charged are reviewed against loss experiences for uncompetitive or predatory pricing practices. As a result, PMI premiums are remarkably similar from MI to MI. One distinction is that certain companies may discount their premiums to lenders whose loss experience is minimal or exemplary. Although the homebuyer doesn't normally get to participate in the decision of to which company the mortgage insurance application should be sent, they should have the opportunity to review all of the premium plans available.

Choosing the Right Plan - Premium Plan Options
The borrower must choose a plan that suits his needs in the same way he chooses a loan plan. The ***"traditional" premium plan*** has existed in its original form since the inception of PMI.

There is an initial premium that is generally higher than the renewal premium. This reflects the fact that most defaults occur within the first year of the loan. The insurer collects premiums annually from the lender, but the lender collects 1/12 of the renewal premium monthly from the borrower and holds it in escrow until due. Until recently there were no other choices.

In 1992, ***"One Time", or single premium, plans*** were offered as an alternative to large up front premiums with monthly renewals. In a single premium plan, the premium may be paid in cash or financed - similar to the FHA MIP. One advantage of this plan is that, if the premium is added to the base loan amount - or financed - the additional interest may be tax deductible, whereas PMI is not. The monthly payments are devoted to Principal and Interest instead of PMI which means that the more competitive the rate, the more affordable premium financing is. A financed premium may result in a lower payment that could enhance qualifying. If the payment is made in cash there is a definite monthly payment savings.

Beginning in 1993, ***Monthly Premium Plans,*** where the insurer collects monthly payments from the lender in lieu of the annual escrow plan, were offered as an additional option. ***Benefits:*** There is no up front, or initial, premium payment, making cash requirements far lighter than earlier plans. This is the only plan that works in conjunction with the higher LTV programs. The premiums are level throughout the life of the loan, which could result in higher payments over time than the "classic" plan.

The most recent innovation is ***"Lender Paid MI" (LPMI)*** where the lender increases the interest rate, but waives collection of premiums. ***Benefits:*** The higher interest payment is tax deductible where PMI is not. A shortcoming is that, while you can petition a lender to cancel PMI, Lender Paid MI means the borrower will pay the higher interest rate for the life of the loan.

Comparing PMI Plans

			Traditional	Single Financed	Monthly	LPMI
Home Price		$ 200,000				
Downpayment		10.00%				
Base Loan Amount		$ 180,000				
Premium			0.65%	2.85%	0.52%	0.625%
Total Loan			$ 180,000	$ 185,130	$ 180,000	$ 180,000
Premium at Closing			$ 1,170.00	$ -	$ 156.00	$ -
Principal and Interest	7.50%		$ 1,258.59	$ 1,294.46	$ 1,258.59	$ 1,336.49
PMI Renewal Escrow	0.34%		$ 51.00	$ -	$ 78.00	$ -
Monthly Payment			$ 1,309.59	$ 1,294.46	$ 1,336.59	$ 1,336.49
Tax Benefits at	28%		$ -	$ 10.04	$ -	$ 21.81
Net Cost			$ 1,309.59	$ 1,284.41	$ 1,336.59	$ 1,314.68

To calculate the mortgage insurance premiums multiply the loan amount by the premium. If the premium is an annual plan, divide the result by 12 months for the premium to be collected monthly. If the premium is a one-time payment, multiply the loan amount by the premium, and if the premium is

PMI Premium Calculation

Loan Amount	$	250,000
Multiply by Premium Rate		0.52%
Premium	$	1,300.00
Divide by 12 for Monthly	$	108.33

to be financed instead of paid in cash, add it to the loan amount.

PMI Underwriting Guidelines

Because MI underwriting is "risk-based," as opposed to underwriting for loan salability or "secondary marketing," it can be subjective. As a result any restrictive guideline set forth may be overridden by compensating factors, depending on the insurer's risk experience with a specific profile.

HPA and PMI Cancellation

Independent of the individual lender's guidelines or property value, The Homeowner's Protection Act (HPA) of 1998 provided for mortgage insurance cancellation once a property achieved these benchmarks.

Guidelines for Canceling PMI
The decision to allow a mortgage insurance contract to be cancelled rests with the servicing lender. However, a borrower may petition to cancel PMI if the following conditions are present: • PMI has been in force > 24 Mos. • LTV is 80% with Principal Reduction • LTV is 75% with Appreciation • Still Owner Occupied • No Late Payments in 24 mos.

- Loan balance has declined so that LTV is 78% of original sales price/value or
- Loan has reached the chronological "mid-point" such as 180 months into a 30 year loan and
- There are no 30 day late payments in the last 12 months or 60 day late payments in the last 24 months

Although VA and FHA loans are not covered by the law, the guidelines for FHA mortgage insurance have been changed to meet the law. Any loan other than conforming is considered a "high risk" loan – including jumbo or other non-conforming loans – and the LTV must be 77% for PMI cancellation.

The Federal Housing Administration (FHA)

The FHA program, as it is referred to, is not a loan program at all, but an insurance program implemented by the government in 1934 to encourage banks to make home loans after the depression. FHA insurance completely protects lenders against potential default. Applicants pay for the insurance through monthly and lump sum mortgage insurance premium plans (MIP). Although banks, savings and loans and other private lenders could utilize this insurance for their own holdings, most FHA loans are sold into the secondary market in GNMA (Government National Mortgage Association) pools. Many tax exempt revenue bond issue loan programs for first-time home buyers will also utilize FHA insurance as well as Private Mortgage Insurance (PMI).

The FHA insurance program bears all the idiosyncrasies of any politically motivated program. Loan amounts and guidelines vary from region to region (See https://entp.hud.gov/idapp/html/hicostlook.cfm). The program is continually changed at a moment's notice contingent upon major loss experiences or scandals throughout the industry (normally existing approvals/commitments are exempted from changes). Underwriting

Insurer - Guarantor   **Federal Housing Administration (FHA)**

LTV Matrix							
Transaction	Owner Occupied LTV	CLTV	2nd Home LTV	Investor LTV	Property Type	Loan Amount	High Cost (87% of FNMA)
Purchase or Rate and Term Refinance	97.75% Low Closing Cost States		N/A	N/A	Single Family, Condo	$ 200,160	$ 362,790
	98.75% High Closing Costs States (<$50,000) * See below		N/A	N/A	2 Unit	$ 256,248	$ 464,449
			N/A	N/A	3 Unit	$ 309,744	$ 561,411
			N/A	N/A	4 Unit	$ 384,936	$ 697,696
Cash Out	95% DU (85%)	N/A	N/A	N/A	SFD, Condo	$ 200,160	$ 362,790
Programs Offered	30-, 20-, 15-, 10- Year fixed (Sections 203b & 234c). 1-Year ARM with 1/5 caps, 3/1 and 5/1 ARM (Sec 251), Rehabilitation/Construction Permanent loan (Section 203k).						

Assumability	Mortgage Origination Date	Assumability Feature
	prior to 12/1/1986	Fully Assumable for $125
	12/1/86 - 12/14/89	Investors must put 25% down
	12/15/89 - present	$500

Mortgage Insurance	Loan Term	Upfont MIP	Monthly Premiums Based LTV		
			90% or Less	90.01 - 95%	over 95%
	30-Year	1.5	None	.5% to 78% LTV	
	15-Year	1.5		.25 to 78%	.25% to 78%

Automated Approval	Yes - "Total Scorecard" / DU/LP
Refinancing	Streamline Refinance - With 12-month mortgage payment history and payment reduction, borrowers do not requalify. No income/asset documentation is required. Loan amount can only be increased for closing costs with new appraisal.
Eligible Properties	SFD, 2-4, Condo, PUD - Condo & PUD Units must be approved https://entp.hud.gov/idapp/html/condlook.cfm

Income Restrictions	
Qualifying Ratios	31/43 ARMs and buydowns qualify at 2nd Year rate if LTV is greater than 95%. Or TOTAL Scorecard, DU or LP.
Documentation Types	FULL and alternative documentation
Non-Occupant Co-Borrowers	No Restrictions - May not be used for qualifying on 2-4 family properties
Self-Employment	Minimum 2 years, recommend 5 Years
Trailing Spouse	Not considered. CAUTION - may only have one FHA insured loan.
Secondary Financing	Discouraged by program because 1.) must still make required down payment 2.) cannot exceed statutory sales price/mortgage and 3.) does not remove mortgage insurance. May use with bond financing

Asset Restrictions	
Cash Reserves	15-days interest.
Gift Letters	Acceptable from any source. FHA "prefers" buyer has 25% of own cash. Donor may borrow (secured) funds for downpayment. Must still verify gift, transfer and receipt of funds.
Seller Contributions	6% of Sales Price, including discount, buydowns and prepaid items.
Required Contribution	Borrower MUST invest 3% cash in transaction, including closing costs or downpayment. If borrower does not have 3% invested, loan amount is reduced.
Borrowed Funds	Must be secured/counted for qualifying.

Credit/Borrower Restrictions	
Credit Scores	Not considered.
Multiple Properties	ONLY ONE PROPERTY WITH minimum down payment.
Non-Resident Aliens	No restrictions
Major Derogatory Credit	Significant derogatory credit may be tolerated with documented extenuating circumstances. Bankruptcy Chapter 7 - 3 Years from discharge; Chapter 13 - 1 Year from discharge. Foreclosure - 3 Years from discharge.

*97.65 percent: For properties with values/sales prices in excess of $50,000 up to $125,000. 97.15 percent: For properties with values/sales prices in excess of $125,000. Borrower must make a 3% down payment regardless of LTV. Loan amounts vary from jurisdiction. AK, HI and territories can be up to 150% of the high cost limits. See https://entp.hud.gov/idapp/html/hicostlook.cfm for current list.

guidelines are highly subjective, with much emphasis placed on helping first time or otherwise disadvantaged buyers. Maximum Loan Amounts are designated as 87% of the conforming loan amount maximum for high cost areas, but are varied from jurisdiction to jurisdiction as determined by the area or field office.

FHA has eliminated the confusing acquisition cost formula (through 12/03) in lieu of standard LTV calculations. As a result, borrowers can make a minimum 3% investment into the transaction or 2.25% down with a minimum .75% contribution to closing costs.

The Direct Endorsement Program (DE)

DE allows approved FHA lenders delegated authority to commit FHA insurance. This speeds the loan process and takes the approval authority out of the government's hands. This also allows lenders to utilize staff appraisers instead of appraisers from FHA's approved list. DE means that, in addition to approving a borrower, the lender is also approving the property. The Substantial Rehabilitation (203(k)) program is not authorized for DE in most regions.

FHA Mortgage Insurance Premiums

FHA is motivated and influenced by the politics of government. Current government insurance rate premiums reflect this. The history is emblematic. When the Single-Family Housing program was enacted by congress under the National Housing Act (the Act), it fell under section 203(b). The insurance provided by this program was paid for through monthly payments by borrowers. In 1973, the Act was amended to allow for insurance for condominiums, since condos were becoming a popular form of property ownership in the urban areas of the country. This section of the Act was called 234 (c).

In 1981, as part of the Reagan Revolution, the Act was changed to require a one time up front premium instead of a monthly premium for FHA insurance. This was good for the government because it got all the cash up front. Borrowers, however, paid the premiums by financing them into their loans. That is, the lenders lent them the money to pay for the insurance on top of the money they needed to buy their house.

Loan Term	Up Front MIP	95% and Over	90%-95%	Below 90%
30 Year	1.50%	.50% - to 78% LTV	.50% - to 78% LTV	.50% - to 78% LTV
15 Year	1.50%	.25% - to 78% LTV	.25% - to 78% LTV	None

Reminder:
- Condominiums and 203(k) loans have up front premium effective 5/2005
- One time MIP still applies to Single Family Refinances of Insurance contracts Originated prior to 4/1/92
- FHA's monthly insurance is a "declining balance" contract, which means the premiums decrease monthly as the loan balance decreases. Monthly premiums are calculated on the amortized balance.

Certain sections of the Act were not affected by the mortgage insurance premium changes - because legislators overlooked them. A simple oversight during this overhaul - that other federal insurance was covered under different acts - meant that 234 (c) and all the other federally insured loan programs were not changed. The result is that single family loans have one insurance schedule while condos (234(c)), substantial rehab (203(k)), coinsurance (223(b)), land development (221(d)), etc., while single family has another. New insurance plans show now that there is a combination of up-front and monthly premiums. However, for the first time there is an incentive to put more that than the least amount of money down.

The FHA Maximum Loan Amount Based on LTV

In 2000, FHA simplified the calculation of the maximum mortgage amount, changing it from an acquisition cost formula to a straight LTV formula. The design of the acquisition cost formula was to ensure that costs associated with the transaction – which vary from jurisdiction to jurisdiction – were considered in determining the amount of high leverage financing could be provided.   As recognition that closing costs are relatively static (the costs of a $50,000 transaction are similar to a $200,000 transaction), FHA tiered loan to values, giving more leverage for smaller transactions. In addition, areas that levied taxes in association with a transaction were considered to be "high cost" – consequently higher-cost areas were accorded more leverage (higher LTVs).

Closing Costs and LTV's		
Low Closing Costs States		High Closing Cost States
Arizona, California, Colorado, Guam, Idaho, Illinois, Indiana, New Mexico, Nevada, Oregon, Utah, Virgin Islands, Washington, Wisconsin, Wyoming		All Others
98.75% if < $50,000 97.65% if $50,000 - $125,000 97.15% if > $125,000		98.75% if < $50,000 97.75% if > $50,000

The FHA Maximum Loan Amount – Borrower's Cash Investment

Calculating the Buyer's Minimum Cash Investment

Sales Price		$	175,000.00
Required investment	3.00%	$	5,250.00
Downpayment investment	2.25%	$	3,937.50
A. Mandatory Investment/Buyer Costs	0.75%	$	1,312.50
Total Closing Costs		$	3,850.00
Seller Paid Closing Costs		$	(2,500.00)
B. Buyer's Portion *		$	1,350.00

*B must EXCEED A - If a negative number reduce base loan amount by this amount $ 37.50

FHA Mortgage Amount Calculator available as a tool with Loan Officer's Practical Guide to Marketing.

While the LTV formula for the maximum loan is the same as for any conventional loan, the borrower is required to make an equity contribution of at least 3% of the sales price towards down payment AND closing costs. This is problematic only when the seller contributes so much towards the buyer's cost that buyer's minimum investment is not met. To avoid pitfalls in this regard, before calculating the maximum base loan amount, insure the borrower has made the minimum investment.

Financing Mortgage Insurance

The FHA Mortgage Insurance Program allows the initial Up Front Mortgage Insurance Premium (UFMIP) to be financed in addition to the base loan amount. Once the base loan amount has been determined, the UFMIP is added to determine the total loan amount.

Financing the UFMIP	
Base Loan Amount	$ 130,000.00
Multiply by UFMIP %	1.50%
Total UFMIP	$ 1,950.00
Loan Amount with MIP Financed	$ 131,950.00

Refund of MIP

Until 2005, FHA allowed refunds of FHA MIP depending on how long the loan had been in place. Now, MIP refunds are only available on FHA to FHA refinances, and are calculated based on the following table.

Upfront Mortgage Insurance Premium Refund Percentages

Year	Month of Year											
	1	2	3	4	5	6	7	8	9	10	11	12
1	80	78	76	74	72	70	68	66	64	62	60	58
2	56	54	52	50	48	46	44	42	40	38	36	34
3	32	30	28	26	24	22	20	18	16	14	12	10

The Refinance Conundrum

There is a puzzle which has daunted loan officers, processors and underwriters alike: When you refinance a FHA-insured loan, there is a refund of the unused portion of

Refinance Mortgage Amount Calculation				
Value			$	125,000
Multiply By LTV				97.75%
Unpaid Principal Balance	$	119,000	$	122,188
Plus Costs*	$	2,500	$	2,500
Less UFMIP Refund	$	(1,904)	$	(1,904)
Maximum Base Loan	$	119,596	$	122,784
*Points, Prepaids, Interim Interest can be financed up to original balance without new appraisal				

insurance. If you are financing the upfront portion, how do you account for the premium in a refinance transaction without "over-financing"? This question is amplified by the ability of FHA borrowers to "Streamline" refinance – reduce the rate without re-qualifying. As a result, to properly calculate the refinance mortgage amount, you must account for and "net out" the amount of MIP refund the borrower would receive. So instead of financing an entire new MIP, the borrower only finances the additional MIP due.

FHA Nuances/Trivia

We used to play a game called Government Loan Trivia. It is ongoing and describes things one can do or are limited by with FHA Financing. Here is an ongoing list.

1.   FHA Veteran (203(b)) Veteran

Compensating Factors for exceeding standard ratios
• Three months reserves - limited debts
• 10% down
• Less than 10% housing payment increase
• Outside income not counted in effective income
• Non-Taxable income
• Temporary/Seasonal Income
• Shorter Mortgage Term by 5 years
• Smaller Family - higher residual income
• Energy Efficient Dwelling 2% Ratio increase
• 25% or more down payment - Ratios not considered important

may have a down payment of up to $750 less than standard borrower.
2.   FHA 203(k) Rehabilitation Mortgage - A construction permanent program wherein an existing 1-4 family owner occupied can be completely renovated according to plans and specs approved by FHA.
3.   You can "Streamline Refinance" an investment property.

The Department of Veteran's Affairs (VA)

VA acts as a guarantor and, in effect, co-signs loans for eligible veterans. The program inception in 1944 was designed to help veterans returning from WWII finance a home purchase with no resources aside from income. (The Act authorizing the program is called the Servicemen's Readjustment Act of 1944) The government guarantees it will pay back the guaranteed portion of a loan on which an eligible veteran defaults.

With mounting losses in the late eighties, due to defaults, congress implemented a formula that VA utilizes to determine how it resolves defaulted loans. VA may buy the house from the lender at foreclosure - for the balance outstanding - and assume the responsibility of disposing of it. Or they may simply pay the lender the amount of the guaranty in cash, at which point the lender is forced to dispose of the property - which is referred to as a "No Bid." The potential of a loss to the lender is much greater since the adoption of the "No Bid" policy and as a result lenders have taken steps to offset this risk. These include charging higher points for VA loans and instituting more conservative underwriting standards than VA itself promulgates.

VA No Bids aside, the VA Guaranty Program still offers the most aggressive lending guidelines available. This is because it is an employee benefit program for veterans and active service people. The philosophy is "let's get the Veteran in the home."

Entitlement and the Maximum Loan Amount

The VA Guaranty program is a kind of employee benefit program. The idea is to help veterans buy homes so that, theoretically, the VA is the veteran's co-borrower. The question is "how much is guaranteed"? Each eligible veteran is given a "loan guaranty entitlement." The amount of this benefit has increased with time as home prices have increased. The trick is that the entitlement is never exhausted. It may be utilized to guaranty a loan on a veteran's home, but as soon as that home is sold and the loan is paid off the veteran has that portion of entitlement back to use again. This is important because of the issue of partial entitlement and the potential for a

A History of Loan Guaranty Entitlement		
1944 - World War II - Inception	$	4,000
After 7/12/50 Increased to	$	7,500
After 5/7/68 Increased to	$	12,500
After 10/2/78 Increased to	$	25,000
After 10/1/80 Increased to	$	27,500
After 2/1/88 Increased to	$	36,000
Increased 12/18/89 for veterans with full entitlement and for purchases over $144,000	$	46,000
Increased 10/13/94 – basic remains at $36,000	$	50,750
Increased 12/01 – basic remains at $36,000	$	60,000
Increased 12/04 - 25% of FHLMC	$	89,913
Increased 12/05 - 25% of FHLMC	$	104,250

veteran to have remaining entitlement even though they may still have a previous home loan guaranteed by the VA. The only way to restore eligibility is to sell the home or have the loan assumed by an eligible veteran who substitutes their eligibility for the original veteran.

Insurer/Guarantor Department of Veterans Affairs

LTV Matrix							
Transaction	Owner Occupied LTV	Owner Occupied CLTV	2nd Home LTV	Investor LTV	Property Type	Loan Amount at 100%	Hawaii, Alaska
Purchase or Rate and Term Refinance	100%		N/A	N/A	Single Family, Condo, 2-4 Family	$ 417,000	$ 625,500
Cash Out	90%		N/A	N/A	Single Family, Condo	$ 417,000	$ 625,500
Refinancing	Streamline Refinance - With 12-month mortgage payment history and payment reduction, borrowers do not requalify. Loan amount can only be increased for closing costs with new appraisal.						
Programs Offered	10 - 30-Year Fixed Rate.						
Mortgage Insurance	VA Funding Fee is in lieu of Insurance. See "Risk-Based" Premium Charts						
Eligible Properties	SFD, 2-4, Condo, PUD - Condo & PUD Units must be approved						
Eligible Borrowers	Servicemen with documented eligibility have at least the following active duty: **90 Days** WWII 9/16/40-7/25/47 Korea 6/27/50-1/31/55 Vietnam 8/05/64-5/7/75 **181 Days** Pre-Korea 7/26/47-6/26/50 Post-Korea 2/1/55-8/4/64 Post-Vietnam 5/8/75 to for Enlisted 9/7/1980 for Officers 10/16/1981 **24 Months** Current Active Duty after 9/7/80 for Enlisted after 10/16/81 for Officers 6 Years Reservists/National Guard Members (Expires 10/99) Also Eligible NOAA Officers; Commissioned Public Health Officers; ESSA Officers; C&G Survey Officers; Veterans discharged prior to eligibility due to service-related disability; surviving spouse of veteran who died as a result of service related injury or disease. **Veterans and their Spouses.** Eligible Veterans have served continuous active duty for at least the time frames listed and have an honorable release or discharge.						
Secondary Financing	Allowed. Note must be at least 5 years in length. Since VA is no money down formula, 2nd mortgage would only be used to exceed the maximum financing of $240,000/$359,650						
Automated Approval	Loan Prospector						
Assumability	$500 Fee and the Borrower must Qualify. No Release of Liability.						
Income Restrictions							
Qualifying Ratios	41/41						
Documentation Types	Full, Alternative Documentation						
Trailing Spouse	Not Considered - Veterans regularly relocate						
Non-Occupant Co-Borrowers	Veterans and their Spouses ONLY. Eligible Veterans have served continuous active duty for at least the time frames listed and have an honorable release or discharge.						
Self-Employment	Minimum 2 Years - Recommend 5 Years						
Asset Restrictions							
Seller Contributions	4% of sales price, not including points. Transaction may be structured so that borrower pays no money at closing, but borrower may not receive cash back at closing.						
Cash Reserves	None Required						
Gift Letters	May come from any source not involved in transaction. Must verify donor, transfer and receipt of gift funds.						
Borrowed Funds	Funds may be borrowed - must be counted for qualifying.						
Credit Restrictions							
Multiple Properties	Number of VA Loans is limited by entitlement.						
Credit Scores	Not considered.						
Major Derogatory	Significant Derogatory Credit may be acceptable with extenuating circumstances.						

The Maximum VA Insurable Loan

The amount of available entitlement a veteran has is important because it determines the LTV or the maximum loan for a property. GNMA requires that its exposure be limited to 75% LTV.

VA Loan Amount Calculation	Example 1: Full Entitlement	Example 2: Partial Entitlement $22,000
Sales Price X 75% + Eligibility = Base Loan Amount Plus Funding Fee = Loan Amount with Funding Fee.	Sales Price $200,000 x 75% =150,000 Eligibility + 60,000 Base Loan $200,000 = Downpayment 0 Note: Even though not all entitlement is used, the maximum LTV is still 100%	Sales Price $100,000 x 75% = 75,000 Eligibility + 22,500 Base Loan $ 97,500 = Downpayment 2,500 Note: Even though the VA Program is 100% Financing this is limited by Eligibility

There are some limitations to the use of loan guaranty eligibility: 1.) Entitlement remains tied to the property it was used to purchase, so cannot be restored until the property is sold. 2.) In high cost areas, the veteran may only use the high cost eligibility (over $36,000) with full entitlement.

This means that the "top" 25% (or riskiest) portion of the sales price must be guaranteed or paid

in cash in order for the loan to be eligible for sale. To determine a veteran's maximum loan, start with the sales price and multiply by the maximum exposure tolerated (75%). Then add the available entitlement to determine the minimum down payment requirement.

The amount of entitlement a veteran has is determined by obtaining a Certificate of Eligibility from the Regional VA Office. It is a little green form - a certificate - that states the amount of entitlement available for loan guaranty. The Veteran MUST have this original form to close on a new VA loan.

The Funding Fee

The VA Funding Fee is not an insurance premium but a one-time charge. It is tantamount to a user fee. VA allows the funding fee to be financed, or added to the base maximum loan amount up to the maximum GNMA Loan Limit, or $359,650. Because of the losses experienced in the program, the fee schedule has been increased to be, in some cases, prohibitive. In addition, newly eligible borrowers - specifically reservists - pay a higher premium than normal veterans. Disabled Veterans are exempt from payment of the Funding Fee – any percentage of disability entitles the veteran to receive this waiver.

Funding Fee Active Duty	Funding Fee National Guard/Reservist	Transaction Type
2.20%	2.40%	Purchase with less than 5% Down or Refinance
3.30%	3.30%	Purchase with less than 5% down with Restored Eligibility
1.50%	1.75%	Purchase with less than 10% Down
1.25%	1.50%	Purchase with 10% or More Down
0.50%	0.50%	Streamline Refinance

Tax Exempt Revenue Bond Issues and First Time Buyer Programs

Affordable housing has long been an "American Dream" paradigm. Promoting homeownership has many benefits. It creates communities, can cost less than renting, but most importantly, the first-time entry buyer is at the bottom of the real estate food chain. Each purchase can create a string of transactions trickling up, so to speak. Federal housing programs are under funding pressure. Higher user fees and insurance have made these programs less attractive than in the past. As a result a number of initiatives promoting homeownership have come from the states as well as private industry.

The Federal Bond Subsidy Act authorized state governments to issue tax-exempt revenue bonds for the purpose of funding loans to low and middle-income home purchasers. (The act also allows the underwriting of loans in apartment complexes that comply with affordable housing initiatives.) The bonds are attractive to investors because the interest from them is generally exempt from federal and state income tax. Because the interest is exempt from income tax, the effective yield to the bond buyer is much higher than the coupon or actual rate of interest. As a result, these types of bonds can be offered at much lower interest rates than comparable taxable bonds and still be competitive in the credit markets. In turn, a first time homebuyer can obtain a lower rate loan.

The Federal Bond Subsidy Act authorized state governments to issue tax-exempt revenue bonds for the purpose of funding loans to low and middle-income home purchasers. (The act also allows the underwriting of loans in apartment complexes that comply with affordable housing initiatives.) The bonds are attractive to investors because the interest from them is generally exempt from federal and state income tax. Because the interest is exempt from income tax, the effective yield to the bond buyer is much higher than the coupon or actual rate of interest. As a result, these types of bonds can be offered at much lower interest rates than comparable taxable bonds and still be competitive in the credit markets. In turn, a first time homebuyer can obtain a lower rate loan.

In order to qualify for tax exempt financing the borrower must meet certain guidelines. Most important, they must

Characteristics of Bond Programs
• Home prices are generally limited to 90% of average home prices. New homes may be categorized differently than existing homes.
• Incomes are limited to 80% of median income for the area for moderate-income households or 100% for low-income households.
• Targeted Areas: May offer lower rates or ignore guidelines for areas in which the economy is worse.
• Targeted Areas: Census Tracts in which the median income of 70% or more of families have income that is less than 80% of the statewide median income.
• At least 20% of funds from each bond issue must be targeted.

be first time homebuyers - defined as not having had an interest in real estate for the past three years. However, there are specific limitations from state to state, depending on economic circumstances in any area.

These programs may utilize FHA insurance, VA guaranty, Private Mortgage Insurance, or the state may offer a Mortgage Insurance fund in which the borrower can participate. In each case, those guidelines supersede those of the bond issuer. If borrower's utilize tax-exempt revenue bond financing, they will be subject numerous covenants and restrictions. One significant aspect is that the borrower may be subject to a penalty or recapture tax if the home is sold before the incentive period expires (between 5 - 10 years/ tax up to 6.25% of original mortgage amount).

ALT-A, Expanded Criteria vs. Sub-Prime (Non-Prime)

ALT-A (Alternative to "A") aptly defines the borrower whose risk profile represents an investment quality ("A" grade) loan, but where there is an aspect of the transaction that makes the loan non-saleable to traditional conforming or Jumbo investors. The higher returns available on non-traditional mortgages have brought an explosion of guidelines and products from capital market investors who use a risk vs. reward pricing rationale. For example, a borrower with a sub-660 credit score who is eligible for FNMA/FHLMC financing, but is ineligible for a traditional Jumbo balance mortgage, would be a perfect candidate for an ALT-A product. The guidelines are expanded to allow the borrower to obtain the loan with a price premium – either higher rate or points.

ALT-A lending is different from Non-Prime (or Sub-Prime) lending. Sub-prime lending has also been called "Equity Lending" because the borrower's equity position in the property, in addition to increased rates, offsets the lender's credit risk. Non-Prime lenders must credit grade – or "Pre-Qualify" - applications before accepting a loan into process. This is because, comparatively, fewer sub-prime applications go to closing. Borrowers often reject a high interest rate. Program LTVs may render the transaction infeasible.

The sub-prime process has made its way into the ALT-A world, with many loan officers choosing to have ALT-A loans pre-qualified by wholesale investors. This process is unnecessary because there is no subjective judgment about the acceptability of the loan. ALT-A lenders have guidelines that borrowers must meet in the same way that borrowers must meet other program guidelines. If the loan meets guidelines, it should be approved. They loan officer must take care to price the ALT-A loan correctly taking into consideration the pricing premiums.

Expanded Criteria and "Price Bumps"

When you study credit scoring and risk grading, you will note there is a correlation between risk and the rate that is charged on a loan. One of the advances that came with the sophistication of the secondary mortgage market is the ability, on certain programs, to add features on an "A La Carte" basis. These features expand "niches" or guidelines that are restrictive in the Generic Conforming Specifications and charge a rate or point premium to offset the perceived risk.

In addition to the major expanded criteria programs, FNMA and FHLMC, and most investors in the secondary market have adopted this methodology for adjusting the price of loan to compensate for specific risk criteria. This makes accurately pricing a loan very challenging and fraught with the possibility of an error. To offset this problem, loan officers should use a price quote worksheet that identifies all possible add-ons. Then the "net price" can be correctly quoted.

When these items are not addressed, they can result in unexpected "price-bumps" for the loan officer and possibly for the consumer. The key is in weighing whether an option on a specific loan could be obtained without a pricing option. When this occurs it is what we call a "pricing event." A pricing event is when a customer knows there is a credit challenge to an area of the loan because other loan officers have told them. Typical pricing events are:

1.)   Inadvertent late mortgage payment in the last 12 months
2.)   Adverse credit references
3.)   High investor concentration in a project
4.)   Self-employment
5.)   Investment Property

It is in situations like this where the professional loan officer can add value to the loan by finding a specific program that allows for the nuance without pricing premiums – such as switching the borrower from a conventional loan to an FHA loan.

Price Quote Worksheet

	Rate	Points	Margin	Explanation
Base Rate	**6.250**	**-0.500**		The base price from the rate sheet
Add on For:				
Loan Amount				Premium charged for larger or smaller loans
Buyup/down Points	-0.375	1.125		Buying up means adding to the rate to reduce
0.375 add to price for				the points - buying down means adding to the
-0.125 in rate				points for a lower rate
Buyout Pre-payment Penalty		0.500		A fee may remove a prepayment penalty
Buydown Points		2.500		The cost of a Temporary Buydown (2-1-0)
Owner Occupied LTV		-0.250		Adjustment for lower LTVs and O/O
Owner Occupied Cash Out LTV	0.125			Price up for Equity Out
Stated Income LTV	0.250			Reduced Documentation loans pricing increases
No Income/No Asset LTV				with LTV
Investor Cash Out LTV				
Investor Purchase LTV				Investment property loans are much riskier than
No Income Investor				owner occupied properties, so as LTV increases
No Income No Asset Investor				and documentation is reduced, price increases.
No Ratio Investor				
2nd Home Purchase LTV				2nd/Vacation homes are slightly riskier than
2nd Home Cash Out LTV				residential properties so the price is higher.
Condo Low/HighRise	0.500			Non-FNMA condos and those over 4 stories
2-4 Family				Multi-Unit Properties
A- Credit LTV	0.500			"Just-Missed" credit is priced up
NO PMI LTV	0.375			The rate premium for waiving Private MI
BK/FC Credit Event				If a Bankruptcy of Foreclosure is in evidence
Long Term Lock				New Construction-Longer Lock=higher price
Escrow Waiver		0.250		Fee to not collect Taxes/Insurance Escrows
Margin Buyup				Just like buying up or down the interest rate, the
0.125 add to price for				lender may accept a higher ARM initial rate for a
-0.125 in margin				lower ARM margin or vice-versa.
2nd Mortgage				Rate/point premium for secondary financing
Streamline Refinance				Premium for reduced documentation refinance
Net Price	**7.625**	**3.625**		

Generic Product Matrix

	FNMA/FHLMC	Generic Jumbo	Generic SubPrime	Generic ALT-A	FHA	VA
Property Type Primary	SFD, SFA, PUDs, Condos Multi 1-4 Units, Coops	SFD, SFA, PUDs, Condos (40% Investor - Limits on HiRise)	SFD, SFA, PUDs, Condos (30% Investor - Limits on HiRise)	SFD, SFA, Condo, PUD, 2-4 Unit	SFD, SFA, PUDs, Approved Condos (49% Investor) Multi 1-4 Units	SFD, SFA, PUDs, Approved Condos Multi 1-4 Units
Second Homes	1 unit only or 2 units with restrictions	1 unit only or 2 units with restrictions	ALT A - A- Only	SFD, SFA, Condo, PUD, NO MI	Case by Case	Only allowed on VA to VA R/T, if property was the veteran's primary
Investment Properties	SFD, SFA, PUDs, Condos Multi 1-4 Units	SFD, SFA, PUDs, Condos Multi 1-4 Units	ALT A - A- Only	SFD, SFA, PUD, 2-4 Unit NO C	Available on streamlines refis w/o appraisal, qualified	Only allowed on VA to VA Rate/Term Refis
Primary Purchase LTVs	95% to $417,000 1 unit - up to 100% LTV on Flex w 720 score and 97% - 100% Community Homebuyer	95% to $400,000 1-2 Units 90% to $500,000 1-2 Units 80% to $500,000 1-4 Units 75% to $650,000 1-4 Units 70% to $1,500,000 1-4 Units	A- 95% w > 580 100% w >620 B 85 - 90% C 75 - 80% D 60-70%	1-2 Units, All PUDs, Low Rise Condos 90% to 400,000 3-4 Units, High Rise Condos 75% to 400,000	$312,895 For High Cost states - Max 97.75 of value loan amounts >50K or 98.75 <50K	$417,000 (FNMA Limit) to 100% of the lesser of sales price or CRV & funding fee. Based on Veteran Eligibility
Primary Rate/Term	95% to $417,000- May Streamline portfolio loans	95% to $300,000 90% to $400,000 85% to $500,000 80% to $650,000	A- 95% w > 580 100% w >620 B 85 - 90% C 75 - 80% D 60-70%		Vary by SMSA, County. Max High Cost is 87% of Conforming. See www.hud.gov/highcost	VA Max Mortgage worksheet must be utilized
Primary Cash Out LTVs	90% to $359,650 - 720 score 80% < 720	95% to $300,00 90% to $400,000 80% to $500,000 75% to $650,000	A- 90% w > 580 95% w >620 B 85 - 90% C 75 - 80% D 60-70%	1-2 Units, All PUDs, Low Rise Condos 85% to 400,000 3-4 Units, High Rise Condos	85% of appraised value plus allowable closing cost. Loan cannot > FHA SMSA loan limits	90% max
2nd Home Purchase	95% to $359,650 w 720 score 90% <720	95% to $300,00 90% to $400,000		80% Reduce LTV from Primary Residence Chart by 10%	Subject to limitations	Not allowed
2nd Home Rate/Term	95% to $359,650 w 720 score 90% <720	95% to $650,000 1 unit	90% Reduce LTV from Primary Residence Chart by 10%		Streamline	VA Fastrach
2nd Home Cashout	90% to $359,650 w 720 score 80% < 720	90% to 80% to $300,000 75% to $650,000	75%		Not allowed	Not allowed
Investment Purchase R/T Refis LTVs	90% to $359,650 w 720 score	90% to $300,000 80% to $400,000 70% to $650,000	80%	1 Unit, All Puds 70% to 400,000 2 Units/low rise condo 65% to 400,000	Allowed only on streamline R/T refis w/o appraisals, assumptions or purchases of FHA-owned property	Not allowed on purchases. VA-VA IRRRL permitted
Investment Cash Out	85% 1-2 units 70% 3-4 units	80% to 300K 75% to 400K	70%	1 Unit, All Puds 70% to 400,000	N/A	N/A
Subordinate Financing Primary Residence	90%LTV/95% CLTV - 1-2 units 100% HTLTV - 1-2 units	80/15/5, 80/20 - Primary	up to 95% CLTV	N/A	Cannot Exceed statutory Loan Limits, must still have MIP	Allowed - 1st and 2nd does not exceed the lesser of the CRV, max mtg amt or appropriate max LTV
Mortgage Insurance	Primary Res w/term > 20 yrs >90-95% - 30% > 85-90%-25% >80-85% - 12%	Primary Res w/term > 20 yrs	N/A	N/A	Dependent on type of loan. UFMIP and monthly MIP to 78% LTV dependent on Loan Term	One time funding fee applies
Fees	Standard Fees	Standard Fees	Standard Fees		Ancillary fees cannot be charged to the borrower (seller can pay).	Ancillary fees cannot be charged to the borrower (seller can pay).
Seller Concessions	95% - 3% 90% - 6%, 70% - 8%	Primary - Standard 2nd Home / Investment > 80% - 3% <80% - 6%	2%		6% max	Seller can pay reasonable discount pts and closing costs w/o limit. 4% max if concessions go towards prepaids, funding
Ratios	28/36 Manual Underwrite-- Can exceed with automated underwriting	33/38 - Dependent on AU if Available	A- 45/45 B - 50/50 C - 55/55	55% Single Ratio	31/43 Manual Underwrite-- Can exceed with automated underwriting	41% Manual Underwrite--Can exceed with automated underwriting or residual income computation
Resident Aliens	Allowed - Standard guidelines	Allowed - FNMA	Allowed with SS#	Allowed	Allowed-must have a social	Allowed
Non Permanent Aliens	Same as US Citizen and Permanent Resident Aliens	Not Allowed	Not Allowed	Not Allowed	Allowed-must have a social security card	N/A
Non-Occ Co-Borrower	Allowed to Max LTV of 90%	Allowed to Max LTV of 90%	Not Allowed	Not Allowed	Allowed	Not Allowed
Gifts	Allowed--Must be from a relative	Allowed--Must be from a relative	Not Allowed	Not Allowed	May be from family member, family type relationship, Non-	Allowed. Donor need not be a blood relative.
Trailing Spouse	Allowed	Allowed	Not Allowed	Not Allowed	Not Allowed	Not Allowed
Self-Employed	24 months min. > 25% Ownership Get Tax Returns	24 months min > 25% Ownership Entity Returns	Standard FNMA	Standard FNMA	5 Years preferred 2 Yrs o.k. Provide Entity Returns	24 mos Min - Provide Entity Returns
Debts Not Counted	Installment < 10 mos excluded	Installment < 6 mos with reserves	Paid Off Debt not Qualified	Paid Off Debt not Qualified	< 6 mos excluded	< 6 mos excluded
Major Derogatory Credit	0x30 Mortgage, Ch 7 4 Years, Ch 13 2 years	0 x 30 Mortgage, 0 x BK, 0 x FCL	Rolling 30's Counted as 1	2 x 30 Rolling 6:1 Ratio Not Past Due at Application Chp 7 - 2 Years from Discharge Chp 13/FCL- 2 Years from Filing	With explanation, subject to UW	With explanation, subject to UW
Credit Scores	620		680 Dependent on Grade	580 - 599	Not Stated - 2ndary expects 580 - 620	Not Stated - 2ndary expects 580 - 620
Post Closing Reserves	Standard 2 Mos PITI - Expanded 6 Mos PITI	6 Mos PITI	Not Stated	Not Stated	15 Days Interest	No minimum Reserves
Documentation	NINA/No Ratio for Expanded (720 score)	Full, Alt, Reduced, Stated	Full, Alt, Lite, No Ratio	Full, Alt, Reduced, No	Full, Alt	Full, Alt

Chapter 4
QUALIFYING
Ratios and Credit History

Understanding Guidelines

Knowing loan program guidelines is critical to loan officer success. You could say that guidelines are the rules by which the mortgage game is played. The strategy of the game is in fitting a borrower into the guidelines. How an individual borrower fits, or fails to fit, those guidelines are the process of qualification. A skilled loan officer isn't needed to process a transaction where the borrower easily qualifies. When there is a problem with an application, the loan officer needs to be able to fix it. Detailed qualifying is problem solving for insufficient income, excessive debts or insufficient assets.

The problem with guidelines is that the rules are only as effective as the information that is applied to them. Seeing if a borrower meets ratio requirements is more than applying income against expenses - the question is what income and what expenses? In this sense qualification is field underwriting that requires judgment about the context of the information the borrower presents.

Abandon Pre-conceived Notions

Qualifying for a mortgage is one of the biggest fears new borrowers experience when approaching a lender to apply for a loan. This is due to the valuable, but conflicting, free advice that is offered to borrowers when a planned home purchase is announced. In general, care should be taken to actually work through the details of an individual transaction - never use "rules of thumb" or broad estimates to determine qualifications. Even if there is some basis in fact to the estimate or generalization, this does not add credence to the assumption. Start by throwing away these:

- Your home shouldn't cost more than 3 times your annual income.
- Your closing costs will range between 3 and 7% of the sales price.
- You shouldn't spend more than one-quarter of your income for your house payment.

The loan officer's job is to make an accurate assessment of borrowing capacity. Unfortunately, no one aspect of qualification is mutually exclusive of another - so that that when we look at qualifying as to income, we cannot ignore assets, credit and other eligibility criteria or vice-versa. Qualifying has to be taken as a whole, so while it makes for an extensive treatment, this chapter will address all specific aspects of qualification beyond the guideline matrix. We will assimilate the information that will be applied against guidelines to see if a borrower qualifies.

Owner Occupancy

The basis behind the underwriting guidelines, how and whether they may be exceeded, is predicated on one critical risk analysis factor - does the individual live in the property? The theory is that a person has more willingness to repay a loan when times get hard if they are supporting their shelter. As a result, guidelines are more flexible for borrowers who are buying a residence. A second home, or vacation home, is viewed more skeptically. Obviously an investment property is the riskiest loan to make from the lender's perspective and so is not likely to be flexible on exceptions to guidelines.

Can a person have two primary residences? There are certain circumstances where this is possible. One we refer to as the Maury Povich/Connie Chung Syndrome. (They are East Coast broadcast journalists - Maury lived in Washington, DC and Connie worked for a network in New York.) Obviously, there were going to be two primary residences in this family. Any individual who spends a predominant amount of time in two separate places may be entitled to two loans utilizing primary residence guidelines. Another instance of multiple primary residences is one where there is a co-borrower situation. This is where one of the borrowers will occupy the property as a home.

Ratios

In today's lending environment, qualifying ratios determine whether a borrower is eligible for a specific loan program. A ratio measures the percentage of gross income that may be devoted to expenses. Each loan program has specific qualifying ratios allowed for underwriting purposes.

Where did ratios come from?

How can a set of numbers be firmly established to apply to a whole population? For instance the "conforming" loan qualifying ratio guideline is 28/36. If these "conforming" guidelines establish industry standards then arguably most homebuyers

As Income Increases Flexibility Increases				
Income	$	4,000	$	10,000
Tax	$	1,120	$	3,300
Family Support	$	3,226	$	3,226
Available for Housing	$	(346)	$	3,474

are expected to meet this test. Ratios may seem arbitrary and may not seem to take into account unique aspects of individual financial structures. Qualifying ratios have evolved to take into account the "general" financial obligations of a prospective borrower.

Their basis is in what people have to spend money on (or pay for), subtracting that amount and analyzing the remainder. The remainder is discretionary - what is referred to as residual income

- the amount left over after family support, housing, taxes, maintenance and debts. This is a cash flow method of seeing what a borrower can afford to pay. The original qualifying test was the "Residual Method" and is the precursor of ratios.

The example on the right shows an "average" moderate income borrower qualifying under the residual method. The family support tables are the Department of Housing and Urban Development's (HUD) estimate of what it costs to live in specific areas of the country. If you compare the results of residual calculation and ratio calculation yields close to the same mortgage payment amount or total debt ratio as conventional qualifying for the low-to-moderate-income borrower. However, a borrower who earns $100,000 per year skews the residual method too greatly. This borrower would have nearly 2 times the amount of money available for a mortgage payment under the residual method as compared to the ratio method. As incomes have grown and housing costs increased, the cash flow approach would be too aggressive as a universal qualifying method. But this is where 28/36 came from - an era dominated by suburban, single income families of moderate means.

Understanding Ratios - The Residual Income Approach		
Gross Monthly Income		$ 4,000.00
Less		
Federal Income Tax	28%	$ 1,120.00
State Income Tax	8%	$ 320.00
Social Security Tax	7.65%	$ 306.00
Monthly Living Expenses		
Food		$ 475.00
Clothing		$ 100.00
Day Care/Tuition		$ -
Car Insurance		$ 40.00
Gas & Oil		$ 60.00
Repairs		$ 25.00
Automotive Insurance		$ 50.00
Other Transportation (Parking, etc.)		$ 10.00
Entertainment		$ 100.00
Telephone		$ 60.00
Health, Medical		$ 125.00
Dining Out		$ 25.00
Laundry/Dry Cleaning		$ 25.00
Grooming/Hair		$ 25.00
Utilities		$ 75.00
Monthly Debts		
Car		$ 225.00
Credit Cards		$ 100.00
Total Family Support Cost		$ 3,266.00
Remaining Income		$ 734.00
Less		
Real Estate Tax		$ 150.00
Insurance		$ 25.00
Private Mortgage Ins.		$ 64.00
Maintenance		$ 55.00
HOA Fees		$ -
Amount Available for P&I		$ 440.00

There are obviously many people who do not meet the typical mold. This is when the loan officer must be prepared to offer the residual/cash flow method to demonstrate how higher than standard-qualifying ratios may be acceptable. If borrowers don't have children, they don't spend as much for food or insurance. If they don't have a car, not only do they not have to make a car payment, but they don't have to pay for collision insurance - the most expensive auto insurance. A borrower earning $200,000 per year would have the same level of family expenses as someone making $50,000 per year, because fixed costs don't increase as income increases. Higher income borrowers have more disposable income.

This illustration is provided as a backdrop to understanding conventional ratios and where they come from. FHA and VA still utilize the Residual Computation to confirm ratio calculations. Conventional lenders do not set forth any guidelines for residual income. However, this is the primary method for justifying higher ratios than generally allowed under conventional guidelines.

The Mathematics of Qualifying Ratios

Income and debt are inextricably blended in the qualification formula. As income increases and debt decreases, the size of payment the borrower can afford grows larger. Because a mathematical equation is involved - numerator and factor - the results of these numbers change as any aspect of a personal financial situation change. Debts are the most important aspect of this equation - simply because of the way qualifying is structured. Understanding liabilities and their effect on income underlines why debts must be analyzed prior to income in the qualification process. This is just because of the way ratios work.

In this example an additional $100 per month in liabilities creates a need for an additional $300 per month in income. In order to qualify for another $100 in monthly debt the borrower's income

Debts are Much More Significant in the Ratio Analysis						
Monthly Debts	$	200	$	300	$	(100)
Housing Expense	$	840	$	840		
Total Debts	$	1,040	$	1,140		
Income Required	$	2,889	$	3,167	$	(278)
Increase in Income				10%		

would have to increase by 10%. Because it is easier to manipulate components of a debt structure than it is to make a borrower earn more money instantaneously, we are going to address monthly obligations in the qualifying analysis first.

Specific Components of the Housing and Expense Ratios

An individual's largest debt or obligation is normally the housing expense. Because having a roof over your head takes precedence over anything else, the percentage of your income devoted to housing expenses is called the first ratio, housing expense ratio or front ratio.

Then there are the other debts that must be repaid, such as credit cards, car loans, other loans for education and debt consolidation. Any other obligation, such as alimony, child support, or regular payments for maintenance of negative cash flows on rental properties or mortgages must also be considered. The total debt is then added to the housing expense in total. The sum of these two obligations, when compared to income is referred to as the second, back, or total expense ratio.

The Housing Expense Ratio

Following are the components of the Housing Expense Ratio, also known as PITI:

- Principal and interest payment
- 1/12 of the annual real estate tax
- 1/12 of the annual premium for Homeowner's Insurance
- 1/12 of the renewal premium for Private Mortgage Insurance
- the monthly homeowner's association fee for a condominium or a townhouse
- payment for any ground lease/land lease

Assume, as a starting point, that the maximum housing expense one can afford is 28% of gross monthly income. The question being answered is, "how much can I really afford to pay monthly for my home?" Numbers are only as good as the information you apply against them. For the loan officer, it is important to understand how to manipulate them.

Playing with Principal

Reducing interest rate/payment is the simplest way to achieve additional qualifying power. The example utilizes 28% as the maximum housing expense. A 2% reduction in interest rate can dramatically increase the maximum loan amount. How do you achieve interest rate or payment reduction?

Illustration of Changing Interest Rate Impacting Loan Size			
Based on Income of		$	4,166.00
Qualifying Ratio %	28%	$	1,166.48
Less Tax & Insurance		$	(250.00)
Maximum Principal & Interest		$	916.48
At rate of	9%		7%
Results in Maximum Loan of	$ 113,902	$	137,754

- Changing program to a lower rate programs: a 7-year or 5-year program may carry a lower than 30 year fixed rate. An adjustable rate mortgage with start rate qualification might achieve the objective. Keep in mind that many ARMs have minimum qualifying rates.
- Subsidizing the monthly payment for a fixed period of time with a temporary buydown.
- Extending the amortization period of the loan from 30 to 40 years.

Playing With Other Components of the Front Ratio

We have shown how reducing the interest rate increases the maximum loan amount. There are other factors that can be considered to achieve the same effect.

HOA/Condo Fees

If financing of a condominium is contemplated, there will be a homeowner's association fee. This fee is for the maintenance of the common elements and for the operation the project. When **unit** utilities are included in the fee, one can deduct the portion of fees devoted to unit utilities from the condominium fee used to calculate ratios. The loan officer can document that utility payments for the common elements can be excluded from the condo fee. To determine the amount to be deducted, analyze the project's current year operating budget. Add all utilities that are shown as line items in the budget. Divide the annual figure for utilities by the annual assessments to be collected from unit owners - do not include amounts from other sources, such as parking, laundry, vending etc. - to arrive at the percentage of condo fees attributed to unit utilities. The unit's fee may be reduced by this percentage for qualifying purposes.

Another tactic in reducing the fee for qualifying purposes would be to have the seller participate in condo fee abatement by pre-paying a portion of the condo fee for a set period of time. If reflected correctly, by the association or property manager, this can reduce the assessment for qualifying purposes.

A ground lease, where the land on which the property sits is not owned, is another component of the housing/front ratio. This may be the same of a cooperative apartment where there may be an underlying mortgage included in the maintenance fee.

Real Estate Taxes

Can the real estate taxes be adjusted for qualifying purposes? If the current tax rate is incorrect or inappropriate for the subject property purchaser, they may be. Often the posted real estate taxes for a property are for a rental unit - thus the property might be taxed at a higher commercial rate.

If qualification is a challenge, it is worth checking to make sure the current assessment is correct. Also, read the tax laws for your jurisdiction - do they offer tax break for primary residences or homestead exemptions? Are there breaks for owner-occupied properties, first-time buyers, senior citizens or low-income borrowers?

Private Mortgage Insurance

Private Mortgage Insurance, or PMI, is generally required whenever the loan to value ratio is greater than 80% (less than 20% down payment). PMI premiums may be reduced or eliminated dependent on circumstances.

1. Can changing from an ARM to a fixed rate reduce the coverage requirement?
2. Premium financing, while increasing the loan amount, can eliminate PMI from the ratio entirely. This will increase the loan amount, but the dollar for dollar savings to the customer will be magnified, because monthly PMI premiums are not tax deductible, while the interest on financed premiums may be.
3. Can PMI be eliminated to the customer's benefit by utilizing a first and second mortgage combination? (See Chapter 2 - Loan Programs)

The Total Debt Ratio

The total debt, back or bottom ratio is the measure of all other obligations a borrower is responsible for in addition to the total housing payment. As an example, if we use qualifying ratios of 28/36 this allows 8% of total income to be devoted to debts. A borrower who has accumulated a large amount of consumer debt can present a qualifying problem. In pre-qualification the loan officer works backward through the ratio analysis to see whether the housing expense will be limited by total debts. To determine this:

1.) <u>Multiply Total Monthly Income by 28%</u>. Enter Result as Total Housing Payment
2.) <u>Multiply Gross Monthly Income by 36%.</u> Enter Result as Total Monthly Obligations. Deduct all debts. Enter Result as Total Housing Payment.
3.) The <u>smaller</u> of these two numbers is the maximum PITI. Subtract all components (taxes, insurance, etc.) from the smaller number. The result is the Maximum Principal and Interest payment.

In the following <u>Example 1</u> the debts **do not limit** the qualification. In <u>example 2</u> the maximum housing expense **is limited - lower** because of higher debts. Some guidelines do not mandate that you compute a front, or housing expense ratio. In any situation a detailed analysis of debts is important. There are many details involved in correct treatment and computation of debts.

Example 1			Example 2		
Step 1	Monthly Income	$ 4,000.00	Step 1	Monthly Income	$ 4,000.00
	x Housing Ratio	28%		x Housing Ratio	28%
	Available for PITI	$ 1,120.00		Available for PITI	$ 1,120.00
Step 2	Monthly Income	$ 4,000.00	Step 2	Monthly Income	$ 4,000.00
	x Total Debt Ratio	36%		x Total Debt Ratio	36%
	Available For Debts	$ 1,440.00		Available For Debts	$ 1,440.00
	Less Actual Debts	$ 100.00		Less Actual Debts	$ 400.00
	Maximum PITI	$ 1,340.00		Maximum PITI	$ 1,040.00
Step 3	Smaller of 1 & 2	$ 1,120.00	Step 3	Smaller of 1 & 2	$ 1,040.00

What is a Debt?

Any required monthly payment that can legally be collected from an individual - that must be paid - is considered in the debt ratio. The payments for credit cards, student loans, car loans, signature loans, rental negative on rental properties, alimony and child support or other support obligations, payments for other mortgages. Items that are elective in nature, such as automobile insurance, health insurance, life insurance, library fees, membership dues, savings plans and others are not considered debts, because you can choose not to pay these, and your privileges will simply lapse. You won't suffer a collection action if you don't pay your parking fees, you just don't park in the lot.

Understanding the nature of each obligation - how it can be repaid in minimum, and how it impacts other aspects of a personal financial situation is - allows the loan officer to develop the maximum qualification potential of a borrower. We will discuss these in depth here - what the obligation is and how the repayments can be minimized for qualifying purposes.

Credit Card Obligations - Credit cards are the single most abused forms of credit available to consumers. This is because many people receive offers to lend money at times when they are inclined to spend it in an ill-advised manner. For example, college students may receive a check from a credit card company saying "just endorse this check." Often college students can not possibly hope to make a payment beyond a minimum. In some circumstances, he or she may not even be able to meet that. What may ensue is a growing spiral of debt in which the borrower continues to borrow money to pay obligations, and supporting a lifestyle deficit - enhancing living expenses - with credit card purchases. In some situations, people in this situation earn their way out of difficulty - their income increases to keep pace with the expenditures. In some cases people discipline themselves to curtail the escalating expenditures. Unfortunately, there is often the sad conclusion where borrowers give up and their credit is destroyed.

Why is this description important? Maximizing a borrower's qualification is appropriate for individuals who have shown that they can manage their credit, despite complications - it is a measure of character. In other words, someone who has managed his or her debts impeccably is an individual for whom qualification maximization is appropriate. Alternatively, someone who has periodically bailed out, or is in the credit spiral, is not necessarily a good person to whom the maximum amount of money should be loaned.

Credit cards are revolving credit lines. Their minimum payments are based upon current balance, interest due and the previous payments. For a thumbnail qualification one would calculate the minimum payment at 5% of the outstanding balance. Actual minimum payments vary from 1 to 10% depending on the cardholder. But think about it. If the credit card company is earning 18% interest on the credit card balance, do they really want you to pay the balance down? Not really, so they encourage you not to make a payment for a month, or allow you to make a smaller than normal minimum payment.

> **Tactics for Handling High Card Payments**
>
> **1.)** A copy of all credit card statements should be brought to loan application. Occasionally, because of fluctuating balances, the correct minimum payment will not be reported to the credit bureaus. Having the statements at application will allow the loan officer to review that the correct minimum payments are reported.
> **2.)** Another strategy involves planning. You may recommend that the borrower make a payment that is slightly higher - approximately 1.5 times the required minimum. Then when the next statement comes, the cardholder may require a smaller than normal minimum payment.

Alternatively, if debts must be paid off for qualifying purposes, it must be determined that the borrowers are not simply going to re-extend themselves with new credit. For this reason, an underwriter may not allow revolving debt to be paid for qualifying purposes. If there is a possibility of paying off revolving debt, the balances should be compared against the monthly payments to get the biggest bang for the buck - so to speak. Payoff the lowest balances with the highest minimum payment.

Car loans/Installment loans: When there are scheduled payments on a loan, unlike a credit card or long-term obligation like a student loan, the loan served a purpose. If it was a car loan, the purpose is obvious. However, if it was a consolidation loan, or a signature loan, watch for the credit spiral. On the other hand, if the debt was established some time ago, there is a likelihood that the debt will be repaid soon. As with any loan, the balance may be refinanced.

> **Installment Loans May Be Excluded**
>
> If an installment debt has less than ten months (6 months for FHA/VA) remaining at the time of application, it may be excluded from qualifying ratios. For example, a borrower considering a home purchase might consider paying the balance on a car loan with 15 or 20 months remaining down to less than 10 months prior to application. This strategy should not be executed at the expense of post closing reserves - a borrower with no reserves might not be granted the leniency of excluding a low balance installment loan.

Car loans may be structured initially with 24- or 36- month payment schedules. This can make the payments troublesomely high. If a short-term car/installment loan is a problem, investigate the terms being offered by banks for similar loans - and the borrower's own bank too. You can refinance home loans - why not refinance all the borrower's loans to

Refinance a Car Loan to Reduce Debt

	Existing	Refinance
Interest Rate	4.75%	8.90%
Term	60	60
Balance	$ 12,500.00	$ 12,500.00
Payment	$ 470.64	$ 258.87
Savings		$ 211.76

get a lower payment?

Student Loans: Recent college graduates almost always have incurred some student loan debt to complete their education. Generally, the repayment terms are fairly favorable. However, student loans also have deferments that can allow a borrower to graduate from college, and wait for **a period of 12 or more months** before beginning repayment. From a qualification standpoint the question is, if the borrower is in a deferment period, can they afford to make the payment after the deferment is over? However loans that begin maturing more than 12 months into the future can be eliminated if the borrower has the assets to offset the payments once they take effect. If excessive student loans are a qualifying issue, Sallie Mae - the major student loan lender - does offer consolidation loans, which may reduce the overall debt service for a borrower.

Rental Properties: Income properties often create problems for potential homebuyers. Aside from the difficulties of managing rental real estate, lenders may have a disparaging view of the impact rental real estate has on the prospective borrower. Restrictions on rental income include:

- Exclusion of 25% of the gross rental income as a vacancy/loss factor. Although a property may carry a positive cash flow, lenders adjust this income significantly to take into account the potential for the property being vacant with no rental income for an extended period of time. This is known as a vacancy/expense factor. While most rental properties experience a 5 - 10% vacancy factor, an additional expense must generally be considered to determine the wear and tear on the property. The exception to this is FHA/VA loans, in which the borrower can demonstrate a lower vacancy factor, or previous experience as a landlord. Then the vacancy expense factor can be as low as 7%. If this is a factor, then examine the actual cash flow of the property. Has it been rented for more than two years? If so, can you examine the borrower's Schedule E, Rental and Royalty income, from their tax returns? Adding the actual income, less actual expenses (depreciation and depletion added in) may result in a more favorable net rental income than a 25% vacancy factor.
- In many lease situations, properties are rented on a month-to-month basis. If this is the case, the tenant must be contacted to provide a letter attesting to the fact that they intend to continue residing in the property.
- How many properties are financed? If a purchaser owns more than four 1-4 family properties that are financed, and the subject property is an investment property, they are generally ineligible for financing on conforming loans.
- Each property's mortgage must be verified. Also, the taxes and insurance must be obtained separately, either by proving that they are held in escrow, or by providing copies of the paid bills for the obligation.

Alimony/Child Support/Separate Maintenance: Ironically, in this case, what is a debt to one person is income to another. Since half of all marriages end in divorce, understanding the financial obligations and legal documentation of marital dissolution is requisite for lenders.

If there is a support obligation, is it either child support or alimony. If it is alimony, it is taxable to the recipient. This means that it is tax deductible for the payer. If this is the case it will appear as a deduction on the front page of the tax returns. This can be viewed **not as a debt, but as a deduction from gross income,** which can drastically reduce the qualifying impact of the obligation. Remember the example of how it takes $3.00 of income for every $1.00 of debts. This is another example of how it is more efficient for a borrower to reduce debt load to qualify for a mortgage than to increase their income. Nothing in the following examples changed except for the treatment of the alimony as a

reduction in income instead of a debt. This treatment results in an additional $220 a month of towards qualification.

> **1.)** While a divorce can work against a borrower who must pay support, the opposite is true of the recipient. This can work to the benefit of the creative loan officer who can add income and remove debts of one borrower by implementing advantageously a divorce situation. **2.)** Be sure to examine tax returns, bank statements and credit histories for evidence of these liabilities. There are many instances in which these debts can easily be concealed by a borrower, which could circumvent the intent of maximizing qualification.

Treating Alimony as an Income Deduction Increases Qualifying Power

	Alimony as a debt				**Alimony deducted from income**		
Step 1	Monthly Income	$	4,000	Step 1	Monthly Income	$	4,000
	x Housing Ratio		28%		Less Alimony	$	(750)
	Maximum PITI	$	1,120		"Net" Income	$	3,250
Step 2	Monthly Income	$	4,000		x Housing Ratio		28%
	x Debt Ratio		36%		Maximum PITI	$	910
	Max Total Debt	$	1,440	Step 2	Monthly Income	$	3,250
	Less Alimony	$	(750)		x Debt Ratio		36%
Step 3	Result	**$**	**690**		Max Total Debt	**$**	**1,170**

- If it is child support, how long will it continue? Are the children going to be old enough so that the obligation disappears soon? If so then an argument can be made for excluding the obligation. Can the balance be paid off or down to reduce the amount owed?
- Depending on the circumstances a legal separation agreement, post-nuptial agreement, divorce decree, court order, and/or property settlement agreement must be reviewed to determine the extent of obligations.
-

Regular Business Expenses/Self Employed Borrowers

Self-employment presents a separate challenge from an income point of view. These borrowers may be able to deduct many of their normal living expenses from their income, they achieve a higher standard of living by reducing their tax burden. Unfortunately, as lenders we believe that you cannot tell the federal government that you earn a certain amount of income and expect your lender to count a higher amount. It is important to get all income documentation and to attribute debts owed by or paid by a business to the business. *If an expense is actually paid by the business, providing 12 months canceled checks will allow the debt to be deleted from the borrower's personal qualification calculation.*

In many situations borrowers extend their personal credit to establish a new business. While this new business may not have been established long enough to have income that can be utilized for qualifying, it may present an excellent compensating factor for someone who looks as if they are caught in the credit escalation spiral, and may compensate for higher qualifying ratios.

When someone is commissioned, they may write off or deduct their business expenses. Do these debts or expenditures reduce gross income or are they simply allowable deductions? This is a delicate question. For instance, you can argue that union dues must be paid to ensure continued employment. This might be construed as a debt. On the other hand, a commissioned sales person might deduct un-reimbursed employee business expenses, such as mileage.

Because these expenses are generally the result of additional efforts to achieve additional income, these are deducted from gross income to determine what the actual net income is or was. However, the actual amount of the expenditure must be evaluated to determine what income was actually earned.

Co-signed Loans

It seemed like a good idea to help your friend or daughter buy that car. The bank just needed a co-signer to make the loan. Surely the original borrower would be responsible for the debt? This is significant. If a borrower has co-signed for someone it must be substantiated that the primary borrower is making the payments in a timely manner. Without this the co-signer is called upon to make the payments. Unfortunately, many of these obligations do not get paid in a timely manner. And the co-signer is adversely impacted.

Credit History

More and more, the most critical aspect of the loan approval process is the review of the credit history. In 1987 the mortgage industry - in a revolt against the massive, time-consuming paper monster created by verifying all aspects of an applicant's personal history - began to trend towards reducing documentation. Dependent on the relative amount of down payment, many loans were approved entirely upon the strength of credit reports. While some lenders made poor decisions by not verifying more information, time has proven that a perfect credit history is the most reliable indicator of future willingness and ability to repay an obligation. A large emphasis on credit is appropriate and, in fact, a credit report is the first thing a loan reviewer sees.

Credit Bureaus vs. Credit Repositories

The credit repositories provide direct reports. This is the report that a car dealer or bank will examine when deciding to grant credit. These reports are referred to in the mortgage business as an "in-file" report. This report is the "raw" data contained in the database. The credit repositories do not make changes to data. Only a creditor or reporting subscriber can change the data recorded among the repositories. Repositories are not very customer friendly.

Credit Bureaus are service providers to the mortgage industry. They assemble data and present it in a "decoded" format merging data from multiple repositories. They will merge and decode 1, 2 or 3 repository reports into one "in-file" report that can give a wider review of an applicant's history. In addition, they may verify employment and check accounts like landlords or mortgages that are listed but not reported. This "decoded" format is referred to as a "Standard Factual Data Credit Report." This format allows huge flexibility for mortgage lenders because, regardless of what data the repositories report, the customer may refute that information. With compelling documentation a bureau can:

1.　　Confirm and eliminate duplicate accounts.
2.　　Delete accounts that appear to belong to someone else.
3.　　Verify that late accounts are misreported.
4.　　Update balances on accounts that have been paid.

Types of Credit Reports

Name	Data Collected	Description	Cost
In-File	One repository	Usually used to "peek" at what the borrower's credit history is like. This preview allows the loan officer to see how the overall credit is without expending substantial cost and affecting the borrower's credit scores with multiple inquiries	$5 - $8 - can be converted to full tri-merge at no cost.
Tri-Merge	three repositories	Data is sorted and merged eliminating duplicate, old and paid accounts. May also include scores.	$15 - $25
RMCR	three repositories direct references	Residential Mortgage Credit Report is used to verify additional data, such as employment, rental history and unverified debts. The RMCR allows the credit bureau to provide third party verification.	$50 - $60

Remember the old adage regarding first impressions? It is particularly true in this respect. An underwriter may be jaundiced in the loan review process if a borrower's credit history appears immediately negative. To present an applicant's credit history in the best possible light the credit bureau can present all of the accounts that were paid timely on the first page. Then, at the end of the report, show negative accounts.

It is important to remember that, no matter how much a borrower accomplishes with an individual credit bureau, the information in the repositories is not updated when a standard factual data report is modified. Only the creditor or subscriber can modify information with the repository directly. This can present a problem if significant modifications have been made and

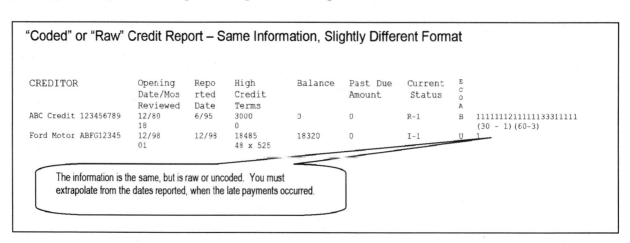

a loan is submitted to a reviewer who compares "in-file" data to the factual reports.

Sample Credit Bureau Report

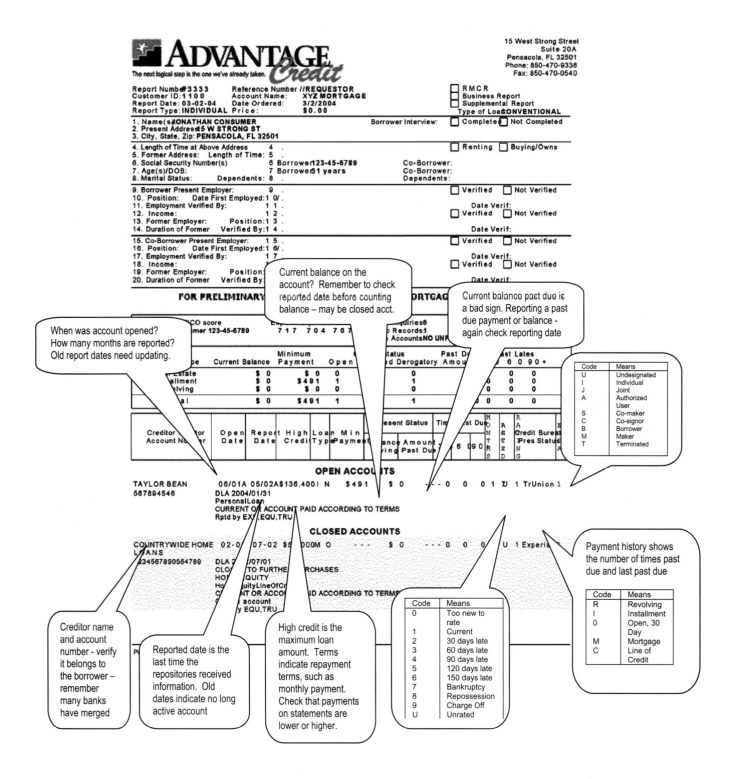

Obtaining a Credit Report

With automation being so prevalent, the ability of the loan officer to obtain a credit report has achieved a high degree of ease. The borrower must provide an authorization for this.

A credit history is like an opinion - almost everyone has one. An immense amount of data is accumulated as you interact with creditors. You report employers and residence addresses when you apply for a loan; lenders report applications, balances, payment amounts and payment histories as you transact business; the courts report any legal actions against you. Credit data is stored among 3 major private companies referred to as "repositories": TRW, Trans Union (TU), and Equifax (CBI). Depending on geography - the South, or East or West of the Mississippi - all consumer credit providers, most mortgage lenders and even some major landlords will report to at least one and perhaps all three of these repositories. They assemble what amounts to a massive, interactive, and open database. This is "raw" credit data.

The credit card application process is a "raw" credit experience. You are analyzed on the data that is contained in the repositories. Period. If you have missed a payment in the past due to extenuating circumstances, or if there are erroneous data in the system, you may be declined. Then your experience can become Orwellian. You don't generally get to talk to a human being and review a negative credit decision. Most consumer credit decisions are based on scoring systems. The scoring is based on the repository information. You are considered guilty if there is a problem and there is very little you can do to prove your innocence.

One of the benefits of the mortgage process is that, as a borrower, you have the opportunity to address and correct items that arise during the process. A negative credit history is like an illness - people don't like to talk about it or admit an error. It is this pain or fear that causes an aversion to dealing with credit issues. Unlike credit card transactions a mortgage application, because of its human element, can be a healing experience. Like jumping into a swimming pool, once you're in the water it doesn't seem that cold. Understanding the process can allay the fear.

Understanding the Ratings - What is "Bad"

We expect that applicants should have "perfect" credit. Perfect credit means **no negative ratings/incidents ever.** Perfect credit is the **basis** for obtaining a loan to be sold into the secondary market and, at least theoretically, the most competitive rates offered. Anything less than perfect credit is considered adverse and is a basis for loan declination.

Generally Acceptable Adverse Credit History	
Mortgage Payments	NO Late Payments in last 12 months
Credit Card/Consumer Loans	TWO (2) 30 day late payments in last 12 months One (1) 60 day late last 2 years
Legal Actions	NO Open Liens, Judgments or Collection Actions
Inquiries	THREE (3) Inquiries in previous 3-6 months prior to application

Beyond perfect is where the credit evaluation process becomes almost purely subjective. We have obtained a consensus definition of acceptable negative ratings to eliminate some subjectivity. A survey of underwriters for major lenders indicates that there can be some lenience in allowing less than 100% perfect credit. (Nobody readily commits to lenience in this regard. To achieve lenience no other negative factors may be present.)

While the loan reviewer places most emphasis on the preceding 12-24 months, **all** negative instances must be clearly explained. Again, this is because the basis, or standard for obtaining a marketable loan is "perfect" credit.

No Credit is **not** perfect credit. Standard guidelines require 3 - 5 pieces of credit maintained for at least 2 years to qualify as "established" credit. There are alternatives to having no commercial credit history. Payment records to landlords for rent, utility companies, and installment purchases, merchandise redeemed from a pawnbroker all can be compiled to develop a repayment history.

> **What is the Problem with Inquiries?**
> It's not the inquiry itself - too many inquiries indicate:
> - A borrower with latent credit problems that cause him/her to repeatedly attempt, unsuccessfully, to obtain new loans to conceal delinquent accounts
> - Someone who is trying to borrow for the down payment
> - Someone who is trying to obtain multiple owner-occupied loans simultaneously
> - Someone who cannot obtain credit or is desperate for credit

Credit Explanations

As discussed, all adverse credit notations must be addressed in writing by the borrower. While it would be naive to think that a credit explanation could change a loan reviewer's opinion to approve or decline an application, there are scenarios that can be effective in addressing serious or recent adverse incidents which could compromise loan approval.

- A logical explanation that compellingly indicates an applicant's efforts to properly handle an account.
- Someone else's fault - documentation that the responsibility of an incident was out of the applicant's control.
- Extreme Contrition - an earnest admission of responsibility and recognition of how to avert future incidents.
- The Big Bang- The event or circumstance that caused the delinquency is no longer a factor.

From Bad to Worse

Unfortunately many Americans fall prey to the lure of easy credit, becoming victims to a tempest of red ink. An understanding of credit status is important because in certain situations a borrower is not eligible for traditional financing any more. If an applicant falls out of the generally acceptable range, or displays any of the following characteristics, they need more help than what a traditional loan officer can offer. We will discuss this later.

Credit Issue	Description	Resolution
Late Mortgage	Over 30 days past due on rent or mortgage in last 12 months; currently past due	**Get direct mortgage verification** or canceled check to refute exact timing; 12 months time elapsed since incident
30 – 60 Days Past Due	If an account has been handled well historically, some creditors are loath to report minor late	**Pay Off Account** prior to application; pay account

Credit Issue	Description	Resolution
	payments. Current 30- or 60-day late references are emblematic of a serious situation arising. Reported as an I-2, R-2, I-3 or R-3.	current; depending on circumstances may require 12-24 months time elapsed since incident.
Over 60 Day Past Due	This indicates a serious unwillingness on the part of the borrower to repay a debt: I-4, R-4 to I-6/R-6	Pay Account Current/**Pay Off**; 12-24 mos. time elapsed
Collection Action	Anyone who can report to credit repositories (collection agencies, doctor's offices, parking enforcement, etc.) can file a collection action against you. All that is required is an unpaid invoice. Normally these are nuisance actions too small to go to the expense of obtaining a ruling via a judge. No action can result from a collection, but it will impede your ability to obtain credit.	Pay off collection.
Charge Off	Means that the creditor gave up trying to get payment from you and wrote the account off as a loss. May become a judgment if charged off account is sold.	Evidence of payment/dispute Must be paid
Judgment	A judgment is a collection action that has been reviewed for merit by a small claim, circuit or district court depending on the amount or size of the claim. A judgment is serious because the party to whom the ruling inures may seize your property, wages and assets to satisfy the obligation.	An attorney may appeal the judgment and, if successful, the ruling may be vacated, or thrown out.
Tax Lien	Federal or state tax liens are more serious than judgments because the government is very good at seizing assets and collecting for money owed. Even though tax liens can come about as the result of legitimate disputes over tax practices, they are viewed primarily as a credit problem.	Release of lien
Consumer Credit Counseling	A borrower enters into a credit repair agreement with a non-profit counseling agency. The account will show up on the credit report as "CCCS account." The account will be CCCS until it is a "0" balance.	Borrower may not have open CCCS accounts. Pay off and close.
Bankruptcy Chapter 7 - Liquidation	A filing under any chapter of the bankruptcy code creates an estate. The Courts act as trustee over the estate. Under Chapter 7 all of a debtor's assets (with some exceptions) and liabilities are liquidated. Unless a creditor objects, all debts included in the bankruptcy are discharged within a few months of filing.	Some lenders will never consider a borrower after bankruptcy is declared. FNMA/FHLMC allow financing 4 years after discharge Chapter 7 and 2 years after Chapter 13 with re-established credit. Chapter 7 is the most negative form, philosophically, because the debtor has walked away from assets and liabilities and let the court force creditors to
Bankruptcy Chapter 13 - Adjustment of Debts by Wage Earner	This chapter allows debtors to pay back creditors in full or in part, based upon income, over a period of up to 5 years. The payments are made to a trustee who begins paying creditors as soon as the plan is approved. You must have less than $350,000 in secured debt and $100,000 in unsecured debt to file	

Credit Issue	Description	Resolution
Bankruptcy Chapter 11 - Reorganization	This plan is available to all individuals and entities, but is intended to allow an ongoing business to restructure its debt. The filing must be accepted by the court as well as creditors	take less money than owed in what is known as a "Cram-Down." Because all debts are discharged this may disguise a previous pattern of debt mismanagement. "Dismissal" means that the court did not approve the filing.

Relief From the Tide of Red Ink

Depending on the seriousness of the situation there are ways to avoid being subjected to intense pressure from creditors.

Non-Standard Credit Mortgages - If you are fortunate to have a large down payment or have built up equity in your home, or in other improved property (not land), you may be eligible for a higher risk mortgage. These are referred to as "Sub-Prime," "Credit-Rated Paper," "B, C & D Paper" (as in, not "A"), and "Equity Based" loans. They are offered under the same terms as the "junk bonds" of the 80's, giving investors a higher rate of return, or yield, than standard investments in exchange for accepting higher default risk. Theoretically, the interest rate premium and the fact that a larger equity position is required offsets the investors risk of default. A standard grading apparatus would show an increasing interest rate and equity requirement as the credit quality deteriorates.

Ways to Improve Credit

Problem	Tactic	Result
No Credit	Obtain secured credit card or work with loan officer to obtain credit cards/loans.	Positive Outcome - establish credit. Could have been a-chieved without credit doctor.
Credit Problems (Minor)	Utilize multiple correspondence addressing each incident and follow up systems to test credi-tors responsiveness. Creditors only have 30 days to respond to written request in writing. If they do not, they must remove the notation under ECOA.	Positive Outcome - there is a chance that the creditor will not be able to respond to some or all of the requests in a timely manner and will have to remove negative references. On the other hand, there is no guarantee - you might do this yourself.
Credit Problems (Major)	New Social Security Number or Tax I.D. number.	Negative - this is highly illegal.

Credit Counselors/Agencies - There are credit counseling agencies which can help borrowers who have over-extended themselves work out repayment plans with creditors, re-arrange financial plans, and arrange consolidation loans. For a local agency, call the National Foundation for Consumer Credit (301) 589-5600, a non-profit organization. As seductive as it may sound, there is no bona-fide way of obtaining a new, completely repaired credit history without dancing around ethical barriers and breaking laws. If a company offers to repair credit and charges a large up-front fee, you are dealing with a "credit doctor." See – Strategies for Improving Credit History for ways to work that may or may not improve the ability to obtain credit.

Credit Counseling is perceived as a negative. This is counter-intuitive to many borrowers' instincts. Their thought is "I'm getting my credit cleaned up!" Our perception is that they gave up on doing it themselves – couldn't handle it – so why are they trying to borrow money again?

There is one positive thing to be said about adverse credit history - it eventually does go away. The statute of limitations for delinquent credit reporting is 7 years. Judgments and liens are removed after 10 years. Often a lender who reported negative ratings will delete them if the account has been reestablished in a positive way. For instance delinquent student loans may have their negative ratings removed once paid. Even though lenders have an obligation to report delinquencies, guaranteed student loans were made available to help the students, not destroy financial futures.

Sub-Prime Lending

The fact remains that, despite some options, there is very little a mortgage lender can do to help a borrower who has poor credit. Some first time homebuyer programs are more liberal in determining creditworthiness, such as FHA, VA and Community Homebuyer programs. If a borrower fails eligibility for any other program, he or she can avail themselves of what is known as "Credit Graded," "B, C & D," "Choice"or" Non-Prime" mortgages. A generic grading system shows the illustrative increase in interest rates and equity requirement as the credit grade deteriorates. While the lines between "Sub-prime A-" and "ALT-A loans" have become gray, true "Sub-Prime" is also known as "B-C-D".

Generic Sub-Prime Grading Matrix				
Rating	Description/Allowable Derogatory	Ratios	Equity (LTV)	Rate Premium
A- FNMA EA1, 2, 3	Mortgage - Current; 2x30, 0x60; Consumer Credit - Generally excellent, no more than 20% of all other accounts report delinquencies; No bankruptcy; No judgments over $100	42/42	80-90	0.00 - 2.50%
B	Mortgage - Current; 4x30, or 2x30 & 1x60; Consumer Credit - Reasonably good, no more than 40% of all other accounts report past delinquencies. No bankruptcy in 24-36 months; No judgments over $250	45/50	75-90	1.50 - 3.00%
C	Mortgage - Slow; 6x30, 1x60, 1x90 - Can be currently past due; Consumer Credit - Significant past problems; Many accounts late; Open judgments; No bankruptcy within last 12-24 months;	50/60	70	2.00 - 6.00%
D	Mortgage - Currently Past Due/Foreclosure; Consumer Credit Serious problems, collections, judgments, delinquencies; active Bankruptcy	60/60	50-60	4.00 - 12.00%

The embrace of the huge profit potential of the ALT-A and non-prime loan business among mortgage companies has had unintended consequences which costs companies more than they realize in lost profits and time. The result, the further erosion of credit analysis and qualifying skills of loan officers, reduces the significance of the role of the originator. In addition, it contributes to the accidental application of predatory lending practices.

How it Happens

The wholesale non-prime business' primary sales focus is to get originators to submit applications for a pre-qualification. The originator faxes a 1003 and credit report to the wholesaler to get a credit grade and indicative rate. The wholesale representative then grades the loan and "stips it out," adding the standard documentation requirements as a condition of pre-qualification. The originator, in turn, contacts the borrower to obtain the requested documentation from the borrower. When the originator follows this process, the wholesale representative enjoys a position of inordinate power in this role, controlling the loan from the minute it arrives. On the face of it, there is nothing different in this process from what a loan officer does with a retail client, so what is the problem?

Problem 1: The Wholesaler's Control

The position of certainty – that is, "don't worry, I'll get this loan done" – occupied by the wholesaler naturally impairs the loan officer's motivation to represent the borrower's best interests. "The loan is done, and I can go on to the next deal." This means that the first representative who gives a positive answer on the loan will likely control that loan for the remainder of the process, whether or not it is the best transaction for the borrower.

Many states legally mandate that a loan originator cannot accept a loan from a borrower if the loan originator does not know whether the borrower will receive a loan. How can the loan officer make this determination if he or she is relying on the wholesale investor's pre-qualification?

Problem 2: The Pre-Approval The verbiage "Pre-Approval" has become substituted for what it is – a "Pre-Qualification." A Pre-Approval, in the context it is used today, means "Approved subject to Approval." Really – it's a "Pre-Qualification" until it is a "Loan Commitment." Unfortunately, many loan officers don't focus on this blatant distinction. They tell their borrower that the loan is approved and use it as leverage to advance the application. This results in an obvious question from the borrower when the transaction ends up not proceeding as planned – "I thought you said the loan was approved." There have been many cases in which borrowers have followed a loan process only to learn that there was no approval. The consequences often are; having to close later, at a higher rate, with a lower loan amount or with a different program.

Many states are now regulating the use of the word "Pre-Approval" to mean that the borrower must in fact apply and be accepted prior to being "Pre-Approved."

For the loan officer, the use of the "pre-qualification as pre-approval" system costs him or her money. If all he or she knows about pre-qualification is "give me your name, social security number and address," the loan officer does not have any tool for developing a trusting rapport with the borrower. Only the most desperate borrowers will end up with this loan officer.

Problem 3: Predatory Practices

Non-Prime loans are already viewed with a jaundiced eye by regulators because borrowers who can least afford to pay higher rates are most often offered these loans exclusively. Some predatory practices are a by-product of the Non-Prime wholesale process:

Bait and Switch – Initially offering a more attractive product and changing the terms at the end of the process is a problem created by the "Pre-Qualification as Pre-Approval" process.
Lending without Regard to Repayment Ability – Wholesalers may encourage loan officers to submit loans as "Stated" income, or change the process from a Reduced Documentation process to a No-Qualifier process without consulting the loan officer in an effort to facilitate the approval. As we know there are many ways to get the loan approved, but should we?

Problem 4: Faulty System

The process of submitting a loan for a pre-qualification from a non-prime lender is no different that submitting a loan to automated underwriting through DU or LP. The approval is really no better than the documentation submitted to support it. The difficulty is that many companies do not force loan officers to take complete applications in advance. As a consequence, individuals – loan officers, processors, managers – spend a lot of time trying to obtain documentation that does not exist or is insufficient. These documentation problems would be revealed immediately with a complete application.

What to Do

These scenarios are in no way an indictment of the non-prime business, which performs a vital function in providing financing to non-standard borrowers. It is a matter of education of the loan officer, and creating a culture of managing the process instead of the process managing us.

With respect to the Sub-Prime lending quandary, we already know where the problems are, and we take the following steps to correct them:

1.) Institute "Defined **Complete** Application", to be taken in before the loan is submitted for underwriting – including all commonly requested loan documents – income, asset and credit.
2.) Assemble Loan Plan Specifications Matrix for top programs – with underwriting guidelines – and selective review and approval of wholesale representatives. All originators, but particularly new loan originators, should be required to use only approved investors.
3.) Institute Processing Flow identifying the specific steps that must be followed by EVERY party in order to deliver excellent customer service.

High-Rate, High-Fee Loans (HOEPA/Section 32 Mortgages)

The Home Ownership and Equity Protection Act of 1994 (HOEPA) addresses certain deceptive and unfair practices in home equity lending. It amends the Truth in Lending Act (TILA) and establishes requirements for certain loans with high rates and/or high fees.

> **Section 32 Loans**
> - A first-lien loan where the annual percentage rate (APR) exceeds the rates on Treasury securities of comparable maturity by more than eight percentage points;
> - A second-lien loan where the APR exceeds the rates in Treasury securities of comparable maturity by more than 10 percentage points; or
> - The total fees and points payable by the consumer at or before closing exceed the larger of $488 or eight percent of the total loan amount. (The $488 figure is for 2004. The Federal Reserve Board, based on changes in the Consumer Price Index, adjusts this amount annually.) Credit insurance premiums for insurance written in connection with the credit transaction are counted as fees.

The rules primarily affect refinancing and home equity installment loans that also meet the definition of a high-rate or high-fee loan. The rules do not cover loans to buy or build your home, reverse mortgages or home equity lines of credit (similar to revolving credit accounts).

The following features are banned from Section 32 high-rate, high-fee loans:

- All balloon payments for loans with less than five-year terms.
- Negative amortization.
- Default interest rates higher than pre-default rates.
- A repayment schedule that consolidates more than two periodic payments that will be paid in advance from the proceeds of the loan.
- Most prepayment penalties, including refunds of unearned interest calculated by any method less favorable than the actuarial method. Unless
  - The lender verifies that your total monthly debt (including the mortgage) is 50 percent or less of your monthly gross income;
  - you get the money to prepay the loan from a source other than the lender or an affiliate lender; and
  - the lender exercises the penalty clause during the first five years following execution of the mortgage.
- A due-on-demand clause unless
  - there is fraud or material misrepresentation by the consumer in connection with the loan;
  - the consumer fails to meet the repayment terms of the agreement; or there is any action by the consumer that adversely affects the creditor's security.
- Creditors may not:
  - make loans based on the collateral value of your property without regard to ability to repay the loan.
  - refinance a HOEPA loan into another HOEPA loan within the first 12 months of origination, unless the new loan is in the borrower's best interest. The prohibition also applies to assignees holding or servicing the loan.
  - document a closed-end, high-cost loan as an open-end loan. For example, a high-cost mortgage may not be structured as a home equity line of credit if there is no reasonable expectation that repeat transactions will occur.

Understanding Credit Scoring

The development of credit scoring has been touted by the banking industry as a panacea to the problem of maintaining consistency in underwriting and assuring quality loans. Credit scoring is the process of numerically grading the overall profile of a

How Good Is My Score?	
700 & Above	Excellent
680 - 700	Very Good
640 - 680	Generally Acceptable
620 - 660	Marginal
below 620	Caution

borrower to ascertain how the profile has historically performed and making a credit decision on that basis. The Fair-Isaacs Company (FICO) developed a predictive model for Experian/TRW that has become the basis for many credit models that now exist. In fact these models have taken on a life of their own. They can be adjusted or enhanced by the ordering party to reflect their particular underwriting preferences.

The scores are designed to predict, based upon past experience, how a customer will repay the loan. These scores, combined with specific risk grading criteria, are how banks have traditionally approved credit cards, auto loans, home equity loans and other minor consumer loans for the past 10 years. "Risk-based" underwriters like PMI companies have utilized the methodology for years. It is the contribution of mainstream commercial banking to the evolution of mortgage banking evolution. However, it is a negative for the mortgage business because in this industry lenders have given traditionally given borrowers a closer look. In the interests of speed, many borrowers may fall between the cracks. The risk score is not supposed to make the decision to approve a loan. But one can't help but think that an adverse credit score is sure to impede the approval, while a positive score is a confirmation.

The basic theory of risk scoring is that there are historical factors that impact a borrower's ability - or willingness - to meet obligations. The factors are, not surprisingly, credit history, source of income, down payment, debt to income ratios, and loan type.

Credit Scoring Models
CBI/Equifax – **Beacon** – Most Conservative Model
TransUnion- **Empirica**
TRW – **Experian** – Most Active in Consumer and Business Reporting

Credit Score Reason Code/Description	CBI	TU	TRW
Amount owed on accounts is too high	1	1	1
Delinquency on accounts	2	2	2
Too few bank revolving accounts	3	n/a	3
Too many bank or national revolving accounts	4	n/a	4
Too many accounts with balances	5	5	5
Consumer finance accounts	6	6	6
Account payment history too new to rate	7	7	7
Too many recent inquiries last 12 months	8	8	8
Too many accounts opened in last 12 months	9	9	9
Proportion of balances to credit limit is too high on revolving accts	10	10	10
Amount owed on revolving accounts is too high	11	11	11
Length of revolving credit history is too short	12	12	12
Time since delinquency too recent or unknown	13	13	13
Length of credit history is too short	14	14	14
Lack of recent bank revolving information	15	15	15
Lack of recent revolving account information	16	16	16
No recent non-mortgage balance information	17	17	17
Number of accounts with delinquency	18	18	18
Too few accounts currently paid as agreed	19	19	19
Time since derogatory public record or collection	20	20	20
Amount past due on accounts	21	21	21
Serious delinquency, derogatory public record or collection filed	22	22	22
Too many bank or national revolving accounts with balances	23	n/a	n/a
No recent revolving balances	24	24	24
Proportion of loan balances to loan amounts is too high	33	3	33
Lack of recent installment loan information	32	4	32
Date of last inquiry too recent	n/a	19	n/a
Time since most recent account opening too short	30	30	30
Number of revolving accounts	20	n/a	20
Number of bank revolving or other revolving accour	n/a	26	n/a
Number of established accounts	28	28	28
No recent bankcard balances	n/a	29	n/a
Too few accounts with recent payment information	31	n/a	31

FICO Model

- 35% overall payment histories
- 30% amount of debt
- 15% length of credit file
- 10% recent history

- 10% mix of credit

Risk Grading

There are numerous risk scoring devices. As the consumer credit business seeks ways to automate and streamline credit approval we add new tools constantly. In mortgage lending, none of these are designed to be exclusive; they are used in tandem with each other. Unfortunately, most of these tools currently take the form of what we refer to as automated underwriting protocols. These "proprietary underwriting models" include FHLMC and FNMA models as well as privately developed models.

There are 3 possible outcomes from Automated Underwriting: Approve, Deny or Refer. *It is loans in the "deny" and "refer" categories where loan officers to earn their money.* Obviously, mortgage companies don't need loan officers if a machine can approve a loan; so knowing the ins and outs of the guidelines is how the lender adds value.

The developers of these programs – not surprisingly - don't give much insight as to how to work within the models. These organizations are purposely secretive about the specific guidelines they set for rendering Automated Underwriting Decisions. If they told us what the guidelines were and how it worked, we could simply tailor every application to meet the system's requirements and it would be relatively easy to manipulate the model's outcome.

However FHLMC has published a manual scoring worksheet – "The Gold Measure Worksheet." The Automated Underwriting that is becoming more prevalent through computer approval programs is merely a risk scoring mechanism where the machine finds enough positive criteria present to eliminate the need for a subjective positive decision. The FHLMC Gold Measure is simply one of many scoring systems. Although it is extremely simple, it has been statistically more accurate than many more complicated models. It is represented by a self-explanatory one-page worksheet. From this one can see where the weight is placed. Each attribute is a positive or a negative. How strong or weak the attribute is in the overall consideration is indicated by how dramatically the overall score can be impacted by the measure. Attributes are ranked in "Risk Units," with the objective of obtaining the lowest possible score. (A minus is a good thing!)

Scoring Positives	Scoring Negatives
• Perfect credit file with 11 or more open accounts • Revolving balances below $500 • Percent of all trade lines with derogatory rankings; 0-10% • 2 years on job • **Good** - 30% down payment • **Best** - down payment of 40% or more • Previous housing expense that is <120% of the proposed payment	• Percent of all trade lines with derogatory rankings; 16-40% >60% • Worst delinquency ever is >30 days • Judgments or collections • More than 3 delinquent public records • **Bad** - 2-3 inquiries • **Worse** - more than 5 inquiries • Less than 2 years work history • Self-employed/commissioned borrowers • Less than 2 months reserves • Over 40% total debt • ARMs • **Bad** - Condominiums and 2 units

• Loan term < 25 years	• **Worse** - 3-4 unit properties

Consider the Impact

It doesn't take long to realize that, utilizing risk scoring, the following transactions won't be easy to approve:

1.) Borrowers with marginal credit
2.) Self-employed borrowers who have creative income approaches
3.) Borrowers with high ratios and little down payment funds
4.) Borrowers who do not have established credit
5.) Any condominium or 2-4 unit property with marginal attributes
6.) Anybody with a total debt ratio of over 42%

A positive aspect of this system is that a greater emphasis is given to down payment. With a large down payment, there is almost nothing that impedes a loan from being approved.
Hopefully there will always be the lender that makes an individual decision on each loan. For years the loan officer has been able to present a case that challenges established guidelines. The loan officer's job in that situation is to argue the case, its merits, support compensating factors, dig for details that can give the underwriter a visceral sense that the case is solid. This process has also helped many individuals gain respect for creditworthiness. By understanding the challenges they present to lenders, borrowers can improve or modify their behavior to make financing easier for them in the future.

Fraud Alerts

When dealing with borrower's credit reports, care should be taken to look for issues that might indicate a borrower is misrepresenting or concealing information. These "Red Flags" can cause problems in the loan process.

CREDIT / CREDIT REPORTS
• No credit (possible use of alias)
• High income borrower with little or no cash (undisclosed liabilities)
• Variance in employment or residence data from other sources
• Recent inquiries from other mortgage lenders
• Invalid social security number
• AKA or DBA indicated
• Round dollar amounts (especially on interest-bearing accounts)
• Borrower cannot be reached at place of business
• High income borrower with no "prestige" credit cards

Gold Measure®—Version 2.3 Worksheet

Freddie Mac

Borrower/Co-borrower Name(s)	Seller/Servicer Name
	Seller/Servicer Number
	Freddie Mac Loan Number (if available)
City, State	Branch Office/TPO
Lender Loan Number	Underwriting Center
Origination Date	TPO Name
Completion Date	Underwriter

Loan Decision Approved ___ Denied ___ Withdrawn ___ File Closed ___

Directions: ■ Following Gold Measure worksheet instructions, circle the appropriate "Risk Units" (RUs) for each applicable worksheet category. Add up the RUs in each section and enter that number on the **Subtotal** line for that section. To calculate the worksheet score, combine the Subtotal for each section and enter that total on the **Total RUs** line. Note that negative numbers such as "-2" indicate risk offsets.
■ It is important to read the accompanying *Gold Measure—Version 2.3 and Worksheet Instructions* booklet and to refer to it for additional information on completing this worksheet.
■ Freddie Mac's Gold Measure worksheet is an Expanding Markets℠ underwriting aid and is not a substitute for the underwriting decision; use Gold Measure in conjunction with your Freddie Mac Purchase Documents.
■ Complete either Credit File A or Credit File B, but not both. Use Credit File A if at least two credit scores are requested from the repositories. Use Credit File B if fewer than two credit scores are requested, or if the scores you receive are not usable for Gold Measure.

I. Credit File A

Directions: Use Credit File A when not using Credit File B, and complete **either** the FICO bureau score **or** the MDS bankruptcy score, but not both. (See instructions)

FICO bureau scores	RUs	MDS bankruptcy scores	RUs
Equifax BEACON℠, Trans Union EMPIRICA® and Experian/FICO (formerly TRW/FICO)		Equifax Delinquency Alert System℠, Trans Union DELPHI℠ and Experian/MDS (formerly TRW/MDS)	
Over 790	-16	150 or less	-12
771 – 790	-14	151 - 200	-10
761 – 770	-11	201 - 240	-4
731 – 760	-7	241 - 300	-3
721 – 730	-5	301 - 320	-1
701 – 720	0	321 - 360	0
681 – 700	6	361 - 420	4
661 – 680	8	421 - 480	8
641 – 660	12	481 - 540	11
621 – 640	17	541 - 620	15
601 – 620	20	621 - 700	18
581 – 600	23	701 - 740	21
541 – 580	25	741 - 840	23
540 or less	32	841 - 960	25
		Over 960	29
No reported score available	14	No reported score available	14

I. Credit File A.
Subtotal of circled **RUs:** _____

II. Income

	RUs
Self-employed **and** earnings exceed area median income (if commissions RUs not circled)	5
Majority of income from commissions (if self-employed RUs not circled)	5
Co-borrower on application with income	-2
Borrower's time on job is five years or more	-2
Co-borrower's time on job is two years or more	-1

II. Income. **Subtotal** of circled **RUs:** _____

III. Loan, Collateral, Assets

LTV or TLTV (including secondary financing*) is	RUs
60.5% or lower	-27
60.6 – 70.5%	-16
70.6 – 80.0%	-5
80.1 – 85.5%	-1
85.6 – 90.5%	0
90.6 – 93.5%	2
93.6 – 94.5%	5
94.6 – 95.5%	8
95.6 – 96.5%	10
96.6 – 98.5%	11
98.6 – 99.5%	13
99.6 – 99.9%	15

Property seller contributions exceed 3% of value	RUs
	5

Reserves are	RUs
Less than 1 month	8
At least 1, but less than 2 months	5
At least 2, but less than 4 months	0
At least 4, but less than 5 months	-3
5 or more months	-6

	RUs
Less than 5 percent down from borrower funds with 95 percent LTV (e.g. Affordable Gold® 3/2) (Do **not** circle for 97 percent LTV loans)	3

III. Loan, Collateral, Assets.
Subtotal of circled **RUs:** _____

*For secondary financing with payments due before the maturity of the Freddie Mac loan, add the amount of the second mortgage to the amount of the first mortgage to calculate the TLTV. For secondary financing with no payments due before the maturity of the Freddie Mac loan, add one-half the amount of the second mortgage to the amount of the first mortgage to calculate the TLTV.

I. Credit File B

Directions: Use Credit File B if not using Credit File A.

If there are **no**
■ Delinquencies
■ Other derogatory tradelines
■ Derogatory public records
and
■ Total number of tradelines (open **or** closed) is

	RUs
11 or more	-3
6 – 10	-2
1 – 5	0

One or more revolving tradelines, **and** total revolving balance is under $500	RUs
	-3

Fewer than 3 tradelines (open **or** closed)	RUs
	2

Percent of all tradelines (open or closed) ever delinquent or worse (30-90 days or more, collection, charge-off, etc.)

	RUs
0 – 10%	-3
11 – 15%	0
16 – 40%	3
41 – 60%	6
Over 60%	8

Worst ever derogatory credit file entry is either

	RUs
■ 30–180 days delinquent **or** ■ Public record (bankruptcy, foreclosure, judgment, lien, garnishment, suit, certain collections), or tradeline reported as over 180 days delinquent, charge-off, repossession or collection	4
	7

Number of derogatory public records	RUs
0 - 1	0
2 - 3	3
Over 3	7

Number of inquiries in the past three months	RUs
0	-1
1	0
2 - 3	4
4	6
5	8
More than 5	10

Age of oldest tradeline (in months)	RUs
0 (no tradelines) – 6	12
7 – 12	9
13 – 24	5
25 – 48	2
49 – 72	1
73 – 120	0
121 or more	-1

If age of oldest tradeline is 13–48 months **and** any one or more of the following
■ More than three inquiries within the past three months
■ More than three tradelines opened in the past year
■ Total open balance exceeds $10,000

	RUs
	4

Spread between total debt and housing ratios (i.e. nonhousing debt ratio) is

	RUs
10 – 15%	2
More than 15%	5

I. Credit File B. **Subtotal** of circled **RUs:** _____

IV. Debt Payment-to-Income Ratios

Debt payment-to-income ratio is	RUs
Less than 32.6%	0
32.6 – 38.5%	2
38.6 – 40.5%	3
40.6 – 42.5%	5
42.6 – 44.5%	6
44.6 – 46.5%	8
46.6 – 48.5%	10
48.6 – 50.5%	12
Over 50.5%	30

Proposed monthly housing expense is less than 120% of previous monthly housing expense	RUs
	-1

IV. Debt Payment-to-Income Ratios.
Subtotal of circled **RUs:** _____

V. Loan/Property Type

Loan type is		RUs
Fixed-Rate	15-Year	-6
	20-Year	-4
	25-Year	-1

		RUs
ARM	Rate-Capped	6
	Payment-Capped	8

Property type is	RUs
2-Unit	5
3- to 4-Unit	11
Condominium	5

V. Loan/Property Type.
Subtotal of circled **RUs:** _____

Total of Sections I A or I B, II, III, IV and V. **TOTAL all RUs:** _____

Freddie Mac Risk Unit Guideline	15 RUs
Guideline if prepurchase counseling	16 RUs
Guideline if postpurchase counseling	17 RUs
Guideline if pre- and postpurchase counseling	18 RUs

Refer to *Gold Measure—Version 2.3 and Worksheet Instructions* booklet for more information.
This worksheet is an aid, not a substitute for the underwriting decision.
Call your account manager for additional information.

© February 1998 Freddie Mac

Chapter 5
QUALIFYING
Income & Other
Restrictions

Understanding Income

The most frequent complaint in qualifying borrowers is that "the ratios are too high." The ratios themselves, though, are simply measurements. Actually, what needs to be analyzed is the information against which the ratios are being applied. In this case qualifying ratios really are only as useful as the information applied to them. Often, then, as lenders we are put in the position of saying "how much income does this person need in order to qualify?" and working from there.

Most people know how much they can afford to spend based on their experience. These people may have income situations that make it hard for them to qualify for the amount they believe they can afford. The loan officer must have a fundamental understanding of the way all different people in all vocations are paid. If everyone were paid a base salary or an hourly wage for a standard workweek, a discussion of income wouldn't be necessary. The objective in addressing income as to qualifying is how much income the lender can count on to be stable and continuing.

"Stable" Income

With individuals who work for a company and are paid a regular salary, there is no ambiguity over the amount of income available for debt service. However, the temptation to utilize a higher level of income exists for borrowers who have variable income or who are self-employed. It is for these borrowers that we must address income.   Each category of income has different

Hourly	Weekly	Bi-Weekly	Semi-Monthly	Monthly
Rate x hours/week X 52 weeks divided by 12	Rate x 52 divided by 12	Rate x 26 divided by 12	Rate x 2	Rate
$8/hr x 40 = $320 x 52 = $16,640 /12 = $1,386.66	$800/wk x 52 = 41,600/12 = 3,466.66	$2,000 x 26 = 52,000 /12 =$4,333.33	$1500 x 2 = $3000	$3000

attributes that affect the manner of treatment. Within each category there are different ways of increasing the amount of income that can be used for qualifying. To determine the manner of treatment we must ask the same basic question again; "How much income is needed for qualification?" because there are conservative, less conservative and aggressive approaches for each category.

Base Income with Enhancements

If the income needed for qualification is higher than what is available from the base alone, the treatment of additional sources becomes important. The biggest question from a qualifying perspective is at what point does the borrower stop being a salaried employee and become technically self employed. The standard definition is that where 25% or more of the income required for qualifying is of a variable nature, the borrower is considered self-employed and is subject to some of the rigors of self-employment qualification including income averaging and an examination of all applicable income documents.

25%

The reason for this is the underwriting concern that a borrower may offset some of the variable income earned with tax deductible expenses reducing the actual income. If the variable income does not result in deductions by the borrower, then there is no problem. However, if the borrower does have significant deductions which adversely affect qualifying every effort should be made to limit the amount of variable income attributed to the borrower for qualifying purposes to less than 25% of the overall qualifying income. One can even include a co-borrower's income to increase the proportion of variable income that can be utilized before invoking the 25% rule.

Getting the most of Overtime, Bonus, & Commissions

Overtime, bonuses and commissions are three areas in which a salaried or base income employee can enhance their qualifying income. The most important aspect of utilizing these is past history of receiving the type of income, the current level, and the probability of its continuance. The circumstances surrounding each are different so its treatment and maximization are different.

Overtime

Overtime may be paid out at a multiple of base earnings (time and a half, for example). The trick in maximizing overtime income

Example - Calculating Overtime for Hourly Workers						
Year	Pay/Hr.	Hrs. Wk.	Base	Overtime	Weekly	Annual
2001	$ 6.50	46 Hrs	$ 260.00	$ 58.50	$ 318.50	$ 16,552.00
2002	$ 6.83	46 Hrs	$ 273.20	$ 61.47	$ 334.67	$ 17,402.00
2003	$ 7.18	46 Hrs	$ 287.20	$ 64.62	$ 351.82	$ 11,258.00
(8 Months in 2003)					Total	$ 45,212.00

is to extract the amount of hours of overtime worked for averaging, as opposed to averaging the dollar amount. **Average the hours - not the dollar amount!** The reason for this is that averaging the dollar amount reflects past earnings, whereas averaging the hours allows you to take advantage of the current rate of pay and utilize income going forward. This takes into account increases in the base or hourly rate as cost of living and other raises are applied.

The most fundamental issue for overtime maximization is establishing the average number of hours worked per week. Obviously, the greater the number of hours worked, the larger the income for qualifying. If; 1.) There is nothing that prevents an employee from working more hours, such as a second job, school, or a demonstrated need to care for a family, and 2.) The employer states that the employee is eligible to work more hours and states an average number of hours of overtime worked per week, then it is possible that there could be additional income available for qualifying.

Two Approaches to Overtime Income Calculation

Approach	Conservative - Average Earnings		Maximized - Average Hours Worked	
Example	Total Income Divided By Number of Months = Qualifying Income	45,212 32 1,412.87/mo.	Current Overtime Rate (7.18 x 1.5) Multiply by Average Hours of O.T. Qualifying Weekly Overtime Plus Base Weekly Income Total X 52 = 18,294/ yr divided by 12 =	$10.77/hr x 6 hours $ 64.62 $287.20 $351.82 $1,524/mo

Bonus, Tips and Commission

With overtime you can establish qualifying income with some certainty; the number of hours and the rate of pay, in addition to a historical performance, can all be demonstrated. The only thing that can be reasonably quantified about Bonus, Tips and Commission income is that it will continue. In these cases a historical average is the accepted method of determining qualifying income. There are some circumstances in which a larger amount of income might be acceptable, depending on whether the situation is compelling and compensating factors are in place. Unfortunately, even under the most lenient guidelines, credence will never be given for income that has not yet been received - referred to as prospective income.

Income Type	Conservative Treatment	Optimal Treatment	Maximized Treatment
Commissions	Average 2 Years Tax Returns	Utilize 24 months exactly. Example: 8 months Year to Date, 12 months past year and 4 months previous year	If there is a trend of increasing commissions, utilize a shorter average. For instance previous full year and year to date. Must show previous earnings were irrelevant/not comparable. (See self-employment.)
Bonuses	Average past 2 years	Use previous bonus alone with letter from employer that future bonus will be higher	Use guaranteed bonus if it can be shown that similar employees received similar bonus.
Tips	Average Past 2 Years	Average previous 24 months exactly, if beneficial for qualifying	Utilize bank statements to show deposits of tips above base. Utilize previous year and year to date.

Other Arguments for Using a Shorter Average

When a borrower needs to utilize a higher level of income to qualify, and using the methods shown above does not provide enough income for the case, another strategy is to show the progression of a borrower's income. A case can be made that the current income (from the previous year's tax return and year-to-date income statement) can be used in the example of a borrower that has income which has increased regularly for 5 years and can provide substantiation that it will continue at least at the same level at a minimum. In the previous example, we assume that the borrower doesn't qualify for the loan requested based on 2001, 2002 and year-to-date income averaged over 30 months ($47,000 + $58,000 + $37,000 ÷ 30 = $4733/mo.). By showing that the income has increased consistently, we can optimize the income by averaging the last 2 years (24 months) exactly, increasing qualifying income by $204. A maximized scenario shows the borrower is increasing income every year, and a shorter average is utilized to show just the most recent 18 months be able to utilize the past year and year to date income ($58,000 + $37,000 ÷ 18 = $5277/mo.), increasing the qualifying income by $544/month.

Using History of Income Increase to Support a Shorter Average

Year	Conservative Approach Income	(%Increase)	Optimal Approach		Maximized Approach	
1997	$ 20,000	N/A				
1998	$ 25,000	25%				
1999	$ 31,000	24%				
2000	$ 38,000	23%				
2001	$ 47,000	24%	$ 23,500	6 months		
2002	$ 58,000	23%	$ 58,000	12 months	$ 58,000	12 months
2003 (6 mos)	$ 37,000	28%	$ 37,000	6 months	$ 37,000	6 months
Total	$ 142,000		$ 118,500	24 months	$ 95,000	18 months
Divided By Months	30		24		18	
Qualifying Income	$ 4,733.33		$ 4,937.50		$ 5,277.70	

Another scenario for using a shorter average might actually be where the lender needs to omit a recent year. If there was a personal tragedy, or the borrower was working on something unrelated, which caused the income to drop it might be unfair to hold the decrease against the borrower. In this case, the same strategy is utilized, except the year that was unfavorable is minimized or omitted. If 2001 was the documented bad year, the traditional approach would yield income of only ($18,000 + $58,000 + $45,000 ÷ 30 = $4033.33/mo.) while going back further and averaging ($50,000 + $58,000 + $45,000 ÷ 30 = $6433.33/mo.) for a borrower whose income decrease was really an anomaly.

Eliminate a Bad Year By Using a Longer Time Frame

Year	Income	(%Increase)		
1997	$ 45,000	N/A		
1998	$ 47,000	4%		
1999	$ 40,000	-15%	$ 40,000	12 months
2000	$ 50,000	25%	$ 50,000.00	12 months
2001	$ 18,000.00	-64%		Eliminated
2002	$ 58,000.00	222%	$ 58,000.00	12 months
2003 (6 mos)	$ 45,000.00	55%	$ 45,000.00	6 months
Total	$ 121,000.00	228%	$ 193,000.00	
Divided by Months/Years	30	6.5	30	
Qualifying Income	$ 4,033.33	35%	$ 6,433.33	

Omitting the income and including year-to-date income greatly enhances the average, or stable, monthly income.

Future Raises

Something that is scheduled to happen in the future is never certain. Things change, as we all know, and this is one of the truths in underwriting. Anything that is proposed is prospective and is automatically discounted. Since prospective income can never really be included for qualifying income, don't ever refer to it as such. Call it something different, like pro-forma income. It means the same thing, but doesn't have the negative connotations. An argument can be made for counting future raises if there is a history of past raises and the new pay will start reasonably soon (within 6 months) of closing. A future bonus may fall under the same category.

There are specific instances where a future raise can definitely be used. Government workers, armed forces servicemen, or employees of institutions which have regularly scheduled cost of living increases which are a matter of record can compellingly prove that their raise will be effective. In this case a future raise can be used as a matter of course. If an employee obtains a copy of a performance review which indicates a promotion, or a grade increase, then it is possible to utilize the higher figure. Again, it is a matter of how compelling the information is.

Income Documentation Requirements Matrix

Employment Type	Standard Documentation	Documentation to Optimize or address extenuating Circumstances
Hourly	30 Days' Paystubs, 2 Years' W-2	For future increase, employer letter
Hourly with Overtime	30 Days' Paystubs, 2 Years' W-2	VOE or employer letter showing hours worked
Salary	30 Days' Paystubs, 2 Years' W-2	For future increase, employer letter
Salary with Bonus	30 Days' Paystubs, 2 Years' W-2	Employer letter stating bonus continuance, VOE
Salary with Commissions	30 Days' Paystubs, 2 Years' W-2	If more than 25%, Federal Personal Tax Return 1040 with Schedule A Attached
		If using shorter than 24 month average, current commissions pending
Commissions Only	30 Days' Paystubs, 2 Years' W-2, 1040 with Schedule A, 2106 Employee Business Expenses	
Tips	30 Days' Paystubs, 2 Years' W-2, 1040 with Schedule A, 2106 Employee Business Expenses	

Dividends & Interest

One frequent income qualification error is the use of assets that are income bearing but will be liquidated as part of the transaction. Just as prospective income cannot be used, income from an asset that no longer exists cannot be used. If a portion of the assets yielding income is to be liquidated, it may benefit the borrower to determine the percentage of assets remaining and then take a percentage of the previous income.

Calculating Dividend/Interest Income		
Mutual Fund Account	$	100,000
Portion Liquidated	$	50,000
Percentage		50%
Income - 2001	$	8,125
Income - 2002	$	13,150
Total	$	21,275
Divided by 24 Months	$	886
Multiply by 50%	$	443

Self-Employment

There exists a quandary for the self-employed borrower. It is based upon the premise of risk and reward. Small business drives economic growth and the entrepreneurial spirit has created many wealthy people. But there are some stunning and sobering statistics:

- Self-employed borrowers are more than 200% as likely to default on their obligations. In Southern California self-employed borrowers are 400% as likely to default.

- 90% of all start-up businesses fail within the first two years.

These are daunting odds and present a special challenge in qualifying, processing and approving self-employed borrowers. The case will be reviewed far more thoroughly than that of the average borrower for a number of reasons:

- The borrower's income stream, even if it appears stable, is based upon the company's performance, which may vary. There are two levels of income to review.
- Self-employment income is taxable on a "net of expenses" basis. Since paying taxes decreases income, one of the benefits of self-employment is deducting expenses from gross income to reduce a tax bill. In this situation the most substantive form of income documentation - the tax return - suddenly becomes the enemy because every conceivable legitimate deduction is utilized to reduce the tax burden.
- In a closely held company, where does the company end and the self-employed borrower begin? Is a company car really the company's? What expenses are really just personal expenses that are taken into consideration by general underwriting guidelines for the populace?

2 Years!!

Because of the high number of failures of start-up businesses someone who is considered self-employed must have been in business for at least 2 years to even be eligible for a mortgage. A case can be made for considering a borrower who has been self-employed for less than two years if there is sufficient documentation to show that the income going forward has a reasonable probability of continuing.

Obviously, if the borrower has been in business for 22 or 23 months, and shows signs of success, it is probably close enough. If a borrower could go back to a salaried position, such as a lawyer, doctor or other professional, the risk is mitigated particularly if the income being used for qualifying is lower than the salary being earned before and the business and clients are the same. One could also make the argument that an existing businesses previous cash flow could be attributed towards the borrower who recently acquired it - if it were a franchise or other established business.

Who is Self-Employed?

An individual who owns 25% or more of a business would be defined as self-employed. In addition to income averaging at this level you must now analyze the business as well as the borrower. The first level of understanding is what kind of a business it is, because this determines what documentation is required and how the income is averaged.

Treatment of Self-Employment Income

One of the primary benefits of self-employment is that expenses (allowable write-offs, deductions, and deferments) can reduce taxable income. The fewer taxes you pay, the more money you keep - simple! Taxable income is net income. Often there is confusion when a self-employed borrower reports gross income, as opposed to net income – the lender will use income net of expenses for qualifying. In addition, companies themselves are vehicles for storing money or assets necessary for operation of the business. This money does not get taken out until it is needed or the business is liquidated.

This is legitimate tax avoidance - not tax evasion. There are many wealthy self-employed people who pay far less in taxes than their employed counterparts. By its very nature self-employment income verification is in direct contradiction to the goals of the loan officer. The borrower wants to show the best possible picture to the lender, but the worst picture to the IRS. The problem here is that both the IRS and the lender have to use the same source of information - the Federal Tax Forms.

Self-Employment and Documentation Types

Type	Description	Document
Sole Proprietor	A 100% individually owned business with no separate legal entity or identity. There is no separation between the individual and the business. The only way to separate the person and the business accounts is if separate bank accounts are maintained. The benefit of this business form is its simplicity.	Schedule C Personal tax return
Partnership	A partnership is created with a legal contract that binds at least two people. There are stratification, or levels, of partnership participation. A general partner makes decisions concerning the operation of the business, and is liable for the business's debts. The general partner may deduct certain items for tax purposes but is limited to the amount of capital that he or she has contributed and the amount that he or she has "at risk." A limited partner does not participate in the operation of business and is liable only to the extent that his or her investment in the partnership is at risk. K-1 will detail ownership interest, general or limited partner, capital contributions.	Partnership return is Federal 1065. Personal income on K-1 and Sche-dule E of 1040's
"C" Cor-poration	A corporation is a legal entity created within a specific state for which shares of stock are issued. The stock may be sold to the public or privately to get money for the business operation. Owner(s) of stock are entitled to participate in the profit of the company. A board of directors controls decisions over the operation of the business. Owners of stock are liable only for their initial investment, not for business debts. The corporation may retain or disburse income at its discretion. In addition, there may be a fiscal year different than a calendar year, which may make year to year analysis difficult.	Corporation tax return is Form 1120. Personal income is W-2-.
"S" Corpo-ration	"S" Corporations are a hybrid combination of partnerships and corporations. Business income must be claimed within a cal-endar year (like a partnership) and cannot be carried forward. However, shares of stock are issued and owners are limited in liability to their initial investment.	1120S Federal tax return, K-1 from 1040
LLC & LLP	"Limited Liability Corporations" and "Limited Liability Partnerships" are recent innovations. From a tax perspective, they will mirror the business form of corporation and partnership. The benefit of this form is that officers and partners will have less personal liability.	1120S or 1065, depending on type
Trader	An individual who buys and sells on his or her own account, such as a stock investor or real estate speculator.	Schedule D 1040
Investor	An individual who owns and rents real estate or other income produc-ing assets.	Schedule E 1040

Because each self-employed borrower is unique, many lending personnel have a phobia of analyzing this income. Every lending manual prescribing varying methods of how to do it exacerbates this phobia. The underwriters at FNMA probably thought that they were helping when they designed 3 different self-employed income analysis forms for lenders to use in assisting evaluating tax returns. In fact the forms themselves raise other quandaries: should I use the "Adjusted Gross Income Method" or the "Schedule Analysis Method?" Why do you need a "Comparative Income Analysis" - can't you just see whether the income is increasing or decreasing? The problem with these forms is that they try and provide the same treatment for all forms of self-employment. So to be comprehensive the worksheet is very long and daunting. In addition, they give the impression that there are some types of income that must be excluded.

The truth is that every self-employed borrower is different. You can't use a pre-printed form and fairly maximize the income. The only method that works is to **actually read the entire tax return!!** The depth of the analysis goes back to the first question asked in this chapter - How much income does the borrower need to show to qualify for the loan they want? If they qualify based on a 2-year average of the adjusted gross income from the first page of the tax returns, you don't need to perform a further analysis. If they are challenged at that level, though, get out a pencil and be prepared to read and write. The philosophy of self-employed income analysis is to find all of the deferred income, deductions, non-cash losses, and duplicative expenses deducted by the business and held against the borrower **and add them on back to, or on top of,** taxable income. The result should be tallied in column form, by year, and averaged for the period analyzed (generally two years) to result in qualifying income.

Start With the Personal Returns

Simple Self-Employed Income Analysis						
		2001		**2002**		**2003**
Gross Inome	$	198,103.00	$	177,654.00	$	204,003.00
Depreciation	$	18,123.00	$	19,175.00	$	20,220.00
Casualty Loss			$	25,076.00		
SEP IRA	$	13,867.21	$	12,435.78	$	14,280.21
Total	$	230,093.21	$	236,342.78	$	238,503.21
Grand Total					$	704,939.20
Divided by # of Months						36
Stable Monthly Income					$	19,581.64

The most frequent complaint we encounter in analyzing self-employed borrowers is the complexity. Like many things, the way to tackle a complex task is to break it down into its components and work from there. Break apart the personal returns from the business as a beginning and begin analyzing where the income comes from. The federal 1040 will be the basis of the income analysis, so always start the analysis here, even though additional information and/or returns may be needed to complete the review. Take a blank piece of paper, or a spreadsheet, make the first column the most recent year, write down the source of each piece of income from the first page. As you note the income from the 1040, see what deductions have been taken that can be added back.

Income Sources & "Add-backs"

The general theory of adding deductions back to the taxable income is based on the fact that these deductions did not actually affect the bottom line of the business. They are allowable "Paper" Deductions. You can almost always add back depreciation. A gray area is the concept of "non-recurring expenses." If, for instance, there is a large deduction for attorney's fees, and the applicant's position is that this suit was settled and won't occur again, how do you know that it won't?

In isolated cases the borrower may have income which is paid to him - a schedule E Property (it may even be a vehicle he leases back to himself) which he pays the rent on. It may make sense to look for an add-back here, but is must be done in the context of which works better for qualifying. If it is added back as a non-cash loss, then there may be a mortgage to be added to debts.

Source	Description & "Add-back" Rationale
W-2, 1099, Tips	Salary & Other Income - Compare to company return for consistency
Schedule B, Interest/Dividends	Asset be verified and remain after closing. Non-Taxable income can be added back in and "grossed-up," if necessary. Notes receivable must continue for 3
Schedule C - Sole Proprietor	Since the borrower and the entity are one and the same, look for duplicative expenses. Car expenses - is a car loan paid by the business? If yes deduct it from the debts. Add back "Business use of the home," and "Depreciation." "Optional" expenses like contributions; and pension/profit sharing can be added back. If there will be a home office and rent will be eliminated, add the rent back.
Schedule D	Capital gains can only be counted as income if there is a history of assets purchased and sold, and if the assets remain. Deductions from gain, exclusions and non-cash losses can be added back.
Schedule E - Rent and Royalty Income	Two Methods: 1.) Ignore tax returns, take rental income supported by leases, deduct 25% and subtract Debt Service. 2.) Analyze Schedule E for add backs - depreciation, anomalies such as tenant evictions, and eliminate properties sold. Newly added properties must utilize 1st method.
	Partnership and S Corporation income is also reported here, but add backs come from the K-1 or business returns.
Schedule F - Farm Income	An active farm may not be eligible for financing. Depreciation, interest payments accounted for in the ratios can be added back.

Partnership and S Corporation Tax Returns and Income Analysis

If the borrower's income is from a partnership or S Corporation the **K-1 Form** will determine the ownership interest. If the interest is more than **25%,** the entity's returns must be analyzed. Unlike C Corporations, Partnerships and S Corporations must operate on a calendar year and their specific purpose is as a vehicle to disburse all income to the owners to avoid duplicate taxation. The K-1 Form itself will give the partners' share of deductible expenses which can be added back - depreciation, charitable contributions, and tax credits. An analysis of the tax returns can reveal other add-backs, non-cash deductions, and non-recurring expenses. A partner would generally not receive a salary from the partnership. If it is referred to as salary, it is more likely that it is a guaranteed draw or distribution. Conversely, an S Corporation can pay its officers a salary. In addition it may not be clear that there is an ownership interest if the borrower does not have a corporate title. Caution must be taken to identify that, if the borrower is an officer, the K-1 statement be requested to determine if there is ownership interest. If there is ownership interest, the borrower is not considered salaried and must submit to income averaging.

Limited partnerships may be treated differently if the purpose of the entity is to provide a tax shelter. These are investments, generally, and do not represent the individual's primary source of income. If there are limited partnership losses that reduce income these should be added back in because the limited partner is only liable up to the extent of his initial investment. In other words, the loss doesn't represent a negative going forward; it is an expression of the deteriorating value of the initial investment.

Analyzing the US Corporation Income Tax Return

One of the unique advantages of the Corporation ("C Corporation" as opposed to "Subchapter S Corporation") is the ability to operate on a fiscal year that is different from the calendar year. This is referred to as "Straddling." Because C Corporations have the highest income tax rate of any form, this straddling allows the company to declare income over two years, or offset a loss in one year against income in another to reduce the impact of taxation. The benefit for the corporation, however, becomes a challenge for the underwriter. This is because the fiscal year has to be reconciled with the calendar year of the individual returns.

The borrower's income will appear under officer's compensation. This is the W-2 income accounted for on the personal tax returns. The corporation's net income is also income to the borrower. To determine how much income from the corporation can be attributed to the borrower, take taxable income and start **adding back non cash losses, depreciation, depletion, duplicative expenses, discretionary or voluntary expenses, and contributions to profit sharing plans.** The result is the corporation income that the borrower can utilize for qualifying. This amount is multiplied by the ownership percentage of the borrower.

Retained earnings are a curious phenomenon. It is income that was previously declared but not paid out and has been added to the corporation's balance sheet. As a result it is possible to count this as income if it can be shown that it resulted in a year that is not being utilized in the income computation. In other words, if you were analyzing 1995 and 1996 returns and there were retained earnings in 1996, and not in 1995, that income has already been accounted for in the average. However, if retained earnings are carried forward to 1995 and not 1996, a case can be made to utilize the 1995 portion, because it hasn't been counted anywhere else.

The **balance sheet** is a part of the corporation return. It shows positives such as retained earnings. But it may also show negatives such as a deterioration of cash position from the beginning to the end of the year. Also, loans that come due within 12 months must be deducted from corporate income.

Borrowers who do not take income from the corporation, but loan themselves money are avoiding tax consequences. The loans may show as assets for the company. This cannot be counted as income. However, if the borrower decides to repay the corporation and it can be documented with copies of the promissory notes, checks payable to the borrower, and a letter from the accountant, it is possible to increase the corporation's income, which would then be attributable to the borrower.

The Profit and Loss Statement

An income statement, profit and loss, or other bookkeeping record is required to cover the period between the ends of the most recent tax period and document the business performance up to the current time - within 90 days. It is a concern as to whether an accountant must prepare the statement. The extent of preparation of this document is contingent upon how much weight the underwriter needs to give the income from this period. If the reliance on the income statement is just to show that the business is on track, it can be self-prepared. If the income is needed for qualification, either because of a short business experience or to document an increasing income stream, an accountant prepared statement is necessary. The same treatment for the profit and loss should be taken, as with the tax returns - non-cash losses, duplicative expenses, and tax treatment deductions such as depreciation, depletion and amortization, as well as any discretionary contributions should be added back to the year-to-date income, for qualifying.

Levels of Profit and Loss (P&L) Statement Preparation

Level	Description
Self-Prepared	The borrower, or internal accounting mechanism ,may prepare the document. It must be signed and accompanied by a perjury statement.
Compilation	An accountant takes the borrower's information, and presents it in proper format, addressing apparent issues.
Audit	An accountant reviews all inflows and outgoes independently and presents a thorough view of the operation's financial condition. Because of the time and expense involved, an audit is not mandatory.

The Balance Sheet

As part of the profit and loss statement of the borrower's company, there should be a section dealing with the assets and liabilities of a company called the balance sheet. There are some useful aspects of this. Since a company is often a vehicle to keep wealth from being taxed, there may be a **large net worth** that can be added to the borrower's net worth. In addition, liquid assets that the borrower might have access to or even retirement funds would appear here. On the other hand, the balance sheet can reveal weaknesses. Most importantly **notes and loans receivable within one year** are counted against the company's income.

Self-Employed Business Credit Reports/Dun & Bradstreet

The use of business credit reports for self-employed borrowers on residential loans has diminished as FHLMC and FNMA eliminated the requirement. The idea was that the underwriter could find out if the business had borrowed money to give to the borrower to meet the down payment requirement. However, the reason they were eliminated was that they were being routinely required for the most prevalent form of self-employment - the Schedule C Sole Proprietor. There is no entity for a sole proprietor to shield debts or borrow money on behalf of. A credit report ordered through a standard credit repository or bureau does not yield that much information anyway and is a compilation of the information provided by the business. However, there are occasions when an underwriter requires them. This could be triggered by signs of business troubles encroaching on the personal financial situation of the borrower, such as business-related judgments or legal actions. For commercial loans it is more prevalent to check a Dun & Bradstreet (800-666-6994) where they specialize in background, licensing and credit checks for businesses.

Verification of Authenticity (4506 & 4506T)

With extensive fraud occurrences among self-employed borrowers where either the lender or the borrower have submitted tax returns that exaggerate income, the industry has moved over the past 4 years to protect itself. The **4506** is the IRS form which allows the beneficiary to receive a copy of the complete return as filed from the IRS. It costs $6.00 per year requested, must be forwarded to the IRS center that was responsible for processing the return, and takes at least 4-6 weeks to receive. Obviously, this is too cumbersome for a timely check of the borrower's tax return authenticity. The **4506T** is the IRS form which allows the beneficiary to retrieve a transcript of the tax form which was filed. This allows the lender to quickly check and assure that the numbers reflected on the return that the borrower submitted match those filed with the IRS. All self-employed borrowers should sign this form, as a cautionary note.

No Income Verification Loans

No income verification loans are often touted as tools for self-employed borrowers who are too busy to meet the documentation requirements of a fully documented loan. The truth is no income verification loans allow loan officers to avoid the challenges involved in qualifying self-employed borrowers. While the documentation burden may often be lifted, there is usually a price to be paid. Normally, borrower who must utilize reduced documentation programs are subjected to higher interest rates, reduced program selection (being limited to 15- or 30-year fixed loans), and larger down payment requirements.

In some cases, the self-employed borrower's income documentation is SO convoluted that a reduced documentation loan is the only solution. If there is a significant down payment and the borrower is willing to pay a slightly higher rate, there are many programs that allow the borrower to utilize stated income for qualifying and not require proof of income. However, the borrower must have 1.) Excellent reserves - at least 6 months' PITI; 2.) Perfect credit; and 3.) The asset verifications, such as bank statements, shouldn't call the income into question. There are also no income verification loans available for borrowers who do not have perfect credit. However, this involves the "Credit-Rated Paper" financing discussed in Chapter 4, which means the program variety is restricted and the rates are significantly higher than similar programs.

Documentation Types and Their Meanings

Type	Description
Full Documentation	Full refers to the process of directly contacting (by mail) the verification source, such as a bank or employer, in addition to the borrower provided bank statements, employment documentation and other materials. Loan officers may NOT hand carry this documentation, so an unfolded Verification form is VERY suspicious. • VOE – Verification of Employment • VOD – Verification of Deposit • VOM – Verification of Mortgage • VOR – Verification of Rent • VOL – Verification of Liability

Documentation Types and Their Meanings

Type	Description
Alternative "Timesaver" Documentation	An alternative to full documentation simply means that the borrower may provide the bank statements, W-2's, pay stubs and other documentation, in lieu of direct written verification. A loan officer can "mix and match" alternative and full documentation items when there is difficulty verifying a specific item with alternative documentation.
Reduced/Stated Documentation "SISA" (Stated Income, Stated Assets)	Reduced, or "stated" income or asset verification indicates that the borrower will not provide documentation to support the income or asset figures provided on the application. However, the borrower's application will be underwritten relying on the information, so ratio calculations and cash sufficiency are still required to meet guidelines. <u>Most loan fraud surrounds the exaggeration of income or assets by loan officers or borrowers to assist in qualifying</u>. If the loan officer isn't certain that the stated information is accurate, the borrower should be encouraged to apply for a non-qualifying loan, even though the rate and down payment requirements may be higher.
No Ratio/No Qualifier "NINA" No Income, No Asset	When a borrower wishes to avoid being subjected to documentation requirements because he or she cannot verify the income or assets required for qualification, he or she can still obtain a loan for which there is no qualifying. This is preferable when a borrower exhibits all other aspects of creditworthiness and a willingness to make a substantial down payment, or if the loan officer suspects that the documentation, if requested by the underwriter, would not support the loan request.

Acronym	Means	Verified	Stated	Qualify	Also Known As
SIFA	State Income Full Asset	Assets	Income	Income and Assets	Reduced Doc, Stated
SISA	Stated Income Stated Assets	No	Income and Assets	Income and Assets	Reduced Doc, Stated
NIFA	No Income Full Assts	Assets	No	Assets	No Doc
NISA	No Income Stated Assets	No	Assets	Assets	No Doc
NINA	No Income No Assets	No	No	No	No Ratio, No Qualifier

What is a Compensating Factor?

If "no income verification" is not an option, there is the school of thought that there may be sufficient compensating factors to allow an underwriter to approve a loan even though the ratios do not meet guidelines. Relying on compensating factors as a manner in which to obtain a loan approval is referred to as "throwing it against the wall and seeing if it sticks." There are various levels of compensating factors that provide various levels of assurance that insufficient income will not cause the loan to be denied.

These are not the only conceivable compensating factors that can be addressed in presenting the case. Query the borrowers as to why they think they can afford the loan if the ratios are high. Have them draft out a monthly income and expense analysis showing how they are planning on affording the payment. This is perhaps the strongest mechanism for approving a loan with higher ratios. If the borrower is mature and has experience in homeownership, there is a good chance that they know what they are doing, so have them explain it.

Co-borrowers

Often, when a borrower cannot afford a proposed home purchase, a co-signer will be added. Co-signing is a bank term and does not really impact the perception of the case from a home lender's point of view. From a mortgage lender's point of view, a **co-borrower** is required. The distinction between a co-signer and a co-borrower is that a co-borrower's application is reviewed as thoroughly as the borrower's, with the same supporting documentation. If a co-borrower will be living in the property, then it is fairly reasonable to include them on the loan and allow the entire regular lending guidelines to apply cumulatively. However, if the co-borrower will not be occupying the property (non-occupant co-borrower - NOOCB) separate guidelines apply. Generally speaking, the NOOCB must be a

> **Qualifying Tip – Co-Borrowers**
>
> When considering adding a co-borrower, to achieve the fullest benefit that co-borrower should at least propose to co-occupy the property. This will only work if it makes sense. A second borrower moving into a one-bedroom condo doesn't make sense, but Grandma could move into the basement unit of a townhouse.

relative or have a family-type relationship. In addition the occupant borrower must qualify on his or her own and have his or her own minimum cash investment. In these cases the NOOCB acts more as a compensating factor, and does not really add to the strength of the case. In addition, NOOCBs shouldn't be seen as a solution to a qualifying problem until all of their income, liabilities and credit have been examined, because they could, in fact, deteriorate the quality of the case. They should also be willing to answer all questions the lender may pose, because their application will be scrutinized as closely as the borrower's.

Unemployment Insurance

Obviously, it is really important for borrowers to have jobs and stable income. There are times when it is impossible to avoid unemployment. Unemployment can be used in an averaging scenario, when the income is variable. In some cases an argument can be made that the unemployment period is temporary and that employment income along former lines can be anticipated. Further substantiation of this can be when a borrower has obtained an offer of employment but has not yet commenced working.

Income "Red Flags"

In some situations a borrower's documentation simply raises questions that have to be addressed. In others, discrepancies may be an indication of a borrower trying to conceal facts or perpetrate fraud. Being aware of these warning signs can eliminate problems later in the loan process.

EMPLOYMENT / EMPLOYMENT VERIFICATION

- Employee is paid monthly
- No prior year earnings on VOE
- Gross earnings per VOE for commission-only employees should not be used (see IRS Form 1040 Schedule C)
- Borrower is a business professional (may be self-employed)
- Answering machine or service at place of business (may be self-employed)
- Prior employer "out of business"
- Seller has same address as employer
- Employer signs VOE prior to date it was mailed by the lender
- Borrower uses employer's letterhead for letters of explanation
- Employment verified by someone other than personnel department
- Pay stubs are not preprinted for a large employer
- Pay stubs are handwritten for a large employer

- Current and prior employment overlap
- Date of hire is weekend or holiday
- Income is primarily commissions or consulting fees (Self-employment)
- Employer uses mail drop or post office box for conducting business
- Change in profession from previous to current employer
- Borrower is a professional employee not registered/licensed (doctor, lawyer, architect, real estate broker, etc)
- Illegible employer signature with no further identification
- Inappropriate verification source (secretary, relative, etc.)
- Document is not folded (never mailed)
- Evidence of ink eradicator (whiteout) or other alterations
- Verification "returned to sender" for any reason
- Inappropriate salary with respect to amount of loan

SELF EMPLOYED

- (Some "red flags" are indicators that someone may be self employed, these are important if a borrower has not revealed themselves to be self employed)
- Business entity not registered or in good standing with the applicable regulatory agencies.
- Address and/or profession does not agree with other information submitted on the loan application
- Tax computation does not agree with tax tables
- No estimated tax payments made by self-employed borrower (Schedule SE required)
- No FICA taxes paid by self employed borrower (Schedule SE required)
- Self employment income shown as wages and salaries
- Income or deductions in even dollar amounts
- High bracket taxpayer with few or no deductions or tax shelters
- High bracket taxpayer does not use a professional tax preparer.
- Paid preparer signs taxpayer's copy
- Paid preparer hand-writes tax return

TAX RETURNS

- Schedule A – Real estate taxes paid but no property owned
- Schedule A – No interest expense paid when borrower shows ownership of property (or vice versa)
- Schedule A – Employee who deducts business expenses (check against Form 2106)
- Schedule B – Amount or source of income doesn't agree with information submitted on loan application
- Schedule B – No dividends earned on stock owned (may be closely held)
- Schedule B – Borrower with substantial cash in bank shows little or no related interest income
- Schedule C – Gross income does not agree with total income per Form 1099
- Schedule C – Borrower shows interest expense but no related loan (business loans with personal liability)
- Schedule C – Borrower takes a depreciation deduction for real estate no disclosed (or vice versa)
- Schedule C – No IRA or Keogh deduction
- Schedule C – No salaries paid on non-service companies
- Schedule C – No "cost of goods sole" on retail or similar operations
- Schedule C – No schedule SE filed (computation of self-employed tax)
- Schedule E – Net income from rents plus depreciation does not equal cash flow as submitted by borrower.
- Schedule E – Additional properties listed by not on loan application
- Schedule E – Borrower shows partnership income (may be liable as a general partner for

partnership's debts)
- Form W-2 – Invalid employer identification number
- Form W2 – FICA and local taxes withheld (where applicable) exceed ceilings
- Form W2 – Copy submitted is not "Employee's Copy" (Copy C)
- Form W2 – Large employer has handwritten or typed W-2

Eligible Borrowers

In order to get a loan on a home, the borrower must be a person, not a corporation. But beyond this, there are many distinctions as to what kind of a person you are. A natural citizen of the United States does not have problems in this regard. This is because there is no way - even if convicted of a crime - which they could be asked to leave the country and, consequently, the property they own. However, because of the dynamic nature of the world and because of massive immigration, more and more foreigners are purchasing homes requiring financing in the U.S.

When we say "natural person" we mean that the borrower may not take out a loan in the name of a corporation, partnership, foreign country, or other entity. They must own the property as individuals.

Resident Aliens

Resident Aliens are de-facto citizens of the United States. They may not vote, but are entitled to live here and enjoy all the protections of the constitutions and benefits of a wealthy society. Permanent resident aliens are eligible for loans just like citizens. There are distinctions between permanent and non-permanent resident aliens. A non-permanent resident alien is a person who is in the some stage of the process of becoming either a citizen or a permanent resident alien. Following are the criteria for determining the difference between a permanent resident alien and a non-permanent resident alien.

Permanent resident aliens should have a "green card" which is issued by the Department of State and shows that they are lawfully residing in the country. If permanent residence has been applied for, the borrower's passport should be examined for the interim Visa that shows this. The document may be stamped in the passport, or a separate form, referred to as an I-551.

Non-Immigrant Visas

Recently, FNMA changed its guidelines on non-immigrant borrowers. Previously borrowers were required to be permanent resident aliens – to possess a green card - in order to qualify for FNMA/FHLMC financing. Now, most non-permanent visas will qualify the borrower for financing. The borrower still must meet the other requirements of the program and specifically must have 2 years of employment and banking/credit history. FHA and non-conforming sources are other sources for non-resident alien financing. While some non-resident aliens are eligible for financing, some cannot obtain financing at all. Specifically, borrowers who have diplomatic visas - Class A, are ineligible because they may be immune from civil prosecution. This would preclude a lender from foreclosing on a defaulted loan.

In general, borrowers who have not resided in this country also present a special challenge because it is difficult to gauge their real earnings and assets. The guideline is that if they have not resided in this country for at least 2 years, and have not established U.S. credit histories and banking relationships, they are ineligible. This is because it is difficult to prove they have not defaulted on overseas obligations; they may have properties overseas that are liabilities that are concealed; or they may have borrowed money from an overseas source. All of these are issues which U.S. lenders would have no way of discovering, which means there is a high potential for latent adverse contingencies from borrower non-disclosure. There are strategies for assisting borrowers like this.

You can perform an in-depth review of overseas accounts, contact their banks and analyze cash flows, and even contract a State Department sanctioned interpreter to translate documents. Even with the extra verification there is little likelihood that an exception to the guideline will be made if there are unexplained facets of the case. A non-permanent alien may hold one of the Visa categories outlined in the table below.

Visa Symbol	Description
A	1.) Ambassador, career diplomat, consular officer, 2.) Other foreign government official or 3.) employee, or attendant, servant or personal employee of someone classified A
B	Temporary visitor for business or pleasure
C	1.) Alien in transit, 2.) in transit to United Nations, 3.) Foreign government official, family, servant, attendant or personal employee
D	Seaman or Airman
E	1.) Treaty Trader or 2.) Investor
F	1.) Student or 2.) Spouse or child of student
G	1.) Principal representative of recognized government, 2.) Other representative of recognized government, 3.) Representative of non-recognized or non-member government, or 4.) Officer or employee of INTERNATIONAL ORGANIZATION
H	1.) Temporary worker of distinguished merit, 2.) Temporary worker performing services unavailable in the United States, 3.) Trainee
I	Members of foreign information media
J	Exchange visitor
K	Fiancée of U.S. Citizen
L	Intra-company transferee
NATO	Member of North Atlantic Treaty Organization

Chapter 6
Qualifying - Assets Down Payment and Closing Costs

Assets, down payment and closing costs are inextricably linked. Accurately assessing the sufficiency of assets to consummate a transaction requires an understanding of the components. This process is called qualifying for assets. Understanding what the costs are made up of allows you to quickly estimate and manipulate the numbers, tailoring the transaction for its requirements. It should be stated that one of the strongest factors in the loan approval process is the level of assets. Often, having a large amount of residual cash can make up for a shortfall in income.

With this thought in mind you should approach the issue of assets and cash sufficiency from two fronts: 1.) How to increase the amount of available assets; and 2.) How to reduce the amount of the cash required. So, like income qualifying, start with the idea of how much cash the borrower needs for closing. But to gauge the amount required, we do not have to perform a written Good Faith Estimate of Closing Costs. The costs can be estimated quickly and refined later with a lender's Good Faith Estimate of Closing Costs.

Understanding Closing Costs

Throw away the pre-conceived notion that closing costs range from 4-7% of the sales price. This is not because they may not be. This is because it is misleading as to the actual numbers. Closing costs can be controlled, mitigated, and adjusted - customized for the transaction. That is not to say that it feels that way at closing. Settlement is actually the money pit - all of the funds are rolled in together and disbursed out by the settlement agent, title/escrow company, or closing attorney. Helping the customer to understand these charges help the customer understand that settlement fees are not all loan charges but are costs associated with the transaction. The loan fee component is quite small.

The Components of a Buyer's Closing Costs

There are four categories of closing costs: 1.) Loan fees or points; 2.) "Hard" closing costs which are fixed transaction fees charged by the service providers to the transaction; 3.) Municipal and governmental charges which are the taxes and fees required by the jurisdiction in which the property is located; and 4.) prepaid items. Within certain categories, charges may be adjusted.

1.) Loan Fees and "Points"

There are many considerations with respect to paying points, some of which have been reviewed in earlier chapters. When cash is at a premium and seller contributions are limited by program guidelines, seller paid points may not be an alternative. By eliminating the loan fee/point component of closing costs

Determining Optimum Cash Utilization							
Sales Price	$	150,000					
Loan Amount	$	142,500		LTV:			95%
		Option 1		Option 2			Option 3
Down Payment	$	7,500	$	7,500	$		7,500
Closing Costs	$	1,500	$	1,500	$		1,500
Points	$	4,275	$	4,275	$		-
Transfer Tax	$	1,650	$	1,650	$		1,650
Prepaids	$	1,500	$	1,500	$		1,500
Total Cash Required	$	16,425	$	16,425	$		12,150
Seller Pays (%)		0		3%			3%
Seller Pays ($)	$	-	$	4,500	$		4,500
Net Cash Required	$	16,425	$	11,925	$		7,650

a borrower can increase his or her leverage. As housing costs increase, purchasers may find that they have the income for a large mortgage, but not the cash for a large down payment and closing costs. A home buyer may find that a "zero point" option can help minimize closing costs, which might allow a larger down payment, or money for other expenses related to a new home purchase, such as furniture, repairs or sundries.

2.) "Hard" Closing Costs

There are many, many necessary services performed in conjunction with the settlement of a real estate transaction. A fee at closing accompanies each of these services. The fees for these services are fairly standard within a range and so will stay roughly *the same for each transaction regardless of size*. This is why you cannot estimate the cost based upon the transaction size. As a real estate or finance professional you

The Fixed Nature of "Hard Costs"				
Sales Price		$ 100,000	$	300,000
Closing/Attorney's Fee		$ 400	$	400
Title Search		$ 125	$	125
Survey		$ 175	$	175
Termite Report		$ 45	$	45
Appraisal		$ 350	$	350
Credit Report		$ 20	$	20
Document Prep/Undewriting		$ 450	$	450
Courier		$ 45	$	45
Tax Service		$ 80	$	80
Flood Certification		$ 12	$	12
Inspections		$ 150	$	150
Sub Total		$ 1,852	$	1,852
Lender's Title Insurance	$2.50	$ 250	$	750
Total with Title		$ 2,102	$	2,602

should consult and become familiar with the HUD Booklet "A Guide to Settlement Costs" for a detailed explanation of what these services and charges represent. While the term "sales price" is used in this chapter, the costs would also apply to refinance transactions.

Title Insurance

Title insurance is designed to indemnify you against your legal fees and expenses should someone else file a legal claim to your property. In the event of a total loss, referred to as a forfeiture or reversion, the policy insures your equity and, theoretically at least, would reimburse you for your loss. There are two types of Title Insurance: **Lender's and Owner's.**

The lender's policy will always be required if there is a loan involved in the purchase - the lender requires it and the borrower pays for it. The owner's policy, however, is a discretionary purchase for the buyer. To understand whether it is an advisable purchase there are some mechanics of the title insurance business that need to be understood.

- Between 70% and 90% of the premium for owner's title insurance is commission that goes back to the title company. This is because the borrower is insuring "equity", not the sales price or value of the property. This is why title companies press so hard for borrowers to purchase owner's title insurance.
- Understanding this, you may now realize that a very small portion of the premium is allocated towards any sort of fiduciary fund to pay claims. So either the incidence of claims is very, very low, or there is very little risk involved in writing this kind of insurance. In fact, both are true. Very few title claims are paid out, although environmental claims do present a risk in some areas. In addition, the risk of a claim is statistically non-existent relative to some of the other risks of loss in real estate ownership. This is because:
  - There is a title search and survey performed which would reveal any unacceptable defects in the title. These would have to be corrected at the owner's expense before the title insurer would issue a policy.
  - Unless there is a problem with the title, properties are conveyed with a "General Warranty Deed." This means that the seller is saying that the property he is selling has a marketable title. If there is a problem with the title, that seller is liable.
  - In most newly developed projects (PUDs, Condos) there are underlying policies of title insurance. If this is the case, then there are many other parties who will be defending a claim along with the buyer, so this is somewhat of an additional indemnity.

States set maximum premiums and fees and establish the laws governing the insurance business. As a result, even though there are many different title insurance companies, the fees do not vary much. Title insurance is also the subject of many debates when purchasers finally start to study closing costs. If cash is at a premium, owner's title insurance is an added expense. At the very least, a negotiation and disclosure should be made over the full amount of commission to be paid.

3.) Government/Municipal Title Related Charges

The Government wants to get its piece of each transaction, whether city, township, county and/or state. Depending on the jurisdiction, these charges may be called transfer tax, recordation tax,

tax stamps, sales tax, etc. Some states or jurisdictions may offer homeownership incentives under which the buyer's portions of these charges are waived, such as homestead exemptions. The charges may be levied against the buyer, the seller or both. Some jurisdictions may simply not levy these charges.

Whatever the case, the charges are triggered by the act that makes our entire system of legal property ownership possible - the recording of a deed of sale. Recording a deed indicates a transfer of ownership or title to a property. The transfer indicates the amount of consideration, or sales price, upon which a levy is based. In addition, there may be a tax levied for recording a mortgage or deed of trust that would be based on the amount of the loan. These fees/taxes are variable depending on the sales price and loan amount. Knowing these charges is important not only for evaluation of the buyer's requirements, but also for computing the costs of selling a home in another jurisdiction when a new purchase is contingent on a sale. Your local settlement company is a good source for this information.

4.) Prepaid Items

As the term implies, a prepaid item is something paid for at closing which will come due in the future. Pro-rated real estate taxes, homeowner's and flood insurance, PMI, and interim interest are among the most common prepaid items. These are also the most confusing component of closing costs because they are not fixed or immutable and can change depending on the closing date and the jurisdiction. The key concept to understanding prepaid items is that interest on a mortgage is always paid in arrears - after interest has had a chance to accrue on the balance. This is why the first payment date on the mortgage is usually at least one month after the closing date.

People who are accustomed to paying rent think they are getting a "free month" because the first day of the next month after closing arrives and their payment isn't due for another month.

In this example, the borrower closes on March 16th. Interest is due at closing from the 16th of the month until the end of the month. The First Mortgage Payment is due May 1 – after the interest has accrued on the balance.

Interim Interest

Also referred to as *per diem*, or per day, this is an adjustment of the interest from the closing date until regular principal and interest payments start accruing under the term of the loan. This is the easiest place to see the interest in arrears concept, because at closing the settlement agent collects interest from the date of settlement until the end of the month. This is where the common misconception of "closing at the end of the month" being a money saving function comes from.

If you close at the beginning of the month, you would pay 30 days of interest. The cost is just a mortgage payment in advance - and this is the only time one would pay interest in advance. Just like staying in a hotel, you pay interest on the loan for the days that you have it. It doesn't mean you are paying more at closing because, more than likely, you are not paying to stay in a hotel, your old home or a rental anymore.

If the cost of the per diem interest is too much to bear it is possible to arrange for an **interest credit** at closing for a closing early in the month. This means that the lender does not collect any per diem interest at closing, but simply moves the first payment date to the first day of the month following closing. The first payment would be the regular principal and interest payment less interest for the number of days that into the month that the closing occurred.

It is important to note that, no matter what the closing date, FHA requires that at least 15 days of interest be included in the closing cost calculation for qualifying purposes.

Insurance Escrow

One of the most frequent complaints about escrows for homeowner's, flood and private mortgage insurance is "why do I have to pay money into escrow when I have already paid the insurance premium for a year?" The key to understanding this is to understand that all insurance requires that the premium be paid in advance - regardless of whether it is financed or not. Again, the regular monthly payment for principal and interest, taxes and insurance (PITI) doesn't come due for at least one month because the

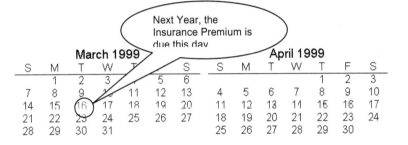

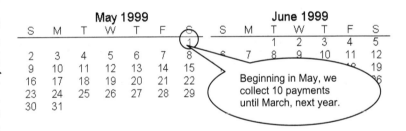

In the same example – at closing the borrower pays for one year of insurance. The renewal insurance premium is still due on the anniversary of the closing. At closing we collect March and April's premium for next year, leaving May through March to be collected over the year.

payment is due in arrears. This has to be reconciled with the fact that the insurance anniversary date is the closing date. Usually there are 10 monthly PITI payments that the lender receives prior to the insurance anniversary or premium due date. The insurer will expect to receive the annual premium that is 12 times the monthly insurance portion of the payment. To make up for the 2 month shortfall, the lender places 2 months insurance into the escrow account so that there will be enough money to pay the premium when it comes due. When there is private mortgage insurance (PMI), it is the same issue. When utilizing PMI under the traditional plan, there is an initial premium paid at closing. The 1 year renewal premium will come due after the borrower has only made 10 regular PITI payments. So to offset the expected shortfall, the lender collects 2 times 1/12th of the renewal premium at closing.

If the PMI is a monthly plan, there is no initial premium, but the premiums must start being remitted from the date of closing. In this case the lender will collect two months of the premium again, to make up for the fact that the first regular PITI payment is not expected for 30-60 days.

Real Estate Tax Escrows

This can be the most confusing prepaid because, on top of the fact that real estate taxes may come due at different times within neighboring jurisdictions, sometimes the real estate taxes are paid in advance, or partially in advance. When this is the case, the lender has to make sure that it collects enough in escrow with the expected PITI payments to pay the taxes when due. The loan officer has to make sure that the borrower understands that they must repay the seller for any

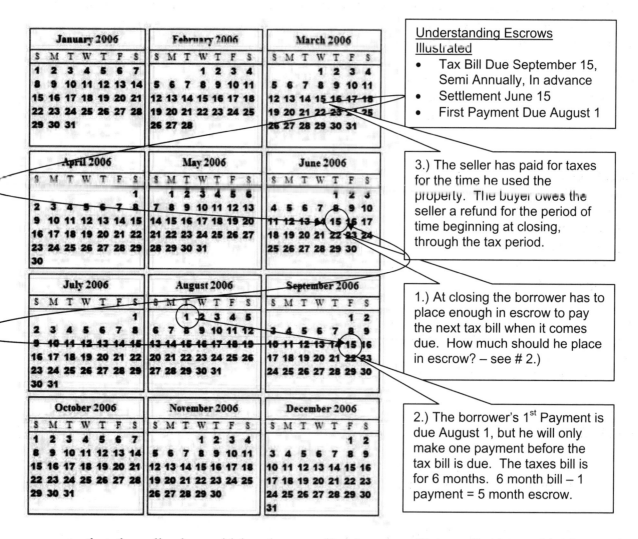

Understanding Escrows Illustrated
- Tax Bill Due September 15, Semi Annually, In advance
- Settlement June 15
- First Payment Due August 1

3.) The seller has paid for taxes for the time he used the property. The buyer owes the seller a refund for the period of time beginning at closing, through the tax period.

1.) At closing the borrower has to place enough in escrow to pay the next tax bill when it comes due. How much should he place in escrow? – see # 2.)

2.) The borrower's 1st Payment is due August 1, but he will only make one payment before the tax bill is due. The taxes bill is for 6 months. 6 month bill – 1 payment = 5 month escrow.

amounts that the seller has paid in advance. For instance, if the seller has paid 1/2 year in advance and the tax bill is based upon an annual assessment, the borrower could pay as many as 14 months real estate taxes at closing; 6 months to pay back the seller, 6 months to the jurisdiction and 2 months into escrow.

O.K., So How Many Months' Taxes are Due?

When and for how many months are taxes due? When is the first payment due? Count the number of months from the 1st payment until the month when taxes are due. Subtract the number of payments the borrower will make from the number of months in the tax period. The shortfall is how many months of taxes to collect at closing.

As in qualifying ratios, it is important to investigate whether borrowers are entitled to any government reduction in tax assessments, such as owner occupancy homestead deductions, senior citizens deductions or deferments.

With new construction, there may be an additional closing cost to take into consideration. Until the property was sold, it was assessed as "unimproved." There may be an improvement levy/tax that the jurisdiction assesses to make up for the fact that they were unable to tax the property until the occupancy permit/certificate of completion was issued.

It is important for the loan officer to measure and fine-tune the impact of the closing costs and prepaid items. Without this a borrower may not have enough funds for closing. Conversely, the need for seller contributions could be overstated which could leave seller contributions under-utilized.

Preparing a Good Faith Estimate

Loan officers should practice preparing Good Faith Estimates (GFE). The form is designed to correlate with the order of appearance of items on the HUD-1 Settlement Statement. The HUD-1 Settlement statement is the final accounting of charges related to closing. The loan officer should compare the GFE to the Settlement Statement for specific transactions. This will aid in refining estimating skills.

Today most GFEs are automated and are generated by loan processing systems. This is a labor savings because GFE preparation is mostly filling in the blanks. From the perspective of the borrower, it is much important to conceptually understand what the estimate includes. In addition, federal regulations require the delivery of a GFE, so it is important to be able to prepare one correctly.

What These Costs Represent

Understanding what the actual costs represent and who they are paid to can also help to explain the Good Faith Estimate and Settlement Statement.

Line	Paid to	Paid By - Description
700. Sales/Broker's Commission	Real Estate Broker	Seller - This is the total dollar amount of the real estate broker's sales commission, which is usually paid by the seller. This commission is typically a percentage of the selling price of the home
800 Section - Items Payable in Connection with Loan. These are the fees that lenders charge to process, approve and make the mortgage loan.		

Line	Paid to	Paid By - Description
801. Loan Origination	Lender or Broker	Buyer - This fee is usually known as a loan origination fee but sometimes is called a "point" or "points." It covers the lender's administrative costs in processing the loan and the costs of commissioned sales people. Often expressed as a percentage of the loan, the fee will vary among lenders. Generally, the buyer pays the fee, unless otherwise negotiated.
802. Loan Discount	Lender	Buyer/Seller - Also often called "points" or "discount points," a loan discount is a one-time charge imposed by the lender or broker to lower the rate at which the lender or broker would otherwise offer the loan to you. Each "point" is equal to one percent of the mortgage amount.
803. Appraisal Fee	Appraiser	Buyer - This charge pays for an appraisal report made by an appraiser
004. Crcdit Roport Fee	Credit Bureau	Buyer - This fee covers the cost of a credit report, which shows your credit history. The lender uses the information in a credit report to help decide whether or not to approve your loan.
805. Lender's Inspection Fee	Lender	Buyer - This charge covers inspections, often of newly constructed housing, made by employees of your lender or by an outside inspector.
807. Assumption Fee	Lender	This is a fee which is charged when a buyer "assumes" or takes over the duty to pay the seller's existing mortgage loan.
808. Mortgage Broker Fee	Mortgage Broker	Buyer/Borrower, Seller, Lender - Often, lenders will not allow brokers to charge an origination fee and will insert the fee as a mortgage broker fee. In some cases, the fee paid to tho brokor is a yield spread premium and does not come out of the borrower's funds at all. If this is the case, the fee may show up as P.O.C. – (Paid Outside Closing)
809. Tax Service Fee	Tax Service Company	Buyer/Borrower – The Tax Service Contract runs for the life of the loan and reports to the lender when real estate taxes go past due. This is important because delinquent taxes allow the government to force the sale of the property without the lender's consent to satisfy back taxes.
810. Flood Certification	Flood Service Company	Buyer/Borrower – Also known as a "Flood Zone Determination" a flood certification is an independent confirmation as to whether a property is in a flood hazard area. If it is, the lender will require Federal Flood Insurance.
811. Other	Lender or Broker	Fees such as Document Preparation, Underwriting, Processing, Document Review, Wire Fees and Application Fees may also appear here, even though they are not pre-printed on the form. These are referred to collectively as "lender or broker fees." Often they are called "junk fees."
Section 900. Prepaid Items Required by Lender to Be Paid in Advance: You may be required to prepay certain items at the time of settlement, such as accrued interest, mortgage insurance premiums and hazard insurance premiums.		
901. Interest	Lender	Borrower – Also known as per diem interest, this is the pro-rated amount of interest from the date of closing until regular principal and interest payments begin to accrue under the terms of the note.
902. Mortgage Insurance Premium	Lender - Mortgage Insurer	Borrower – Lenders require that the first year's private mortgage insurance premium or FHA Mortgage Insurance Premium, be paid in advance. Even if the premium will be financed, it will still appear as a charge here – the increased loan proceeds cover the cost.

Line	Paid to	Paid By - Description
903. Hazard Insurance Premium	Hazard Insurance Company	Buyer/Borrower - Hazard insurance protects against loss due to fire, windstorm, and natural hazards. Lenders often require the borrower to bring a paid-up first year's policy to the settlement or to pay for the first year's premium at settlement.
904. Flood Insurance	FEMA	Buyer – If the flood certification indicates a flood hazard, the lender will require flood insurance.
1000. Section - RESERVES DEPOSITED WITH LENDER		
1001. Hazard Insurance 1002. Mortgage insurance 1003. City property taxes 1004. County property taxes	Insurer or Municipality Collected by Lender	Buyer – Lines 1000 – 1008 are Escrow Account Deposits. These lines identify the payment of taxes and/or insurance and other items that must be made at settlement to set up an escrow account. The lender is not allowed to exceed a cushion of 2 months.
Section 1100. Title Charges: Title charges may cover a variety of services performed by title companies and others to conduct the closing. These costs for these services/items may vary widely from provider to provider.		
1101. Settlement or Closing Fee	Title, Escrow Company or Attorney	This fee is paid to the settlement agent or escrow company. Responsibility for payment of this fee should be negotiated between the seller and the buyer.
1102-1104 Abstract of Title Search, Title Examination, Title Insurance Binder	Title, Escrow Company or Attorney	The charges on these lines cover the costs of the title search and examination, so that the closing agent can perfect the clear title for the property.
1105. Document Preparation	Title, Escrow Company or Attorney	This is a separate fee to cover the costs of preparation of final legal papers, such as a settlement statement, mortgage, deed of trust, note, transfer or deed
1106. Notary Fee	Title, Escrow Company or Attorney	A Notary Public takes oaths and, in the case of the real estate closing, attests to the fact that the persons named in the documents did, in fact, sign them.
1107. Attorney's Fees	Title, Escrow Company or Attorney	An attorney is traditionally required to review any drafting of legal documents. Since most loan documents are pre-printed forms, an attorney may not be required for the closing. Attorney's fees are, however, compensable settlement services. Occasionally, a vendor may place their Closing or Escrow fee here.
1108. Title Insurance	Title, Escrow Company or Attorney	Lender's Title Insurance covering the loan amount, is a normal requirement of a lender. Owner's title insurance, which insures the owner's equity based on the sales price less the loan amount, is not. The charge is variable based on the size of the policy.
Section 1200. Government Recording and Transfer Charges		
1201. Recording Fee	Jurisdiction Courthouse	Buyer/Borrower- The fees for accepting for record the new deed and mortgage/trust. Normally a per page charge.
1202 and 1203. Transfer Taxes, Tax Stamps	State/Local Government	Buyer/Seller/Borrower - Transfer taxes may be collected whenever property changes hands or a mortgage loan is made. These are taxes on the transaction and are set by state and/or local governments. These may be referred to as tax stamps, recording stamps, recording taxes or other names.
Section 1300. Additional Settlement Charges:		

Line	Paid to	Paid By - Description
1301. Survey	Surveyor	Buyer/Borrower – Technically part of the title insurance, a survey examines whether any property line violations exist that could impact the marketability of the title.
1302. Pest and Other Inspections	Inspection Company	Termite or Wood Destroying Pest Inspections assure there is no active infestation or damage. Well/Septic for non public water/sewer property. Final Completion for new construction or repairs.

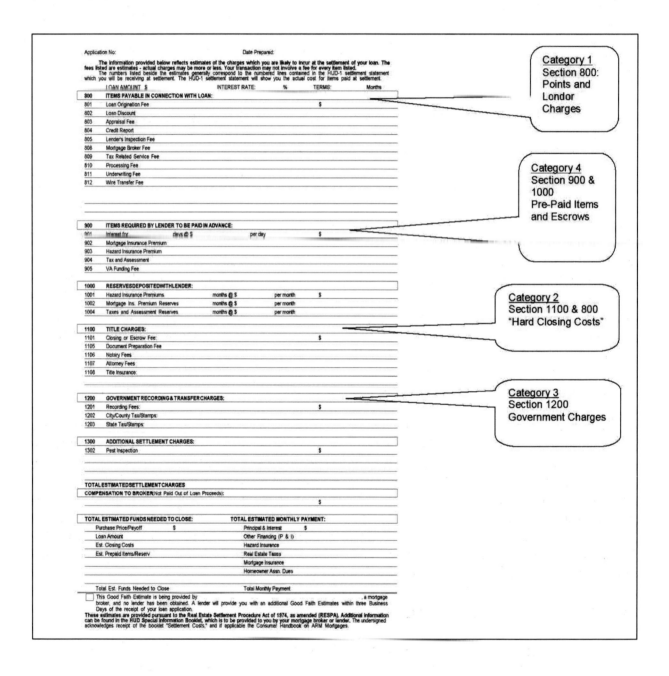

Seller Contributions

Depending on the loan program, a seller may assist by paying for closing costs on behalf of a buyer. This is called a contribution because it is a standard practice and pays for actual costs normally incurred by a buyer. This is acceptable because the lender still assures that the borrower is making an equity contribution in the form of a down payment.

Contributions Help Buyer Pay for Costs		
	No Seller Paid Help	3% Seller Paid Help
Sales Price	$ 200,000.00	$ 206,000.00
Down Payment	5%	5%
Loan Amount	$ 190,000.00	$ 195,700.00
Closing Costs	6000	6000
Seller Paid Costs	0	6000
Cash Requirement	$ 16,000.00	$ 10,300.00

There are limitations as to what the seller can pay for. The reason for this is that excessive seller contributions may artificially inflate the sales price. Excessive contributions are called concessions. For instance, a seller trying to sell a house without a swimming pool to a buyer who wants a swimming pool agrees to give the

Concessions Erode Buyer Equity	
Sales Price	$ 200,000.00
Maximum LTV	95%
Loan Amount before Concessions	$ 190,000.00
Repair Allowance	$ 6,000.00
Effective Sales Price after Concession	$ 194,000.00
Effective Borrower Equity	$ 4,000.00
New Maximum Loan Amount	$ 184,300.00
New Borrower Down Payment Required	$ 15,700.00

buyer $10,000 to pay for a swimming pool to be installed. The reality is that the house price is being inflated to pay for a swimming pool that does not yet exist. The danger in an inflated sales price is that the financing is based upon a certain amount of equity contribution - or down payment - from the buyer as a personal investment. The seller's concession may erode the buyer's equity contribution to the point where the loan balance is greater than the value of the house. As a result concessions may be allowed, but the underwriter/lender should make a downward adjustment to the loan amount to compensate for a lower equity contribution.

It may seem a contradictory technicality that a seller contribution of 3% of the sales price towards closing costs is acceptable, but a 3% decorator's allowance is not. To a certain extent it is, because everyone accepts the fact that seller assistance is based upon a certain amount of price inflation. From the seller's perspective it is all the same. A sales price of $100,000 in a transaction with no contribution as opposed to a $103,000 sales price with a 3% contribution nets the seller approximately the same amount of money. The distinction is one of valuation. If the contribution is traditional in the marketplace, and the inflated selling price is supported by other comparable sales, then the lender has some certainty that the borrower's equity contribution/down payment is bona fide.

Avoiding Problems with Seller Contributions

- **Watch for concessions**, especially on transactions where a reduced sales price could have an impact on the loan approval. An 80% LTV loan with a concession could push the loan into a PMI requirement. Decorator/repair allowances are concessions.
- **Don't specify what can and cannot be paid** with the seller contribution. Specify a flat

dollar amount. This allows the buyer the maximum flexibility in structuring financing. In addition, this will avoid disputes at closing regarding who is responsible for paying certain fees.

- **Avoid over-leveraging**. A seller contribution is tantamount to financing of certain costs. Even in situations where contributions are limitless - like the VA Guaranty Program - the contribution at closing will be carried for the entire ownership of the home.

- **Avoid exceeding the listing price** of the house to finance a seller contribution. Even if the sales price is justified, it would be hard for an appraiser to justify a valuation that was higher than the seller's.

How it can Work

Combining the closing cost tailoring and allowable seller contributions are the most effective ways of reducing the cash requirement. First, throw away the pre-conceived notion that closing costs range from 4-7% of the sales price. Not because they don't, but because this statement can automatically turn a buyer off from investigating the actual numbers. The closing costs can be controlled, mitigated, and adjusted - customized for the transaction. They must be analyzed number by number to

Manipulating Closing Costs				
		"Typical"		"Structured"
Points	$	2,850.00	$	-
Attorney's Closing Fees	$	940.00	$	940.00
Lender's Fees	$	810.00	$	810.00
Government Charges	$	1,100.00	$	1,133.00
Prepaid PMI	$	1,028.00	$	118.00
Hazard & Real Estate	$	574.00	$	574.00
Total Costs	$	7,302.00	$	3,542.00
Seller Contribution	$	-	$	3,090.00
Down payment	$	5,000.00	$	2,060.00
2 Mos Reserves	$	1,734.00	$	-
Cash Required	$	14,036.00	$	2,512.00

assure potential buyers that <u>they can do it!</u> In this example we are able to take a typical $100,000 standard transaction and reduce the cash required from $14,000 to less than $3,000.

Don't pay points	If cash is an issue, a difference in $50 per month is far less dramatic than $3000 at closing.
Use Monthly PMI	The traditional plan can add at least 1 point up front. Monthly PMI takes this away.
Get the Seller's Help	Increase the sales price enough to cover at least a 3% blanket contribution to closing costs. It's all the same to them if they are netting the same amount of money.
Community Homebuyer Program	The borrower can obtain 3% of their down payment in the form of a loan from a credit union or the lender! Also the reserve requirement is waived.

Assets for Down Payment, Closing Costs and Reserves

The borrower may have saved cash over time, or may be selling a current home and reinvesting the proceeds. In fact, the borrower may have waited until he or she has a surplus of cash beyond what is needed to close and if this is the case, a discussion of assets isn't really necessary. It is when the borrower doesn't have the appropriate sufficient funds that a loan officer earns the commission. Here is a listing of some possible alternative sources of down payment funds.

Source	Description/Treatment
Gift	Gifts from family are an acceptable source of funds. With FNMA/FHLMC financing, the borrowers must document that they have 5% of the sales price of their own funds invested into the transaction. If the down payment is 20% or more, the 5% limitation does not apply. FNMA/FHLMC requires that the source, transfer, and receipt of the gift be verified. "No income verification" loans do not generally allow the use of gift funds. FHA/VA does not limit the amount of the gift and does not care who the source is, provided there is no business relationship. SEE GIFT TIPS!
Sale of Asset	If a borrower has any property that could be sold, such as coin or stamp collection, jewelry, used cars, artwork, rugs, or anything of durable value, this can be used as a source of funds for closing. A sales receipt is required, along with a copy of the payment to authenticate the sale. The asset may also be used to meet post closing reserve requirements, if a reputable dealer ascertains the item's value and what the dealer would pay for it - to demonstrate its liquidity. An insurance policy stating the value of an asset is also substantiation of value.
Borrowing	Borrowing against an asset is an acceptable source of down payment funds. Loans include 401(k), life insurance policy or other retirement savings plan loans that provide for partial liquidation in emergency or home purchase. Pawnshops are excellent sources of secured loans, lending on everything from musical instruments, technical equipment, jewelry, cars, silverware, or anything of durable value, and you get a receipt. Many stock accounts have margin options, which is a loan secured by stock. A credit union may lend you money on an unsecured basis and take something of value as security for the purposes of a home loan. With the exception of VA, loans for down payment and closing costs must be secured. FHA/VA - Borrowing is not an acceptable way of making up the difference between the sales price and appraised value. **YOU MUST ALWAYS QUALIFY CARRYING THE LOAN PAYMENT!**
Side Jobs	If a borrower needs to make up a small cash shortfall to meet the requirement to provide 5% of the funds, consider performing some personal services, such as house sitting, painting, dog walking, lawn mowing, catering, etc. Because these are not subject to withholding taxes, and because they are paid immediately and usually by personal check, these funds can quickly absorb cash shortfalls. These cannot be counted as income, but are acceptable sources of cash if documented properly. Handicraft sales can achieve the same goal.
Rental/ Deposits	Often the rental security deposit is overlooked as a source of cash reserves. A letter from the landlord stating that a security deposit refund is due can substantiate the amount of money underwriting may use as a reserve.
Repayment of Personal Loans	You lent someone money 5 years ago, but have been letting it go because you are friends. They didn't sign a note, but you wrote them a check. Get them to pay you back, at least partially. A letter from the borrower, a copy of the original check and copy of the repayment are required.
Gambling Earnings	When you gamble and win a large amount of money, a casino may write you a check in lieu of cash. Again, while this is not a source of income, it can be acceptable documentation of funds.

Borrower's Own Funds

The guideline that the borrower must have 5% of his or her own funds is a reflection of the fact that as lenders we want to show that the borrower has some attachment to the property. If they are leveraging a purchase to the point that they do not have any real investment of money and are receiving all gift funds, then there is little inclination for the borrower to sacrifice and make the payment of the mortgage a priority. Some Community Homebuyer programs allow as little as 0%, 2% or 3% of the borrower's own funds to be invested into a transaction. The portfolio performance of borrowers having less than 5% of their own funds invested into the property is roughly 300% worse than traditional 95% LTV programs. Expect that this is an issue that is heavily scrutinized when the borrower's funds situation is very close.

Reserves

One of the last trip wires you may encounter in qualifying is that there are insufficient funds in reserve. Reserves are moneys lenders require to offset any unseen cash shortfalls and to show that, after the transaction, the borrower isn't broke. The standard guideline is to have 2 months' PITI remaining after all down

> **Qualifying Tip:** To offset any projected qualifying cash shortfall, consider adding the borrower's name to a relative or friend's bank account. The statements can be shown and counted towards cash or reserves as long as a letter is obtained stating that the borrower has complete access to those funds.

payment, closing costs and prepaid items are met. This is because there are costs outside of the transaction (moving expenses, necessary sundries like shower curtains and garbage cans, inspections, etc.) that will absorb some cash flow ordinarily devoted to making the payment. Any of the sources mentioned above would suffice for reserves and wouldn't have to be liquidated. FHA requires only 15 days of interest in reserve. VA doesn't care and some Community Homebuyer programs waive the reserve requirements if the case is strong.

Lender Credits for "Above Par" Pricing Towards Closing Costs

You can use the "above par," rebate, or yield spread towards some of the purchaser's closing costs, prepaid items, or other fees. In certain cases, the amount of the premium is limited to the amount of the seller contribution allowed under the specific loan plan.

Using Yield Spread to Contribute to Closing Costs

Sales Price	$ 100,000
Loan Amount	$ 95,000
Down Payment	$ 5,000
Closing Costs	$ 1,500
Total Cash Required	$ 6,500
Price on Loan Sale ("above par")	103.50%
Cash from "Yield Spread"	$ 3,325
Less Lender Cost of Loan	$ 1,425
Cash Available to Borrower	$ 1,900

Tips for Gifts

The gift letter form is designed to state the intention that funds received are a "bona fide" gift, and that there is no explicit, or implicit, requirement for repayment. To substantiate that there is no implicit repayment required and to confirm that the funds received are, in fact, gift funds and not funds from another source, we require that the following documentation be provided in addition to the actual gift letter:

Donor's Ability to Give	This shows that the person giving the gift actually has the funds to give. This can be accomplished two ways. • The donor can provide a complete bank statement showing that the funds are available in their depository institution, or • The donor can take the gift letter form, when Section A is complete, and have the depository institution complete Section B.

| Proof of Transfer | The "paper trail" of funds must be established to document that the funds received are actually from the donor and not an undisclosed or borrowed source. To do this the following must be provided:
1. Proof of withdrawal of funds from donor. This can be accomplished by providing
    a. A copy of the cancelled check from the donor,
    b. A copy of the withdrawal slip from the donor's account,
    c. Copies of the wire transfer advice. If a broker or 3rd party is liquidating funds on behalf of the donor, copies of this transaction must be made (i.e., debit memo, inter account transfer, etc.).
2. Proof of receipt of gift funds. This can be provided in the form of
    a. A copy of the recipient's deposit slip,
    b. A copy of the wire transfer advice or
    c. A copy of the credit memorandum from the bank |
| Verification of New Balance | Once the gift funds have been received, we need to prove that the funds, now received, are sufficient to complete the transaction. To accomplish this, when the gift is deposited, please have your bank provide a letter with the following verbiage:

PLEASE BE ADVISED THAT $_____ (gift sum) HAS BEEN DEPOSITED INTO THE ACCOUNT OF _____ (recipient's name) ACCOUNT NUMBER _____ (recipient's account). THIS DEPOSIT IS IN ADDITION TO THE CURRENT BALANCE OF $ _____ (recipient' s current account balance). THIS WILL RESULT IN A NEW BALANCE OF $_____ (gift deposit combined with current balance)

Signature of Depository, Date |

Shared Equity

The concept of shared equity is a partnership between an individual who has cash and an individual who is able to make the mortgage payments. The intention of shared equity is to allow an individual who has no cash, but is able to afford the monthly payments to buy a home with the help of a partner. The buyer would get the tax write off for the mortgage interest and, when the home appreciates, a portion of the equity. The equity partner would receive the appreciation, or the equity. There are numerous problems with this approach.

First, there is a legal ownership agreement that divides the ownership interest of the property. The lender does not care if there is a joint agreement, but revealing that there is an agreement could jaundice the approval process. More problematic is the fact that shared equity partners must sign all the closing documents and be obligated on the transaction. They are de facto non-occupant co-borrowers and then the transaction is subject to those limitations. While the occupant borrower may qualify for the loan, there may be problems such as the number of properties financed for the shared equity partner.

"Red Flags" for Assets and Deposits

Review the asset portion of the borrower's application closely for inconsistencies. Asset documentation is one of the most difficult to track areas in the mortgage process. These warning signs can help you avoid pitfalls in the loan process.

VERIFICATION OF ASSETS /DEPOSIT / BANK STATEMENT

- Regular deposits (payroll) significantly at odds with reported income
- Earnest Money Deposit not debited to checking account
- NSF items require explanation.
- Large withdrawals may indicate undisclosed financial obligations or investments
- Lower income borrower with recent large accumulation of cash
- Bank account is not in borrower's name (business entity, trust funds, etc.)
- Evidence of ink eradicator (whiteout) or other alterations
- Verification "returned to sender" for any reason
- High income borrower with little or no cash (undisclosed liabilities)
- IRA is shown as a liquid asset or a source of down payment
- Non-depository "depository" (escrow trust account, title company, etc.)
- Credit union for small employer
- Borrower's funds are security for a loan
- Illegible bank employee signature with no further identification
- Source of funds consist of (unverified) note, equity exchange or sale of residence
- Cash in bank not sufficient to close escrow
- New bank account
- Gift letters must be carefully reviewed (canceled checks, bank statements)
- Borrower has no bank accounts (doesn't believe in banks)
- Document is not folded (never mailed)
- Young borrower with large accumulation of unsubstantiated assets
- Young borrowers with substantial cash in bank

Chapter 7
The Home Financing Process

The Loan Application

It has been said that there is no substitute for experience as a teaching tool. There was one instructor who had an unorthodox but effective method to initiate new recruits - he staged public "mock" loan application appointments assigning seasoned loan officers to role play as borrowers and real estate sales professionals. The new loan officer would walk in completely cold and, in front of a full complement of branch personnel and peers endure the contrived "worst case" customers that the experienced pros created. The result was the overt, general humiliation of the new recruit. This was the instructor's intention - very few of his loan officers went into their next "real" loan application without being sure they were prepared. He knew that the key to a successful loan process was at the beginning - a great loan application.

In the vernacular of the business, "taking a loan application" is the loan application interview. The interview can be conducted in person, via mail, fax, or over the telephone and the purpose is to collect all of the information and documentation that will be required to obtain a loan approval. Note that a mortgage related application does not begin for disclosure timing purposes until there is a property. Then there are the forms -- lots of them and many different varieties from lender to lender. None, however, are as important for the processing of the loan as the application form itself.

Understanding The Home Buying Process

Select Real Estate Sales Professional: The real estate sales professional helps the buyer to determine their needs, select an area, and understand the buying process.

A recent survey sponsored by the National Association of Realtors revealed that over 80% of all loan applicants were referred to their lender by their real estate sales professional. This gives you a sense of how much influence the real estate agent has in the transaction. Among other things, real estate sales professionals will recommend a number of lenders with whom they have worked successfully. The sales community has a huge amount of leverage over lenders in the performance of their commitments, since lenders rely on them for repeat business. The real estate sales professional is counting on them not to jeopardize their commission as much as anything else, so from a pure self-interest point of view the lender a real estate sales professional recommends is a good bet.

Aside from ingratiating themselves to real estate sales professionals, a loan officer can perform a useful service in the early stages of the home selection process by pre-qualifying or pre-approving a borrower before a property is selected. A "Pre-Qualification" is based upon the borrower representations of their financial situation. The lender then states, based upon the information provided what type of financing the borrower can qualify for. A "Pre-Approval" is a review, by an underwriter, of the supporting documentation, including a credit history that verifies the stated information. Because this is an actual approval it holds more weight than a "Pre-Qualification." With a "Pre-Approval," the borrower can proceed directly to closing with a satisfactory appraisal. In some cases a pre-approval can offer interest rate protection as well.

Making an Offer: The offer specifies the price and contingencies such as financing and home inspection. It also specifies the down payment, settlement time, and costs the seller is to pay.

Once pre-qualified or pre-approved the borrower can proceed with identifying a home and negotiating a price. Again, the real estate sales professional is critical in acting as an intermediary and in providing information regarding recent home sales that will help establish a fair price. The offer sets forth the sales price, how much the down payment will be, what the terms of the financing are and whether the seller will assist with closing costs.

The down payment will be determined, in part, by the kind of financing selected. Generally there is a deposit of a portion of the down payment with the contract or offer. This is referred to as an "Earnest Money Deposit" and represents the buyer's good faith in presenting an offer.

The Loan Application Process

Offer Acceptance: Once accepted the offer becomes a contract. The buyer orders a home inspection and selects a settlement agent. If the loan was pre-approved, now we can order the appraisal.

A pre-application checklist, kit or other format for collecting the loan documents necessary to obtain approval should be provided to the buyer or borrower at the earliest possible convenience. This Pre-Application Kit will help speed the loan application interview and the loan. **It cannot be overstated how important it is to collect all of the information required on the application checklist prior to the application interview** with the loan officer.

A Pre-Application Kit Can Save Your Life!

Getting the information required for the loan in advance of the application can save your life, especially when you are new to the business. It allows data to be reviewed at leisure, in the context of overall qualification, and if you have questions about the borrower there is time to get them answered.

Why You Should Use a Pre-Application Kit

When you use a pre-application kit you can

- Screen unverifiable information that would be detrimental to loan approval
- Identify missing or contradictory information or documentation prior to application
- Allow the borrower the opportunity to volunteer additional information not requested supportive of additional assets or income
- Preview credit information, by obtaining a credit authorization
- Spend time in the application interview discussing loan programs or solutions to problems instead of filling out forms or collecting documents
- Put the responsibility of providing all application documentation on the borrower.

In the event that the borrower is unwilling or unable to provide the pre-application kit, and the supporting information, the loan officer can still brief him or her to bring the basic documentation to the application interview. The same information is required on every loan application and is as easy to remember as 1-2-3.

REMEMBER THE BASICS – EASY AS 1-2-3

1 Month of Pay stubs	If salaried - most recent pay stubs covering 30 day period If self employed - year to date income and expense statement (profit & loss) and balance sheet
2 Years of Income Document ation	If salaried – all W-2 forms for previous 2 years If self-employed - Federal Tax Form 1040 (with all Schedules attached) for previous 2 years (Please note: If you are a commissioned sales person, have any bonus income, rental income, or income from other sources, these forms are required even if you do not consider yourself self-employed) If owner or partner in business federal corporate tax returns Form 1120 or 1120S or partnership returns Form 1065 (with all Schedules attached) for previous 2 years, or applicable 2 year fiscal years.
3 Months Assets	3 most recent months bank statements - all pages. Please include savings, checking, investment, stock, mutual fund, 401(k), IRA and Keogh Accounts.

With this information and a copy of the sales contract or other property information, the loan officer has enough information to begin the process. This information does not necessarily constitute a complete application.

The Application Interview

Each individual loan officer develops a unique way of interacting with customers - explaining, questioning, developing an accurate profile of the borrower. This initial interview is critical, because during the first meeting customers tend to be more compliant and receptive to requests for additional information or explanations. The loan officer is in control and can manage the customer's expectations. One of the most frequent complaints customers have with lenders is that they receive frequent requests for additional information. The application interview is the loan officer's last opportunity to ask for information without the customer providing resistance, so it is important to be thorough.

Get Right Into It

If this is a true application interview, the terms of the mortgage have already been arranged. After a review of the Good Faith Estimate, commence the information collection process immediately by setting out the application form to be completed (or the lap top) alongside an "additional items needed" checklist. The application form actually works like a tickler, SO FILL IN ALL THE BLANKS! If something can't be filled in, you are missing information!

Sections 1 & 2 of Application

If you are sitting with the customer, share any concerns with them as they come up. This is the reason a face-to-face interview can be so critical. Rather than recording incorrect information or data that will confuse or detract from the loan approval, clarify it now. Property issues frequently are revealed here: Is the property a condominium? Can you offer this type of loan on a condominium? Is the down payment appropriate?

This can be a good segue into the asset part of the application. Read the sales contract now. How much is the earnest money deposit? Record this information not only on Section 6 Assets, but also in section 11, Details of Transaction. Did they bring the copy of the earnest money deposit check? Ask for it now! Every time something is missing, **put it on the checklist**!

Section 3 – Personal Information

Here we analyze whether the borrower has any potential areas of discrepancy. If they have moved a lot, there may be numerous landlords or mortgages to verify. If you are collecting their previous address, GET THEIR rental data – write down the name, address and phone number of the landlord so that you can have the credit bureau verify it later.

Borrower	III. BORROWER INFORMATION		Co-Borrower	

Borrower's Name (include Jr. or Sr. if applicable)

Co-Borrower's Name (include Jr. or Sr. if applicable)

Social Security Number	Home Phone (incl. area code)	DOB (mm/dd/yyyy)	Yrs. School	Social Security Number	Home Phone (incl. area code)	DOB (mm/dd/yyyy)	Yrs. School

☐ Married ☐ Unmarried (include single, ☐ Separated   divorced, widowed) | Dependents (not listed by Co-Borrower) no.   ages | ☐ Married ☐ Unmarried (include single, ☐ Separated   divorced, widowed) | Dependents (not listed by Borrower) no.   ages

Present Address (street, city, state, ZIP) ☐ Own ☐ Rent _____ No. Yrs. | Present Address (street, city, state, ZIP) ☐ Own ☐ Rent _____ No. Yrs.

Mailing Address, if different from Present Address | Mailing Address, if different from Present Address

If residing at present address for less than two years, complete the following:

Former Address (street, city, state, ZIP) ☐ Own ☐ Rent _____ No. Yrs. | Former Address (street, city, state, ZIP) ☐ Own ☐ Rent _____ No. Yrs.

Section 4 – Employment Data

While collecting employment data verify the income documentation. Check the names, addresses and social security numbers against the documents provided for information that doesn't make sense such as:

- A W-2 from an employer that is not listed.
- A missing W-2 for a listed employer.
- If there is a job that has been going on all year with a very small year-to-date income number.
- A 1099 instead of a W-2 – indicating self-employment.

Section III & IV - Borrower Information & Employment
☐ Borrower's Complete Name, Jr., Sr. ID Variance?
☐ Social Security Number Match
☐ 30 Days' Pay stubs
☐ 2 Years W-2's
☐ Self-Employed at least 2 years?
☐ Two Years 1040's/1120/1065
☐ Non-Schedule C business credit report necessary?
☐ Any Job Gaps/Different Employers? get letter

Incongruent information caught early can save trouble down the line. These are all substantial examples of items that can be caught at the time of application.

Borrower	IV. EMPLOYMENT INFORMATION		Co-Borrower	

Name & Address of Employer ☐ Self Employed | Yrs. on this job | Name & Address of Employer ☐ Self Employed | Yrs. on this job

| | Yrs. employed in this line of work/profession | | Yrs. employed in this line of work/profession

Position/Title/Type of Business | Business Phone (incl. area code) | Position/Title/Type of Business | Business Phone (incl. area code)

If employed in current position for less than two years or if currently employed in more than one position, complete the following:

Name & Address of Employer ☐ Self Employed | Dates (from-to) | Name & Address of Employer ☐ Self Employed | Dates (from-to)

| | Monthly Income $ | | Monthly Income $

Position/Title/Type of Business | Business Phone (incl. area code) | Position/Title/Type of Business | Business Phone (incl. area code)

Name & Address of Employer ☐ Self Employed | Dates (from-to) | Name & Address of Employer ☐ Self Employed | Dates (from-to)

Section V - Income & Housing Expense

In the employment section we check dates. Here, we need to check the numbers. The borrower may state a certain income, but may intend to tell you the net income after taxes as opposed to the gross. They may offer additional income such as benefits, which cannot be counted. Again, there is space for all types of income to be noted, SO NOTE THEM. As to the housing expense, if they are currently renting, ask for the name, address and phone number of their landlord. Is the mortgage on the credit report? If not, get 12 months checks!

Section V - Income & Housing Expense
❏ Examine Pay stub
❏ Salary evident from pay stub?
❏ Yr. to Date Higher/Lower than base salary? - Document/Explain
❏ Deductions - Any Loans? Shown on Credit Report? if not request rating
❏ Retirement? - Get Statement
❏ Bonus/Overtime/Commissions 25%
❏ Rent amount? - Get Landlord Name & Number
❏ Mortgage Amount - Shown on Credit Report? - if no, need 12 months checks

Remember

❏ **NO Income/NO Ratio Verification Loans.** Do not state income here or anywhere else on the application.

❏ Rental Property – Put primary housing expense where PITI goes

V. MONTHLY INCOME AND COMBINED HOUSING EXPENSE INFORMATION						
Gross Monthly Income	Borrower	Co-Borrower	Total	Combined Monthly Housing Expense	Present	Proposed
Base Empl. Income*	$	$	$	Rent	$	
Overtime				First Mortgage (P&I)		$
Bonuses				Other Financing (P&I)		
Commissions				Hazard Insurance		
Dividends/Interest				Real Estate Taxes		
Net Rental Income				Mortgage Insurance		
Other (before completing, see the notice in "describe other income," below)				Homeowner Assn. Dues		
				Other:		
Total	$	$	$	Total	$	$

* Self Employed Borrower(s) may be required to provide additional documentation such as tax returns and financial statements.

Describe Other Income   **Notice:** Alimony, child support, or separate maintenance income need not be revealed if the Borrower (B) or Co-Borrower (C) does not choose to have it considered for repaying this loan.

B/C		Monthly Amount
		$

Fannie Mae Form 1003   07/05   Page 3 of 5   Borrower _____   Freddie Mac Form 65   07/05

Section VI - Assets & Liabilities

Collecting asset and liability information is critical for the success of the application. If there are liabilities listed here which are not verified on the credit report, verifying them may become a chore later. Anything listed or disclosed on the application must be verified, so listing inconsequential accounts can lead to wasted time tracking verification. This is why we always want

<table>
<tr><td colspan="2">**Section VI - Assets & Liabilities**</td></tr>
<tr><td>❑</td><td>Copy of Earnest Money Check - Agrees with Contract?</td></tr>
<tr><td>❑</td><td>Review Bank Statements</td></tr>
<tr><td>❑</td><td>Funds for Closing Evident? - When received & What</td></tr>
<tr><td>❑</td><td>Any large withdrawals, deposits? - Explain & Document</td></tr>
<tr><td>❑</td><td>Net Worth Business? Self-employed P&L</td></tr>
<tr><td>❑</td><td>Cars owned free & clear? Titles?</td></tr>
<tr><td>❑</td><td>Other assets? Anything? Anything?</td></tr>
<tr><td>❑</td><td>Liabilities Reported not reported or verified?</td></tr>
<tr><td>❑</td><td>Credit explanations needed?</td></tr>
<tr><td>❑</td><td>Proof of Payoff?</td></tr>
<tr><td>❑</td><td>Real Estate Schedule - Rental Property on Tax Returns?</td></tr>
<tr><td>❑</td><td>Leases for Rentals</td></tr>
</table>

to take a credit report with us prior to the application interview. In addition, this is your only real opportunity to really question large deposits or other transactions on the deposit verifications – bank statements. It is tedious, but before you write anything down check to make sure you review all pages of any document BEFORE you commit it to the application.

The "Schedule of Real Estate Owned" is a continuation of Section VI – Assets and Liabilities. It presents an opportunity and a challenge. If the borrower has sold an existing property, and there is a question about net proceeds, the amount of the sales price should be inflated to keep the underwriter from minimizing net proceeds. In addition, if a property is pending sale, and may be

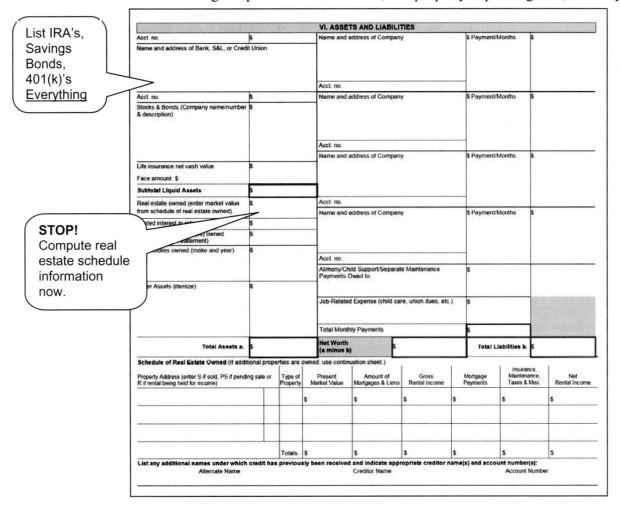

List IRA's, Savings Bonds, 401(k)'s <u>Everything</u>

STOP! Compute real estate schedule information now.

rented to allow the customer to qualify for a new mortgage, the borrower should be advised now that the amount of the rent will be reduced by a vacancy/expense factor of 25%. To offset the vacancy factor the borrower must rent the property for a higher amount - at least 125% of the mortgage payment is required to negate the effect of not having sold the property.

Section VII - Cash Requirements and the First Disclosure - The Good Faith Estimate

VII. DETAILS OF TRANSACTION	
a. Purchase price	$
b. Alterations, improvements, repairs	
c. Land (if acquired separately)	
d. Refinance (incl. debts to be paid off)	
e. Estimated prepaid items	
f. Estimated closing costs	
g. PMI, MIP, Funding Fee	
h. Discount (if Borrower will pay)	
i. Total costs (add items a through h)	
j. Subordinate financing	
k. Borrower's closing costs paid by Seller	
l. Other Credits(explain)	
m. Loan amount (exclude PMI, MIP, Funding Fee financed)	
n. PMI, MIP, Funding Fee financed	
o. Loan amount (add m & n)	
p. Cash from/to Borrower (subtract j, k, l & o from i)	

From the Good Faith Estimate

Sufficiency of assets for closing is a critical concern. The borrower will receive many differing accounts of how much cash they need to bring to closing. At this point you can set them greatly at ease by accurately completing the "Good Faith Estimate of Closing Costs."

Essentially, you are adding all of the costs and coming up with the total transaction costs. Then you subtract all of the items that will be paid for by the seller, the funds from the loan transaction and items, like the deposit that the borrower has already paid. This results in the borrower's net cash requirement for closing. Hopefully the borrower has sufficient funds for closing. In a refinancing transaction and closing costs are being financed, you will go through this process to determine what the appropriate loan amount should be.

Loan File Set Up

Once the application is complete, it helps to place the file in order and use a two hole fastener to place the documents in a legal folder. Using a "Standard File Order" helps to re-review the file to assure that nothing was missed.

While putting the file in order, make notes on a conversation log of some sort regarding the unusual circumstance revealed through the application process. A checklist of items needed to complete the application, which resembles the initial application checklist is given to the customer to inform them of anything remaining to be provided for processing.

There is nothing operations personnel hate more than having to spend significant extra time piecing together a new loan file. It is especially important if you are a new loan officer to do everything you can to make the job of the operations staff easier. All of the comments, notes, qualification information, customer contacts, and special instructions should be included on a conversation log. In addition, having the file in order will allow the processor to more quickly analyze problem areas and prepare the file for submission to underwriting for approval.

Loan File Set Up

Standard Loan File Set Up Order – Two Hole Fastened	
Left Side From Top to Bottom	**Right Side From Top to Bottom**
❑ Conversation Log ❑ Loan Registration ❑ Appraisal Request ❑ Customer Pre-qualification Calculations ❑ Copy of Application Deposit/Appraisal Fee ❑ Pre-Application Kit ❑ Contact information for case ❑ (Upside Down) Customer Supplied Documents not needed for loan approval	❑ Original Application ❑ Application Supplements, Green Cards, Reason for Refinance ❑ Credit Report ❑ Credit Related Information, Explanations, Payment Histories ❑ Income & Employment Information ❑ Asset Information ❑ Divorce Decrees ❑ Leases ❑ Sales Contract for Purchase, Deed ❑ Refinance, Construction Contract or ❑ Costs for Construction Permanent ❑ Disclosures

At the outset of the process the case is "opened" or "set-up," generally performing the data entry and preparing disclosures required before the file is given to a processor to submit. One of the first things that the file opener does is prepare and deliver all disclosures as required by law. The most critical one to the borrower and the loan officer alike is the Truth-in-Lending disclosure.

Red Flags in the Application Process

The application process reveals more information about the borrower than any other common experience in our culture. It is therefore quite understandable that individuals seek to conceal certain facts. It can also be amusing to see borrowers attempt to conceal information, because as lenders, our job is to reveal all aspects of a borrower's creditworthiness. In addition to each item that was recommended to be checked, these issues may cause problems in the application process.

APPLICATION
• Invalid social Security number
• Significant or contradictory changes from handwritten to typed loan application
PURCHASES
• New housing expense exceeds 150% of current housing expense
• Escrow closing check drawn on different depository from VOD
• Escrow receipt used as verification (may be a personal check or NSF)
• Fund paid outside of escrow (pre-existing trust relationship)
• Borrower lives with parents or relatives
• Borrower pays no rent at current residence
• Is the source of the down payment consistent with assets available?
• All recent increases in the bank accounts, as verified on a bank statement or VOD, must be

---

explained.
- Sources of closings funds such as gifts, sale of assets, and stock liquidation must be verified with a "paper trail". The source of the funds (gift letter and copy of check) and the receipt of funds (copy of deposit slip and verified new balance) must be documented.

Understanding Truth-in-Lending

Loan officers receive more calls with regard to the Truth-in-Lending Disclosure than any other form. The Federal Reserve Regulation Z was authorized by the "Truth-in-Lending" Act of 1969. The intent of the law was to create a uniform method of calculating the cost of credit by developing an APR - Annual Percentage Rate. The APR weighs the monthly payments against the non-interest finance charges on a loan. It also gives borrowers the right to cancel a transaction that results in a lien against their primary residence - a Right of Rescission.

One impetus of the law was to provide for "early disclosure" of the APR. This means the disclosure must be delivered to the applicant within 3 business days. The purpose of early disclosure of the APR was to allow a consumer to comparison shop and avoid "hidden" finance charges. If this is the reason for the disclosure, it seems contradictory that it would be delivered after a borrower has submitted an application. Every borrower receives the form, though, so it is important to alert them ahead of time. Without the warning the loan officer can expect an angry or panicked call from a customer within the first week of the application process demanding an explanation for what they perceive are changes in the terms of the loan.

The confusion stems from words. Annual Percentage Rate and interest rate mean the same thing to a borrower - but they refer to two different concepts. When the APR appears on a form and is higher than the interest rate discussed during the application there is understandable concern. From the consumer's perspective the APR is the interest rate, because most consumer loans, credit cards and car loans carry a simple rate with no fees and APR here refers to the rate. Likewise, the phrase "Amount Financed" sounds like lender jargon for the loan amount, but is invariably lower than the amount applied for. "Why was my loan reduced?" is the question. There are 4 boxes on the form: The "APR," "Finance Charge," "Amount Financed," and "Total of Payments." Then there is a "Payment Schedule," followed by a number of other disclosures describing the loan terms.

To understand the Truth-in-Lending disclosure (TIL), start with the concept that it is only a theoretical measure of the cost of credit. For example: If you borrow $100, but there is a $1 charge for the loan, then you really have only received $99 in usable cash. However, you will still make payments on the loan based upon the $100 principal balance. The TIL determines what the theoretical rate on the loan is considering the fact that there was a fee due to make the loan - that is the APR. The $1 in this example is a finance charge.

Keystrokes to Compute the APR for a Fixed Rate Loan			
Enter Loan Amount	100000	PV	100000
Enter Interest Rate	7.75%	"I%"/12	0.646%
Enter Term	360	N	360
Compute Payment	CPT	PMT	$716.41
Compute Prepaid Finance Charge	1836		
Subtract from Loan	100000	1836	98164
Enter Result as PV	98164	PV	
Compute Interest	CPT	"I%"	0.662%
Multiply by 12 for APR	0.662%	x 12	7.943%

The APR Formula

Being able to prepare a TIL for a customer would illustrate the calculation, but this is rarely practical. As in the $100 illustration, the first step in determining APR is to subtract the prepaid finance charges from the loan amount. The result is the "Amount Financed." Then the full principal and interest payment (including PMI) is applied against the "Amount Financed" as if it were the loan amount. The resulting interest rate is the APR. There are some nuances.

Determining the Amount Financed - What are Finance Charges?

Everything that one must pay for in exchange for obtaining a loan (charges you wouldn't incur if you were paying cash for the property) is considered a prepaid finance charge. This includes loan fees such as discount points, origination fees, private mortgage insurance; miscellaneous fees such as tax service, underwriting, document preparation, and lender review fees. In addition, prepaid items such as per diem interest and escrows for PMI or prepaid PMI, FHA upfront MIP, and the VA funding fee are considered finance charges. Interestingly, appraisal fees, credit reports, termite reports and other inspections such as completion inspections (except for construction loan draw inspections), well and septic inspections that are required by lenders are not considered finance charges. Neither are fees for recording a deed of trust. These are excluded from the amount-financed calculation because a buyer or borrower would incur them regardless of whether a loan was involved. Appraisal and credit report fees are "passed through" to service providers.

There is a catch. Any item that the borrower does not pay for is not included in the calculation. This would be the case when a property seller is contractually obligated to pay the fees, or in a lender funded closing cost situation.

APR (Annual Percentage Rate) The cost of your credit as a yearly rate.	FINANCE CHARGE The dollar amount the credit will cost you.	AMOUNT FINANCED The amount of credit provided to you on your behalf.	TOTAL OF PAYMENTS The amount you will have paid after you have made all payments as scheduled.
❹	❸	❷	❶
%	$	$	$

1.) Compute **total of payments** by multiplying payment schedule, including PMI by amount of payments
2.) **Amount Financed** is the loan amount, less points, prepaid interest, PMI, and lender fees.
3.) **Finance Charge** is the **Total of Payments** less the **Amount Financed**
4.) Compute the **APR** by dividing the **Total of Payments** by the number of payments and apply that against the **Amount Financed**, as if it were the loan amount. (See Keystrokes to Compute APR)

Payment Schedule

The payment schedule is the second half of the APR equation. If you borrow $100 and you have

$99 to use, how are you repaying the $100? On a fixed rate loan, the payment schedule is quite simple - the monthly payment is the same through the life of the loan. Variable payments are also a factor when there are changing payments on the loan as in an ARM, Buydown, GEM, or GPM. The payment schedule varies in these situations. To determine the payment amount to apply against the amount financed divide the total of payments by the number of payments and utilize this average payment.

PMI is considered a finance charge. The initial PMI premium, MIP or Funding Fee must be considered in the amount financed. If there is money placed in escrow for PMI or MIP, this is considered in the amount financed as well. When the PMI premium changes monthly – it is acceptable to use a range (varies from – to).

The APR on ARMs can change, based on future interest rate changes. Buydowns, GPMs and GEMs have fixed payment schedules, so the APR on these loans will not change.

Finance Charge

The APR, amount financed and total of payments have been calculated as explained above. What is the total finance charge? The difference between the total of payments and the amount financed represents the cumulative total of all interest and prepaid finance charges accrued on the loan. Subtracting the amount financed from the total of payments reveals this number.

Program Disclosures - work in tandem with the Truth-in-Lending statement and should be given in conjunction with the TIL. They explain more fully the historical performance of the ARM, when the consumer has applied for one. All programs should have disclosure describing fully how the payment schedule works, whether there is any prepayment penalty, late charges, tax and insurance escrow treatments, due on sale clauses and any other nuances of the program.

The "Refund of the Prepaid Finance Charge" - Again terminology can cause confusion between the intended meaning of a phrase and how the consumer interprets it. In the context of the TIL, this applies to prepayment and mortgage insurance. In the event that there is prepaid mortgage insurance, such as the "Up Front FHA MIP", monthly FHA MIP or traditional prepaid or financed PMI, if the loan is paid off early the consumer may receive the cancellation value of that insurance. Consumers sometimes equate the "Finance Charge" box from the TIL with this statement and assume they will still be obligated for the interest under the loan, even though the loan is paid off.

Recording Fees/Security Interest - Even though they are not included in the finance charge, fees to record a deed of trust in the jurisdiction are shown. All mortgages loans are secured by a property, the address of which should be shown.

Late Charge - Stating what the late payment percentage is, when the payment is considered late, and that it is based on the principal and interest portion of the payment only.

Assumption - States whether the loan is assumable. While there are no new unconditionally assumable loans being made institutionally, some loans are assumable with the new borrower's approval by the existing lender. However, even if assumption is allowed, many lenders will change the terms to reflect the current market or disallow the assumption.

Insurance – If insurance is required as a pre-condition of the loan approval, the lender must give the terms of the insurance.

Regulation Title	Regulator	Practical Application	Disclosure	Highlights/Features of the Law
Real Estate Settlement Procedures Act **RESPA Regulation X**	Department of Housing and Urban Development – HUD (also supervises FHA, GNMA, Housing Programs)	Application	• Good Faith Estimate of Closing Cost • Special Information Booklet - HUD Guide to Closing Costs	Residential Only. < 25 Acres, Lot Loans, Commercial Exempt. Deliver to customer within 72 Hours. Customer uses special information booklet to shop for services
		Business Practices	Section 8 - Anti-Kickback Provision	No "thing of value" in exchange for referrals. Payment for referral when no service is rendered is considered Kickback. Gifts must be given to all. Penalty – up to $10,000 per
		Business Practices	Controlled/Affiliated Business Arrangement Disclosure	Interested parties must disclose nature of business relationship at time of sale
		Closing	HUD-1 Settlement Statement	24 hours prior to closing borrower may inspect HUD-1
		Application/Servicing	Transfer of Servicing/Servicing Practices	Signed disclosure within 3 days. Borrower has right to 1.) Annual analysis, 2.) 15 day notice of loan sale from seller and buying lender 3.) Max "cushion" 3 months (2+1)
Truth-in-Lending Act **TILA Regulation Z**	Federal Reserve Board	Application/Closing	APR Disclosure	Truth in Lending delivered to borrower within 3 days of application and again at closing. Owner Occupied Only. Discloses cost of credit, prepayment, late charges and other loan terms.
		Application	ARM Disclosure "Consumer Handbook on Adjustable Rate Mortgages" (CHARM Booklet) "When your Home is on the Line"	If loan is an ARM, borrower receives ARM disclosure (terms, index, history and CHARM (Consumer Handbook on ARMs) Booklet. HELOCs— Borrower receives "When Your Home is on the Line" booklet
		Business Practices	Advertising	Advertised interest rates must give APR at same size. Quoting rates – must quote APR before contract rate.
		Closing	Right of Rescission	Owner Occupied Refinance only. Borrower has 3 day right to cancel transaction. Each borrower must receive 2 copies.
		Application/Closing	Home Ownership Equity Protection Act (Section 32 – High Cost Loans) Disclosure and Truth in Lending.	Loans with rate > 8% (10% for 2nds) over Treasury, > 8 points are considered "High Cost". NO 1.) Negative Amortization. 2.) Balloons < 5 years 3.) Prepayment Penalties 4.) Demand/Call provision 5.) 50% DTI, 6.) Lending without regard to repayment. 7.) HOEPA to HOEPA refi within 12 months, 8.) HELOCs exempt, but may not structure loan as HELOC to avoid. Borrower has 3 days PRIOR to closing + 3 days after Closing to Cancel.
Equal Credit Opportunity Act **ECOA Regulation B**	Bank - OCC Mortgage Banker/Broker - FTC	Application	Non-Discrimination Disclosure Decisioning Guidelines	No discrimination on Race/Ethnicity, Gender, Childbearing, Age. Cannot discourage applicant from applying. Must give written notice of status within 30 days. Credit report, app. pre-qualification starts timing. Borrower has right to appraisal copy.
		Processing	Fair Credit Reporting	State ALL reasons and provide all sources for adverse information. Borrower may receive copy of credit report.
Home Mortgage Disclosure Act **HMDA Regulation C**	Federal Reserve Board	Application	1003 Data Collection	Reporting Data to identify discriminatory practices. Request Borrower Data – Must guess if borrower refuses. State "Lender Designation".
Gramm-Leach-Bliley – Financial Privacy Act	FTC	Application Servicing	Financial Information Sharing	Consumers must be given option to "opt out" of information sharing. Prohibits "pretexting" – calling to for permission to share personal information under the guise of needing it for the purpose of a transaction.

How to Process a Loan

There may be occasions in your career when you are called upon to process your own loans. Your pipeline is just starting to swell when your processor is involved in a serious car accident. You feel sorry for your processor – but your troubles haven't even started yet. If the loan application is perfect, processing is where the

Basic Steps in Emergency Processing
• Order appraisal • Order credit report - if not already done • Review file for completeness • Type application and submit to underwriter

home loan sequence begins to reveal its nightmarish realities. Under normal circumstances, it is the processor's duty to complete the verification process, assure regulatory compliance and prepare the case for presentation to the underwriter, loan committee or other decision-maker. It seems simple enough, but here is where the effect known as "I am not sure if this is completely clear" kicks in. You may have to know how to process to a small degree, to help fill in during an emergency. This isn't a lesson how to process. It is a lesson in what to do in an emergency – first understand the process.

What seemed apparent to the loan officer isn't so apparent to the processor. If it isn't apparent to the processor, it isn't going to be apparent to the underwriter either. In an ideal situation, the processor and loan officer work together to identify "critical" items that could cause the loan to be denied and ascertain whether they can be fixed. Working together and with the borrower it is unlikely that any adverse information can't be refuted. Then there are non-critical items - things that the loan can be approved "subject to" or as a condition of the approval - "nickel & dime" conditions.

The problem comes when a processor doesn't segregate the level of importance of various documents and mails a simple list of outstanding documents to a borrower. Suddenly an inconsequential bank statement or other innocuous pieces of information are as important to the borrower as a critical document, such as proof that a delinquent account is incorrectly attributed, or the current year's tax return. The borrower receives the list and puts everything together, except for the critical document, then sends it in. The mail gets reviewed a week later and suddenly - nearly 1 month into the loan process - there is a huge problem. Welcome to mortgage banking. This is why a complete application is so important!

The loan officer is a "field underwriter," and should not allow the processor to dictate what information is needed prior to submitting a loan to an underwriter. Conversely, the loan officer should not burden the processor with the duty of trying to qualify a borrower.

The Approval Process - Who is this Underwriter?

It is ironic that approval timing and contingencies are still the biggest problem in the mortgage business. The approval process is a relatively short period of time. If a human underwriter is reviewing the loan, the documentation review and credit decision usually take place in the space of an hour. The average underwriter can review between 5 and 12 cases a day. The remainder of the underwriter's time is spent clarifying conditions of approval, mitigating problems with approvals, answering challenges to the initial decision, and determining that subsequently submitted documentation meets the requirements of the initial approval.

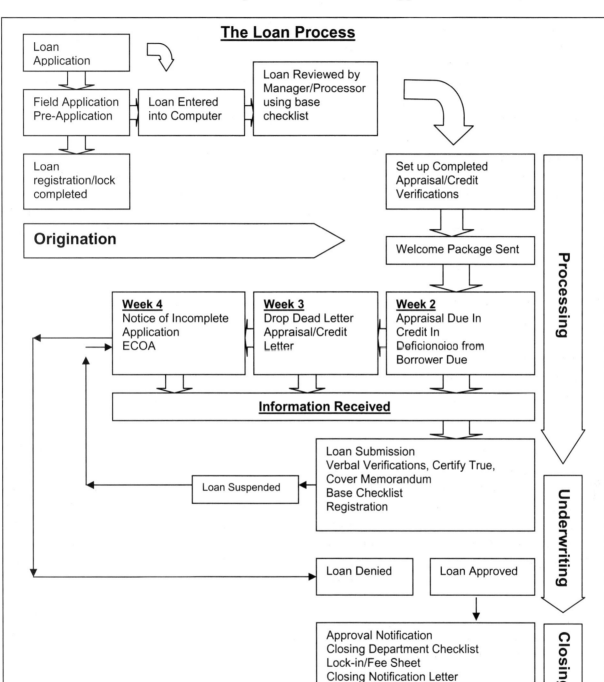

In the case of Automated Underwriting via Desktop Underwriter or Loan Prospector, the decision engine normally responds within 5-15 minutes, but the exhibits of the loan package – the income, asset and credit documentation – are subject to review and interpretation by a human underwriter. For this reason, a loan which is credit approved through Automated Underwriting in 5 minutes may still be held in underwriting or processing for much longer while the documentation is reviewed.

Depending on whether an investor on a whole loan basis is purchasing the loan, or being sold off into a security by a mortgage banker, the underwriter may be an employee of the company or an employee of another company. There may be more or less leniency as a result of this. It may impact the amount of time it takes to obtain an approval. In addition, depending on the loan size, there may be a loan committee or a pool insurance underwriter. Most underwriting today is what is called compliance underwriting - assuring that the loan meets guidelines. The approval process isn't very subjective if the loan meets guidelines - it meets the guidelines, it's approved. If the loan doesn't meet guidelines then there comes the process of determining whether there are sufficient compensating factors to approve the loan. It is the loan officer's job to intervene in a situation where there is difficulty and act as the borrower's advocate.

If there is mortgage insurance, the PMI Company will also have to approve the loan. PMI underwriters generally underwrite on a risk basis. They look both subjectively at whether they have a good feeling about the case and whether the case meets risk profiles established in their risk scoring systems.

Government Agencies (FHA/VA and state bond programs) do approve loans directly, and in some cases must, approve loans directly. FHA allows approved underwriters to approve loans through the Direct Endorsement program. VA offers the same thing called the "Automatic" underwriting program. State agencies have their own underwriting, or may accept a FHA Direct or VA Automatic approval.

A new trend in underwriting is the "contract" underwriter. This may be a PMI underwriter who is authorized to approve loans for various lenders, saving the lenders the expense of maintaining a large staff of underwriters.

The bottom line is the same. The underwriter is a person who is subject to the pressure of balancing the need to make loans and the need to make loans that will not default or be ineligible for purchase in the secondary market. Even one default or one non-saleable loan can be a huge problem for a small or mid-sized lender.

Desktop Underwriter and Loan Prospector

Many people projected that the era of the traditional loan officer would be over when the mortgage process evolved into a fully automated system. Those people did not understand the business, as it exists on a practical basis. Automation only eliminates the underwriter. The loan still needs to be structured correctly. The customer also needs an advocate in process. Most importantly, automated underwriting only provides acceptable initial results in about 25% of all applications because:

- The supporting documentation varies from what was entered into the system initially. Automated Underwriting relies on the information that humans enter into the model. If that information does not conform to the documentation requirements, the loan is denied and must be manually underwritten or re-submitted to Automated Underwriting
- The program specifications require manual underwriting.

- The loan does not meet eligibility criteria for other reasons, such as credit, loan parameters, or other factors.

If you have access to automated underwriting it can simplify the process tremendously. Even though Automated Underwriting protocols sometimes reduce the documentation required for approval, this does not mean that you should not collect as much application documentation as possible. If simply to give a borrower the opportunity for a better rate through another source, or to cover tracks in case a further review of information is required, there is no excuse for not collecting as much information as possible from the borrower. Remember that once the borrowers sign applications, they think they are done. Don't put yourself in the position of chasing conditions simply because it was easier to get the application in the door. Ultimately, the complete application remains the "Holy Grail" of the mortgage business. Strive for complete applications.

Conducting Pipeline Review

We "prove" excellent customer service by providing the results of conducting a weekly pipeline review. The written reports resulting from the review show the customer that the loan officer is in control of the pipeline. Referral sources receiving weekly reports do not badger support staff for status on their transactions. Delivering weekly reports is also an excellent opportunity for the loan officer to generate additional business. Finally, a weekly status review is a time management tool for the loan officer and processor alike. A loan officer, who conducts status weekly, instead of every time a customer asks what the status is, controls the number of interrupting telephone calls received by himself and his processor. Pipeline review is an amazing time management tool for production and production support personnel.

Management has even more critical reasons to insist on loan officers performing a weekly review. By insisting on this as part of the corporate culture, the company is not directly responsible for the smooth outcome of a transaction – it is the loan officer's responsibility. In addition, the company can assure that the employee is reviewing each case appropriately by requiring a copy of the weekly pipeline review. When a problem arises on a case, the company's first question should be "has the loan officer properly managed this case?" by reviewing status logs.

The temptation is to allow customers to access loan status via the internet. This is particularly true when there has been a significant technology investment on the part of the company. The availability of status reports through an internet portal does not preclude the need for the loan officer to conduct a weekly status review.

Conducting Weekly Status Reviews

Responsible Party	Description
Loan Officer	Schedules meeting with each processor handling cases. Time allotted for meeting should be 2-5 Minutes for each case in process

Responsible Party	Description
Processor	Assembles all of the loan officer's files regardless of status, in the order defined by the processor. The file should not be "prepared" for status. The loan officer should witness the actual condition of the loan file.
Loan Officer/Processor	Meet at the scheduled time to review all cases in process. Either processor or Loan Officer is charged with the responsibility of completing the status log.
Loan Officer	Assumes responsibility for external related documentation on case 1. Customer contacts for additional information 2. Referral source calls for items required on the transaction 3. Any qualification issues must be resolved by the loan officer 4. Loan Program or lock-in issues are the loan officer's responsibility.

Processor	Assumes responsibility for internal related documentation on the case
	1. Closing Department or closing agent related documentation
	2. Underwriting Department flow related issues, condition/stipulation satisfaction
	3. Vendor issues
	  a. Credit Report ordering/correction
	  b. Appraisal ordering/correction
	  c. PMI
	  d. Flood Certification
	  e. Insurance Policy

Processor	During the week, incoming loan documentation is fastened on top of the file. During the loan status meeting, loose (received) documents are reviewed together with the Loan Officer and marked on the status report to determine whether document is sufficient or if 2nd request is necessary.
Loan Officer/Processor	Take completed Status Log and make one copy for loan officer, processor and branch manager.
Loan Officer	Take copies of each individual loan's updated status report and deliver to all referral sources the following day.

Sample Status Log

Status Log
Loan Officer _____
Processor _____
Date Completed _____

Status Logs, Status Reports and Detailed Status Process is available in the "Loan Officer's Practical Guide to Marketing at www.lendertraining.com

(Repeated blocks: Borrower | Processor to Handle | Loan Officer to Handle | Checklist: Appraisal Ordered, Credit O.K., Lock Expiration, VOE O.K., VOA O.K., Complete Application Docs In?)

"Congratulations! Your loan is approved"

This is the best part of the process. If it was a difficult case, it may proceed quite rapidly to closing. Understanding the mechanics of closing will allow you to "grease the runway" for a case that has been languishing in underwriting. Settlement requirements are quite simple. These are the items that must be obtained in order to assure the borrower's and lender's interests in the property being purchased.

> **Settlement Preparations:** Mortgage Approval means "begin to prepare for settlement." Get the homeowner's insurance policy, termite report, title binder, survey and final inspections.

The Closing and Requirements

As you prepare your borrower for an approaching settlement, it is useful to remind them of the information that will be required for closing. Every case requires the same information and documentation for closing. The "Final Four" items allow the case to proceed to closing.

> ### The "Final Four"
>
> ❑ Title Binder
> ❑ Survey
> ❑ Hazard/Flood Insurance
> ❑ Termite/Inspections
>
> Four items you can always count on having to get.

Settlement Agent

A settlement agent is also known as a closing attorney, title company or escrow company. The settlement agent is responsible for scheduling settlement and provides; 1.) a title binder – the commitment to issue title insurance, 2.) a survey, showing the house location on the lot and 3.) The "Insured Closing Protection Letter" that indicates the lender is indemnified for a specific closing agent.

1. *Title Insurance* At settlement, buyers are offered the opportunity to purchase OPTIONAL Owner's Title Insurance to protect the equity in the home being financed. This policy is in addition to the **mandatory** lender's policy. This "Owner's Policy" is not required by the lender. If the transaction is a refinance and there is a Title Insurance Policy in force, the owner should provide the settlement agent with a copy as soon as possible. There is a possibility of savings by reissuing an existing policy. In addition, with the old Title Policy, a full title search may not be necessary - a present owner "bring down" simply researches the title from the date of the last title search.

2. *Survey:* A house location survey shows the location of the property improvements relative to the lot lines. It may not be necessary to obtain a new survey if 1.) The title is insurable without a new survey, and 2.) No changes have been made to the exterior of a house (the borrower must sign an affidavit stating this). If these requirements can't be met an existing survey may be re-certified as a cost savings. Surveys are not required for condominiums

3. ***Homeowner's Insurance Policy:*** The basic standards for Homeowner's (Hazard/Fire Insurance) are that the company should be Bests Rated A- or better and meet the following:

   - Dwelling Coverage in the amount of the Loan
   - Dated within the same month, but prior to the date of settlement
   - Paid receipt for the first year's premium
   - Correct property address
   - Names shown as they are shown on the loan application or property title
   - Mortgagee/Loss Payee Clause
   - Investment Properties must carry rent loss coverage equal to 6 months rent.

4. ***Condominiums:*** The management company provides a certificate of insurance showing the borrower's names, the condominium unit number and Loss/Payee clause. The settlement agent may procure this. If the borrower is purchasing a property, the agent is responsible for this. If it is a refinancing, the borrower is responsible.

5. ***Planned Unit Developments:*** If there is a Homeowner's Association collecting fees for maintenance of Common Elements, such as roads, recreational facilities, or other amenities, your property is in a Planned Unit Development (PUD). We require evidence that the association maintains the common elements. A letter from the association or Management Company is sufficient. In addition, they must provide evidence that the association carries liability insurance in an amount of at least $1,000,000 per occurrence. If the borrowers are purchasing, the agent is responsible for providing this. If they are refinancing, this is the borrower's responsibility.

6. ***Flood Insurance:*** If a flood certification firm determines the property to be in a Flood Zone "A", flood insurance must be obtained. If the flood certification cannot make a determination of the flood zone location of the property, a risk assessment must be obtained through FEMA. Sometimes, a house location survey will identify the 100-year flood plain on the property, and if the improvements are located outside of this zone, the Flood Insurance requirement may be waived.

Flood Zone Determinations Requiring Flood Insurance

Zone Designation	Description
BA	Areas of 100-year flood, base flood elevations, and flood hazard factors not determined
AO	Flood depths of one to three feet (usually sheet flow on sloping terrain) average depths determined, area of alluvial fan flooding, velocities determined
AH	Flood depths of one to three feet (usually areas of ponding), base flood elevations determined
AE,AI-A30	Areas of 100-year flood, base flood elevations, flood hazard factors determined
A99	To be protected from 100-year flood by federal flood protection system under construction, no base flood elevations determined
IV	Areas of 100 year coastal flood with velocity (wave action), base flood elevations, flood hazard factors not determined
VE, VI,V30	Areas of 100 year coastal flood with velocity (wave action), base flood elevations, flood hazard factors determined

7. ***Termite Report:*** A termite report, showing no damage or infestation, is required.

Refinances MAY be exempt from this requirement. The original form dated within 45 days of settlement must be provided. Condominiums MAY be exempt from this requirement, if the association shows a line item in the budget for pest control. New Construction requires a soil treatment certificate.

8. ***Well/Septic Certification:*** If your property is serviced by a well and/or septic system a certification from the local health authority as whether the water is potable is required. If a Termite Soil Treatment is performed, water potability must not be affected and a certification to this effect is required. Refinances MAY be exempt from this.

9. ***New Construction:*** A Residential Use Permit (RUP), Certificate of Occupancy or Completion is required from the code compliance authority in the jurisdiction is required. When the property is complete we must be notified so that we may order the final inspection from the appraiser.

10. ***Floating Rate:*** Floating rates must generally be locked 5 days prior to closing.

A Word on Titling

When you buy a house, you get a title to the property. This may be referred to as a Deed of Bargain and Sale, General or Special Warranty Deed, Fee Simple Deed, or a Title. This is the original document that is recorded among the local land records in the jurisdiction where the property is located. You notice that on the first page of the application there is a section that requests "Manner in which title will be held." There are 4 common forms of ownership. In addition, the type of deed that you receive may affect the owner's interest. A General Warranty Deed conveys the property with the seller's guarantee that the title is good. A Special Warranty Deed is basically a statement from the seller of the property that as far as he knows, the title is good. A Quit-Claim Deed sets forth some probability of a problem with the title - the seller only warrants that they are selling the property and will not pursue a claim against it. For instance, in Massachusetts much of the eastern part of the state is subject to Indian tribe land claims. If ever enforced, there is a possibility you lose your title. Thus, by accepting a Quitclaim, you are releasing a seller of any liability in the event of forfeiture.

When encountering property rights, it is important to know what kind of community property laws your region has. Common Law States give spouses rights of Dower & Curtsey that may have to be addressed at closing.

Common Forms of Titling

Joint Tenants with Right of Survivorship means that when one owner dies, the survivors automatically become the owner of the property.

Tenants by Entirety is a form of ownership reserved for married couples. The property reverts to the survivor but shields the owner from claims of individual creditors

Tenants in Common allows the owners to assign percentage of ownership to each owner. When one owner dies, it creates an estate that will be distributed under the terms of the owner's will

Sole & Separate means there is no other titleholder

Lender Sends Loan Instructions to Settlement Agent

The lender will not normally go to settlement, but sends closing instructions to the settlement agent who will prepare a settlement statement. This is an exact summary of the costs of the transaction. Once prepared, the settlement statement will show exactly what you will be required to pay at closing. Borrowers should bring a certified check for the remainder of the down payment (if any) and closing costs. Loan officers are encouraged to read all of their company's closing documents as well as attend a number of settlements to become familiar with the mechanics of real estate transactions. Some people recommend that loan officers attend settlement as a customer service and sales opportunity. Loan Officers should not attend a settlement that is anticipated to be difficult.

Closing "Red Flags"

Incidences of fraud or misrepresentation are often discovered at closing. While not every instance represents intentional fraud, knowing about these problems will allow the loan officer to correct them before settlement and prevent possible delays.

TITLE REPORT
• Income tax or similar liens against borrower on refinances
• Delinquent property taxes
• Notice of default recorded
• Seller not on title (double escrow)
• Modification agreement on existing loan (s)
• Seller owned property for a short time with cash-out on the sale
• Buyer has preexisting financial interest in property

ESCROW INSTRUCTIONS
• Cash paid outside of escrow to seller
• Down payment paid into escrow upon opening
• Reference to another (double) escrow.
• Related parties involved in the transaction
• Unusual credits with no economic substance (see HUD-1 settlement statement)
• Right of assignment (who is the actual borrower?)
• Power of attorney used (why can't borrower execute document?)
• Business entity acting as the seller may be controlled or related to borrower
• Change of sales price to "fit" the appraisal
• No amendments to escrow
• "Fill in the blank" escrow instructions
• Purchase not subject to inspection
• Unusual amendments to the original transaction
• Demands paid off to undisclosed third parties (potential obligation)
• No real estate commission (possibly related parties)
• Actual settlement charges exceed "Good Faith Estimate" by 10%

It is at the closing that questions may be raised about the disparity of fees disclosed on the Good Faith Estimate and the total charges on the settlement statement. Of course no one is concerned when the fees are lower. When they are higher, however, there is usually a panicked call to the loan officer to explain. Obviously the good faith estimate is just that - an estimate. Look at all the numbers. Isolating the lender's charges from the overall closing costs can often defuse a situation where a borrower is attributing the higher number to variances in the closing costs.

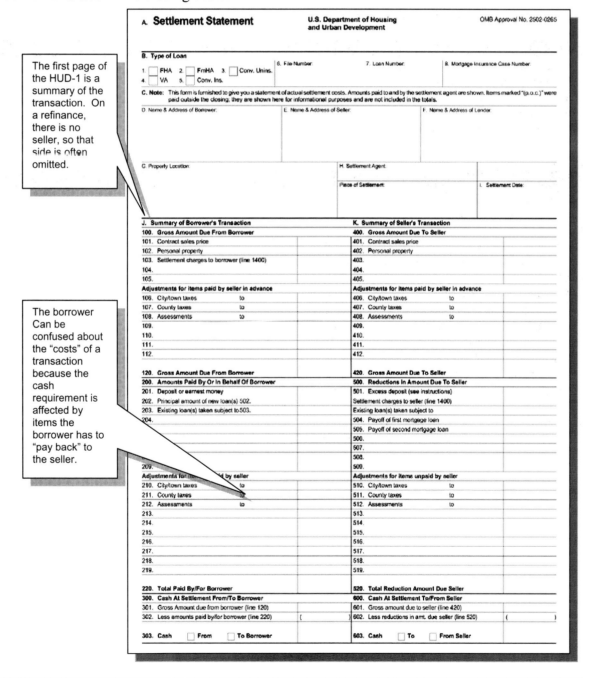

Closing Cost Anomolies
Pro-rated Condo Fees
New Construction Assessments/Partial Levy
Termite Treatment
Reimbursement of Seller Paid Real Estate Taxes
More Days of Per Diem Interest
Optional Owner's Title Insurance Purchased
Refinance - Most recent payment not accounted for in Payoff

The first page of the HUD-1 is a summary of the transaction. On a refinance, there is no seller, so that side is often omitted.

The borrower Can be confused about the "costs" of a transaction because the cash requirement is affected by items the borrower has to "pay back" to the seller.

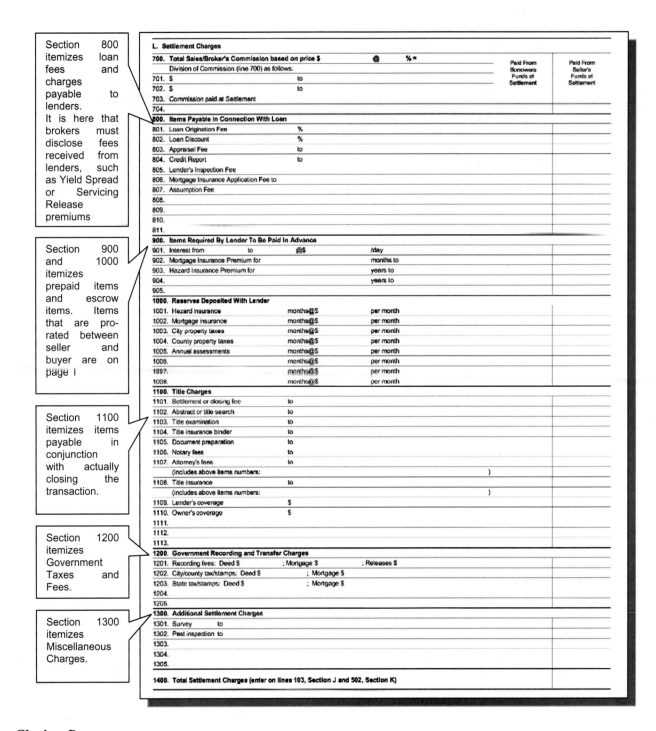

Section 800 itemizes loan fees and charges payable to lenders. It is here that brokers must disclose fees received from lenders, such as Yield Spread or Servicing Release premiums

Section 900 and 1000 itemizes prepaid items and escrow items. Items that are pro-rated between seller and buyer are on page l

Section 1100 itemizes items payable in conjunction with actually closing the transaction.

Section 1200 itemizes Government Taxes and Fees.

Section 1300 itemizes Miscellaneous Charges.

L. Settlement Charges				Paid From Borrowers Funds at Settlement	Paid From Seller's Funds at Settlement
700. Total Sales/Broker's Commission based on price $		@	% =		
Division of Commission (line 700) as follows:					
701. $		to			
702. $		to			
703. Commission paid at Settlement					
704.					
800. Items Payable In Connection With Loan					
801. Loan Origination Fee	%				
802. Loan Discount	%				
803. Appraisal Fee	to				
804. Credit Report	to				
805. Lender's Inspection Fee					
806. Mortgage Insurance Application Fee to					
807. Assumption Fee					
808.					
809.					
810.					
811.					
900. Items Required By Lender To Be Paid In Advance					
901. Interest from	to	@$	/day		
902. Mortgage Insurance Premium for			months to		
903. Hazard Insurance Premium for			years to		
904.			years to		
905.					
1000. Reserves Deposited With Lender					
1001. Hazard insurance		months@$	per month		
1002. Mortgage insurance		months@$	per month		
1003. City property taxes		months@$	per month		
1004. County property taxes		months@$	per month		
1005. Annual assessments		months@$	per month		
1006.		months@$	per month		
1007.		months@$	per month		
1008.		months@$	per month		
1100. Title Charges					
1101. Settlement or closing fee	to				
1102. Abstract or title search	to				
1103. Title examination	to				
1104. Title insurance binder	to				
1105. Document preparation	to				
1106. Notary fees	to				
1107. Attorney's fees	to				
(includes above items numbers:			)		
1108. Title insurance	to				
(includes above items numbers:			)		
1109. Lender's coverage	$				
1110. Owner's coverage	$				
1111.					
1112.					
1113.					
1200. Government Recording and Transfer Charges					
1201. Recording fees: Deed $	; Mortgage $	; Releases $			
1202. City/county tax/stamps: Deed $	; Mortgage $				
1203. State tax/stamps: Deed $	; Mortgage $				
1204.					
1205.					
1300. Additional Settlement Charges					
1301. Survey	to				
1302. Pest inspection to					
1303.					
1304.					
1305.					
1400. Total Settlement Charges (enter on lines 103, Section J and 502, Section K)					

Closing Documents

In addition to the HUD-1 Settlement statement, the borrower signs a multitude of documents at closing.

Promissory Note

There is only one loan document that the borrower MUST sign. A Note is simply evidence of a debt. The mortgage note sets forth the terms of the loan and evidences the borrower's promise to repay the loan. The promise itself is not enough to secure the lender's interest. Mortgage notes are secured by collateral agreements which dictate that the lender may reclaim ownership of the property should the borrower fail to repay.

The Mortgage or Deed of Trust

A mortgage is a document that secures the borrower's promise to repay. There are fifteen states which use both mortgages and deeds of trust. A deed of trust states that the title to the property that secures the loan is held in trust by a third party (such as a title company or an escrow company) until the borrower repays the loan and title is conveyed to him/her. In the event of the borrower's default on the loan, the lender can file a notice of default and the trustee who is holding the deed may begin legal proceedings for foreclosure if delinquent payments are not made.

The borrower is giving a mortgage – the mortgagor
The lender is receiving a mortgage – the mortgagee

Final Truth-in-Lending Disclosure, which states the annual percentage rate, the loan terms, and the number of payments

Initial Escrow Statement, which includes estimated taxes, insurance premiums, and other charges which the borrower will pay from the escrow fund during the first twelve months of the loan. When the closing is completed, the lender will record the lien (for mortgages) or the deed (for deeds of trust) in the public records.

Wet and Dry Settlements

The "Wet Settlement" Act requires that actual cash, or "good funds" be at the closing table. This is designed to assure that all the accounting be based on actual receipts and disbursements so that the settlement agent may accurately disburse all funds at the closing. The settlement agent acts as a conduit for all of the funds accounted for at the transaction. So the settlement statement is a bucket where all the money goes and comes out of. When all the parties meet at the closing table, this is referred to as a round table closing. In certain parts of the country, closings are conducted in escrow. This means the same thing, basically, except that not all parties are at the table at the same time - and the buyer doesn't usually know what the seller's summary is, and vice versa.

The Right of Rescission - Refinances

Although this information is not an early disclosure requirement, it affects any extension of additional credit on a borrower's primary residence. This is part of the Truth-in-Lending Regulation and it provides a 3 full-day "right to cancel" the transaction. Because of this, on refinance and home equity loans, documents are signed but funds do not disburse until after the period expires.

Other Disclosures

- **Good Faith Estimate** *(HUD)* This must be accompanied by the HUD *"Settlement Costs Booklet"* that describes the charges associated with closing and defines them specifically. It also illustrates how the settlement statement works.
- **Good Faith Estimate Addendum Required Service Providers** *(HUD)* – As a lender you must provide a listing of providers that the borrower must use for certain services if they do not have any choice in the matter. Credit Bureaus, Appraisers and Title or Settlement Companies are usual candidates.
- **ARM Disclosure** *(Federal Reserve)* – The "Charm Booklet," also known as the "*Consumer Handbook on ARMs*" accompanies the Truth-in-Lending and ARM disclosures on an ARM Product.
- **Equal Credit Opportunity Act** *(Federal Trade Commission)* – Advises consumers of their rights under the regulations including: 1.) They may not be discriminated against on any basis; 2.) That they have recourse and who to call.
- **Transfer of Servicing (HUD) – Most lenders sell** their loans. The transfer of servicing disclosure tells borrowers how the loan may be sold, and what their rights are under these laws
- **Borrower's Certification and Authorization** *(FNMA)* – The form acknowledges the borrowers' receipt of a perjury statement. It also says that the lender has the right to change the documentation requirements for the application. The form also serves as a credit authorization and signature release.
- FHA disclosures
- VA disclosures

Loan Officer and Processor Time Management Techniques

The loan process is a very detailed progression and assembly of paperwork. Sloppy or incomplete documentation is the single largest cause of problems in the process. To avoid issues with loan processing, every loan officer should have systems in place to manage a caseload. These systems insure that the loan officer spends time generating business, not following up on individual loans. Systems also reduce interruptions for processing. Interruptions are a processor's largest time management challenge.

System 1 - The Complete Application System for Loan Officers

Despite the advances in automation, missing documentation is the biggest problem loan officers' face. The problem begins when a loan officer accepts an application that is missing information. This puts the responsibility of obtaining the documentation on the loan officer, instead of the borrower. The loan officer, who is now in a defensive position, begins the process of mostly undocumented follow-up.

Even though a borrower may be aware of additional documentation requirements, once the application is submitted, there is pushback for providing more. The borrower says, "I thought I sent you that." Then, when the loan officer receives the missing documentation, it raises other questions - such as a pay stub that shows variable income, a bank statement with unexplained deposits or other problems. When this happens there is a question as to whether the loan can be granted. A negative feedback loop begins as the referral source may become involved, and documentation requests are followed by more documentation requests. The customer becomes frustrated or angry. This situation is caused by the incomplete application

The solution is obvious – don't accept incomplete applications. Loan Officers must have a complete application system.

A Pre-Application Kit, or other open ended information collection device, such as the one on the following page, can meet this need. When utilizing this system, the loan officer can arrest the application process until he or she is satisfied that there is enough documentation to proceed. With this in hand, the loan officer can turn in a complete application and not have to revisit the loan until it closes. This frees the loan officer to originate loans and make more money, not chase documentation.

Pipeline Review

Weekly pipeline review may seem redundant in an era of automated approvals and fast decisions. You can simply forward an e-mail that the loan is approved or the appraisal is in. What else is there to check? As this book shows, there are many things that can and do go wrong in the process.

As loan officers, we are responsible for the loan process. When a customer or referral source calls and asks what the loan status is, the loan officer will typically call or e-mail the processor. The processor has to stop what he or she was doing and investigate the status. This interruption can cost the processor 15 minutes of productive time. In addition, because the loan officer doesn't know what the status is, the customer or referral source isn't convinced of the loan officer's professionalism. It also creates a time management issue for the loan officer, because returning phone calls takes 15 minutes of productive time. In this case, one phone call costs 75 minutes of time for the loan officer and processor.

Loan Status Calls Waste Time	
Action	Minutes Spent
Customer Call to Loan Officer	15
Call to Processor	15
Investigation	15
Call back to Loan Officer	15
Call back to Customer	15
Total Time Per Call	75
vs Loan Status	
Minutes Per Loan	5
Status Meeting with Client	15
Total Time Per Loan	20

Instead of reacting to customer requests, move pro-actively to deliver loan status reports to interested parties. This is a sales opportunity for the loan officer. The pipeline review meeting saves the processor's time by avoiding interruptions. The loan officer saves time by staying out of the return phone call loop.

PRE-APPLICATION KIT
Complete this form and provide the information requested on the Completed Application Checklist to expedite your approval Process.

Personal Information

BORROWER	C0-BORROWER
Name_____	Name_____
Social Security Number_____	Social Security Number_____
Age_____ Years of School_____	Age_____ Years of School_____
Current Address	Current Address
City_____ State___ ZIP___	City_____ State___ ZIP___
Own[ ] Rent[ ] Years at_____	Own[ ] Rent[ ] Years at_____
Telephone Number_____	Telephone Number_____
(If at this address for less than 2 years please provide addresses and dates for full 2 Years)	*(If at this address for less than 2 years please provide addresses and dates for full 2 Years)*
Previous Address	Previous Address
City_____ State___ ZIP___	City_____ State___ ZIP___
Own[ ] Rent[ ] Years at_____	Own[ ] Rent[ ] Years at_____
Marital Status [ ] Single [ ] Married [ ]Separated	Marital Status [ ] Single [ ] Married [ ]Separated
Childrens' Ages ____, ____, ____	Childrens' Ages ____, ____, ____

Employment Information

Current Employer	Current Employer
Address_____	Address_____
City_____ State___ ZIP___	City_____ State___ ZIP___
Work Telephone_____	Work Telephone_____
Hire Date_____	Hire Date_____
Title/Position_____	Title/Position_____
Years Employed in this line of Business____	Years Employed in this line of Business____
Base Income $_____ [ ]Yr. [ ] Mo. [ ] Hr.	Base Income $_____ [ ]Yr. [ ] Mo. [ ] Hr.
Other Income $_____	Other Income $_____
Source_____	Source_____
(Note: If you are commissioned, self-employed, or have any income, including rental income, which is variable in nature you will be required to provide 2 years Federal Tax Returns, and year to date income and expense summary.)	*(Note: If you are commissioned, self-employed, or have any income, including rental income, which is variable in nature you will be required to provide 2 years Federal Tax Returns, and year to date income and expense summary.)*
If employed in current job for less than 2 years, please provide previous employers for a two year period.	**If employed in current job for less than 2 years, please provide previous employers for a two year period.**
Previous Employer	Previous Employer
Address_____	Address_____
City_____ State___ ZIP___	City_____ State___ ZIP___
Telephone Number_____	Telephone Number_____
Dates Employed (From)_____ (To)_____	Dates Employed (From)_____ (To)_____
Position/Title_____	Position/Title_____
Income $_____	Income $_____

Borrower's Certification and Authorization

Certification

The undersigned certify the following:

I/We have applied for a mortgage loan from Metro Capital Corp. In applying for the loan, I/we completed a loan application containing various information on the purpose of the loan, the amount and source of the downpayment, employment and income information, and assets and liabilities. I/We certify that all of the information is true and complete. I/We made no misrepresentations in the loan application or other documents, nor did I/we omit any pertinent information.

I/We understand that Metro Capital Corp. reserves the right to change the mortgage loan review process to a full documentation program. This may include verifying the information provided on the application with the employer and/or financial institution.

I/We fully understand that it is a Federal crime punishable by fine or imprisonment, or both, to knowingly make any false statements when applying for this mortgage, as applicable under the provisions of Title 18, United States Code, Section 1014.

Authorization to Release Information

To Whom It May Concern:

I/We have applied for a Mortgage Loan from Metro Capital Corp. As part of the application process, Metro Capital Corp. may verify information contained in my/our loan application and in other documents required in connection with the loan, either before the loan is closed or as part of its quality control program.

I/We authorize you to provide Metro Capital Corp., and any investor to whom Metro Capital Corp. may sell my mortgage, any and all information that they request. Such information includes, but is not limited to employment history and income, bank, money market, and similar account balances, credit history, and copies of income tax returns.

Metro Capital Corp., or any investor that purchases the mortgage may address this authorization to any party named in the loan application.

A copy of this authorization may be accepted as an original.

Your prompt reply to Metro Capital Corp., or the investor that purchased the mortgage is appreciated.

Borrower's Signature	Social Security Number
Borrower's Signature	Social Security Number
Borrower's Signature	Social Security Number
Borrower's Signature	Social Security Number

Assets & Liabilities

This section of your application is designed to evaluate the sufficiency of your assets to consummate the transaction and the impact of other obligations on your ability to repay the loan for which you have applied.

ASSETS

Bank Accounts (Checking, NOW)

Institution	Account #	Balance

Savings Accounts (Statement, CD, Money Market)

Institution	Account #	Balance

Stocks & Bonds (Including Broker Accounts)

Security or Broker	# Shares/Acct #	Value

Life Insurance

Face Amount_____ Value_____
Retirement (401k, IRA, CSA, Etc.)_____

LIABILITIES

List all Loans, Charge Accounts, Revolving Debts, Credit Cards, Installment Loans

Institution	Account #	Balance / Payment

Real Estate Loans

Institution	Account #	Balance / Payment
1.		
2.		
3.		

Landlord (For Past 12 Months)

Name_____ Address_____ Payment_____
Phone #_____

Real Estate Schedule (Attach Separate Schedule if more appropriate)

Property Address	Sold/Rent	Property Type	Market Value	Mortgage Balance	Rental Income	Taxes & Insurance
1.						
2.						
3.						

List Year Make & Value of Autos: _____
List Other Property: _____

COMPLETED APPLICATION CHECKLIST

Use this Checklist to assure that you have provided all the information necessary to approve your loan application.

____ 1. **For Purchases** 1.) Fully Ratified Sales Contract and all Addendums
Purchase Price_____
Loan Amount Requested:_____
Real Estate Agent Name & Number:_____
For Refinances 1.) Copy of Deed, Survey & Title Insurance Policy
2.) Homeowner's Insurance
3.) Most recent Statement from current Lender(s)

____ 2. Most Recent 30 days' Paystubs

____ 3. Last Two Years' W-2's or 1099's

____ 4. Last Two Years Complete, Ratified Federal Individual and Corporate Tax Returns (if self-employed or commissioned, if income is variable, or if any rental property is owned)

____ 5. Year to Date Profit and Loss (Income/Expense) Statement, within 90 Days (if self-employed)

____ 6. Current, Ratified One Year(s) Lease(s) for Investment Properties

____ 7. Proof of any Other Sources of Income

____ 8. Three Months Most Recent Bank Statements (please include all accounts even if not being utilized, including managed stock funds, CDs, checking, savings, mutual funds, stocks - all pages are required)

____ 9. Gift Letter, Proof of Donor's Ability to Give, Proof of Receipt and Deposit of Gift Funds with new balance in recipient's account.

____ 10. Proof of of Any Other Source of Assets needed to Complete Transaction (i.e., sales contract current home, wire advice for transferred funds, liquidation confirmation, or other documentation)

____ 11. Relocation Agreement and Benefit Summary (if Applicable)

____ 12. Mortgage/Rental Payment History (12 Month Cancelled Checks, Computer Generated Printout of Payments, or Letter of Reference)

____ 13. Child Care Statement, Divorce Decree, Separation Agreement (ratified), and Proof of any Other Liabilities

____ 14. Car Title for Cars less than 4 Years Old (With no Loans Outstanding). Deed of Release for Real Estate Owned with no Lien

____ 15. Check For Application fee in the Amount of $360.00. This non-refundable application fee will be credited towards closing costs ($300 - Appraisal / $60 - Credit Report - actual fees may be higher or lower). Lock-in, Float Down Option Requires 1/2 Point Application Deposit.

PRE-APPROVAL PROCESS
1.) Complete the Pre-Application Kit (does not have to be typed) and fax back to 301-738-6523 *This begins your pre-approval process*
2.) Assemble applicable documents requested on checklist and forward via overnight mail
3.) Firm Loan Approval issued within 72 hours of receipt of documents
4.) Formal Application documents will be mailed to you upon receipt of documents. Sign & Return.
5.) Upon ratification of sales contract, appraisal is ordered and closing preparations are made

---

To obtain your own "Pre-Application Kit" to customize and use with your own process, visit www.quick-start.net and buy "The Loan Officer's Practical Guide to Marketing."

Chapter 8

Property Types

When I first started as a loan officer I took every loan I could. I immediately learned that none of the other loan officers I worked with wanted to take condominium loans. They were small transactions and many questions had to be answered - on top of whether or not the borrower was qualified - before the loan could be taken. Needless to say, I ended up with many condo loans. If I was to survive these loans I needed to understand all of the guidelines associated with condominiums. I did, and it was not long before underwriters were calling me to discuss project approval questions. Each market has its own unique concentration of property type. The professional loan officer has to become an expert on those properties to succeed.

Understanding Property Types

We have learned that different types of borrowers present special risks. The loan program, down payment or other characteristics may be reasons a loan may not meet guidelines. One major facet of risk is the type of property being given as security or collateral. Primarily, there are two sources of risk that drive property underwriting:

1.) What kind of risk is the lender taking if they have to re-sell the property after a foreclosure?
2.) What kind of risk is the borrower accepting by living in a certain property type?

Usually, property risk begins when the density of units increases. When someone buys a single-family house, with public streets and no common areas, there is limited risk as to outside forces impacting the borrower. However, risk increases when the property is part of a Homeowner's Association that is responsible for maintaining common areas such as roads, pools, tennis courts, landscape, etc. In a situation like this, for instance, someone might slip and fall on a community road, and sue the homeowner's association. If the association lost the suit and there wasn't sufficient insurance, they might go bankrupt which would adversely impact property values.

There are numerous forms of property ownership, each impacting the risk of the individual loan. In addition, within each type of property ownership, there may be sub-types of property, which impact the risk, such as a mobile home project, a log cabin or historic home, or a condominium with a commercial/retail influence.

Property Types by Ownership Form

Property Type	Description
PUD (Planned Unit Development)	This refers to a property comprised of Single Family Homes, Town Houses or Condominiums. The individual homes and land are privately owned, but common elements such as roads, open areas and recreational facilities are owned and maintained by a mandatory Homeowner's Association. Individuals owners in PUDs are required to be members in and pay for the Homeowners Association.
Condominium	A Condominium is created out of vertical air space. Instead of owning a parcel of land, you purchase a subdivided piece of space contained within a condominium regime, which might be an apartment or a townhouse. The walls, common elements and all improvements are owned and maintained by the condominium.
Cooperative	A cooperative is a corporation that owns real estate. To purchase a cooperative unit the owner actually purchases a pro rata share of the corporation stock. The corporation is responsible for paying real estate taxes, underlying mortgages, and maintenance of all common elements.
Leasehold	A leasehold estate is a long-term ground lease. Renting land out for unencumbered use instead of selling creates a ground lease. At the end of the lease term the land is returned, in its improved state, to the landlord.
Fee Simple	Also referred to as SFD (single family detached) property, this means that the land is unencumbered by any covenant requiring ownership in an association. An attached home can be Fee Simple as well.

Why Condos are Hard to Finance

Like many forms of property ownership, the development of condominium ownership and the lending guidelines surrounding it have evolved to reflect the industry's experience. Condominium ownership creates a high density of individually owned units. The risks and guidelines are based on common sense. Unlike a Planned Unit Development, where the owner maintains each individual house, the owner's association maintains a condominium building. Unlike a cooperative, where the board of directors of the corporation can be selective about who can live there, condominiums cannot have restrictive covenants. They cannot exclude people who might default on the maintenance obligations (a condominium unit that is owned by an investor who rents out the unit would have less of a vested interest in project maintenance) such as absentee owners. Because project maintenance relies on owner's contributions, a project's soundness is impacted by the overall ability of the unit owners to pay for the operation of the condominium.

Conforming Guidelines

Keep in mind that, just like in underwriting a loan, a project underwriter may decide that a project has superior factors and merits an exception. As a result, particularly with new projects, the agencies may make exceptions to their standard guidelines. FNMA and FHLMC both have guidelines for condominium projects. The classifications address the level of risk and approval.

Effective 5/1/05 FNMA has eliminated the approval classifications known as A, B, and C. It has replaced these approval criteria with new processes. The announcement was met with much elation, but a closer examination showed that the guidelines were only moderated somewhat. Most importantly was a slightly lower pre-sale and investor concentration requirement. A major modification was the release of FNMA's Condo Project Manager (CPM) program which automated the approval process and allowed lenders to save time in managing condominium project lists and documents.

Condominium Classifications by Agency

	FNMA	**FHLMC**
New Project	**"Formerly" Type C** - Direct FNMA approval required. 1028 - is a form issued by FNMA that indicates project phase has been underwritten and approved by FNMA. Form 1027 is conditional project approval. Requirements for approval: 1.) 50 % of units within a phase must be sold or under contract to settle. Unit appraisals must address market absorption and sales plan (Addendum A) and budget adequacy (Addendum B). 2.) Attorney's opinion letter addressing condominium documents. 3.) Conversions require engineering structural survey. CPM approval is valid for 6 months	**Class I** - Direct FHLMC approval required. Requirements for approval: 1.) 70% of units within a phase must be sold or under contract to settle. Of those 70% must be sold to owner-occupants. Unit appraisals must address market absorption and sales plan (Addendum A) and budget adequacy (Addendum B). 2.) Attorney's opinion letter addressing condominium documents. 3.) Conversions require engineering structural survey.
Existing Project Not Fully Sold Out	**"Formerly" Type B** - Project is 1.) Complete and no additional phasing 2.) 60% Sold and 70% of those are owner occupied/2nd homes. 3.) Still under developer control. 4.) No more than 10% of units owned by single entity. **Required for Approval:** Attorney's opinion letter; Addendum B.	**Class II** - Project is 1.) Complete and no additional phasing 2.) 70% Sold and 60% of those are owner occupied/2nd homes. 3.) Project turned over to Owner's Association **Required for Approval:** Attorney's Opinion letter; Addendum B.
Existing Project	**"Formerly" Type A** - Project is 1.) 100% completed, no additional phasing, 2.) Owner's association is in control for one year, 3.) 90% sold/50% owner occupied, 4.) No entity owns 10% or more **Type A - Limited Project Review** - For down payments of 25% (20% for DU) or more - Project is 1.) 100% Complete 2.) No other restrictions	**Class III** - Project is 1.) 100% completed, no additional phasing, 2.) Owner's association has been in control for two years, 3.) 90% sold, 4.) 90% individual unit owners - multiple sales to one owner counted toward % of individual owners. 60% owner occupied.
FHA Approved	**Type D** - Project is 1.) On FHA Approved Condo List 2.) 51% Owner Occupied 3.) No entity owns 10% or more 4.) Project is not otherwise ineligible	

As this table demonstrates, as a project becomes more established, the guidelines for approval become less rigorous. This is because the lender's risk is mitigated as the project proves that it is acceptable in the marketplace and people continue to buy units there. You will note that there is considerable influence placed on the percentage of owner occupants within a project. There are two reasons for this:

1.　　Owners who live in a project tend to have a greater "pride in ownership," and thereby - theoretically - will take better care of the project. They will vote to spend money for items that may become necessary to maintain the project such as a special assessment. An absentee owner would only care that the rent charged covered the expenses.
2.　　If the economy turns down, investors would not necessarily make the sacrifices required to maintain mortgage payments, resulting in defaults and foreclosures that would adversely affect the market value of other units within the project.

For instance, if there were a project with 100 units and the monthly assessment fees were $100, and one individual owned 30 of these units, what would happen if that person went bankrupt? Monthly revenue for project operation would go from (100 x $100 = $10,000) to (70 x $100 = $7,000) for a $3,000 per month shortfall. In order to keep the project viable, the association would have to spread the $3,000 shortfall out over the remaining 70 units ($3,000 divided by 70 = $42.85/mo additional levy). This is an increase of nearly 50%! Such a dramatic increase could create a domino effect where other unit owners could no longer afford the maintenance obligation and collapse the entire project.

Private Mortgage Insurance

While the agencies have established guidelines for condominiums, so have the Private Mortgage Insurance companies (MIs). During the introduction of condominium ownership, many MI's did not evaluate condominiums any differently than individual home loans. As a result, some companies became over exposed insuring large percentages of units within individual projects. It was the MI's that were significantly hurt when the real estate market softened dramatically with the rise in interest rates in the early 1980's. As a result, many of the MI companies have developed guidelines that are even more restrictive than agency guidelines (as with all guidelines, exceptions can be made). To summarize there are a number of specific rules which may apply:

- Square footage limitations - Efficiency condominiums are cheaper to buy and require a smaller down payment investment than a house. In addition, the smaller the unit the more difficult it is to sell (a phenomenon which may be linked to the fact that the agents involved can only earn a small amount of commission). Finally, because the equity investment is so small, there is more chance of the lender taking a loss. As a result, the smaller the condominium, the more likely the owner is to walk away from the initial investment during bad economic times. Minimum square footage is considered to be approximately 600-square feet, or one bedroom.
- Owner occupancy - Because condominium apartment projects mirror the appeal of rental apartments, they hold investment potential. These tend to turn into largely investor-held buildings - and because many MI's hold to the belief that pride in ownership is a critical part of risk analysis - investor concentration in condominiums is a huge issue for MIs. Twenty to Thirty percent investor to owner occupant ratio is generally acceptable, with some higher concentrations allowed for established projects.

- Risk exposure - The MI's track exposure in projects and will only accept a certain number of units or a percentage. Always check ahead of time to assure a slot remains. In addition, the PMI Company may perform its own project review prior to insuring the first loan.

- There is currently a movement in underwriting away from traditional subjective underwriting guidelines toward the process of predictive credit scoring. In cases such as this project eligibility may not be an issue. Several of the insurers have stipulated that with scores of over 700, no other underwriting criterion needs to be met.

Regardless of project status, the following information will always be required in conjunction with condominium financing:

Documentation Required for Project Approval

Legal Documents	___ Recorded Declarations, By-Laws, Amendments ___ Covenants, Easements and Restrictions ___ Horizontal Plat/Survey
Insurance	___ Master Policy Declarations ___ If Professional Management firm handles Association funds Fidelity Bond equal to 6 Months HOA fees, naming Management Company as insured and HOA as payee ___ If HOA handles funds, Director's & Officer's Liability ___ If High Rise, Elevator Insurance ___ Certificate of Insurance for specific unit being given as collateral
Financial	___ Current and Past Years' Budget

Treatment of Condominium Fee for Qualifying Purposes

When you are using income and debt ratios in trying to qualify someone to buy a house, do you add in the amount they would be paying for utilities such as electricity, water, gas, sewer, heat and air conditioning? These are not factors in normal underwriting, but they can be large components of the housing expense for a condominium. In fact you can "net out" the utility portion of the condominium fee from the amount used for qualifying. To do this, analyze the project's budget to determine the percentage of the total budget attributed towards utilities, and subtract that percentage from the total fee for qualifying. The appraiser may make your job easier by indicating the percentage of utilities included on the report on page two, project information.

Approved Lists

FHA and VA do approve each individual condominium phase and unit. Project approval through FHA requires an attorney's opinion letter, budget, engineering report, environmental impact analysis and 51% owner occupancy. When a project or phase is FHA or VA approved, it appears on the "approved list." When there is an existing project where it is unlikely that the association will go to the expense of complying with the FHA/VA requirements, it is possible that the individual units could qualify for "spot loan" financing. No more than 10% of the units (20% for projects with less than 30 units) are eligible for spot financing, and the project must still meet the 51% owner occupancy percentage.

FNMA publishes a "list" of condominiums that it has issued 1028 and 1027 approvals for. Until recently, they required the lender to prove that a project, other than a newly approved project, was eligible. FNMA has release Condo Project Manager (CPM), a portal which allows lenders to investigate and request approvals on condominium projects.

> When a project has a high investor concentration according to the Management Company, consider seeking alternative sources of information. Tax records, appraiser's data sources, even direct mail campaigns within projects can be a good way to override management company statistics. Second homes are considered owner occupied.

FHLMC issues a list of condominiums that it has purchased loans in and for projects that it has declined project loans. These lists, however, do not necessarily mean that financing is available. Having a loan in a project that is on a "list" indicates that there is a better chance that the project meets guidelines, but is more useful for locating projects in which a declination has been issued. On most loans in existing condominiums it is up to lenders to "warrant" or guarantee that the condominium meets the agency guidelines.

Termite Reports - If the condominium budget shows a line item for pest control, often the requirement for a termite report can be waived. In addition, because termites need water to digest wood, units above the 3rd floor are normally considered exempt from this requirement. This is because the industry has determined that termites can only climb about 3 floors before they have to turn back to get a drink. However, if a specific unit has a fireplace or wood storage area, a termite report might be prudent to determine if any wood destroying insects have been introduced by imported firewood.

Owner Occupancy Ratios/Individual Unit Owner Concentration

Normally, the person who completes the pre-sale questionnaire has done so repeatedly and often. It is a mundane task. Often the individual may memorize certain responses or may not update pertinent information. This may be detrimental to the ability of a lender to obtain financing. Press the individual for the source of their information regarding this and how recently it was compiled. There are a number of additional questions to ask beyond the standard responses.

> **Standard Condominium Questionnaire**
>
> 1. How many units are in this condominium?
> 2. How many units are sold?
> 3. How many units are closed?
> 4. How many units are owner occupied?
> 5. How many units are second homes?
> 6. How many units are rented?
> 7. Are all units and common areas completed?
> 8. When was the control of the condominium turned over to the unit owner's association?
> 9. What percentage of the monthly association fees are more than one-month delinquent?
> 10. Are there any special assessments now planned or have there been in the past year?
> 11. How many individual unit owners, other than the developer, exist in this project? In other words, how many different unit owners are there? (If there are 10 units, and one person owns 2 units, there would be 9 individual owners.)
> 12. Does any one individual own more than 10% of the units?
> 13. Is there any additional phasing or annexation for the project?
> 14. Is the project leasehold?
> 15. Is the project a party in any legal actions?
> 16. Is the project a conversion? If so, was the conversion in the last 3 years?
> 17. Are there short-term rentals, or rental desks within the project?
> 18. Are there cleaning services provided to the unit owners?
> 19. What percentage of the project is devoted to commercial space?
> 20. Is the project professionally managed or self-managed? If professionally managed, does the management contract have a 90-day right to cancel with no penalty?

1.)   Are any of the non-occupant units second homes or occupied by the unit owners for at least two weeks of the year?

2.)   Consult the tax records - Are tax bills still being sent to the property? If so, there is a chance that current owners intend to return and a compelling argument for a lower investment owner ratio.

3.)   Is the current unit a rental being purchased by an owner occupant?

4.)   If there is a concentration of units owned by an individual or firm, are the units being actively marketed? Perhaps the underwriter can meet a pre-sale requirement instead of a owner occupancy requirement.

PUD/Classifications & Requirements

There are fewer risks relative to Planned Unit Development Financing. Obviously if the project is complete, there is less risk. Concerns arise from the failure to complete a project, examples of which abound. The impact then is on the marketability of the units that are complete, when common elements aren't finished or do not materialize. Again, FHLMC, FHA, VA and FNMA all have varying requirements.

	FNMA	FHLMC	FHA	VA
New Projects, Proposed or under Construction	50% pre-sold for attached housing. All common areas must be complete. No 2-4 family units. Project may not be a conversion. Fidelity and liability insurance required. Fee simple ownership, budget review. Project may not be otherwise ineligible. 1028 - Project approval is acceptable in lieu of meeting warranties.	No pre-sale requirement May not be a conversion, contain commercial or multi-family or 2-4's. Liability, flood and hazard insurance required. No fidelity. Need comparables outside project.	Approved list	Approved list
Existing Projects	Control of HOA turned over to owners association. Not ineligible. Liability/fidelity Insurance.	Same as FNMA.	Fee simple - no requirements.	Approved list

New Construction- Construction Permanent

With new homes there are other considerations for the loan officer. Aside from the project approval issues above, the financing process is very different when there is no developer present. In this case, the buyer or borrower becomes the developer and the loan officer is the construction lender and the permanent lender.

Mortgage lenders do not generally make construction loans because they are inherently short-term loans - intended for the construction period (usually 3-9 months) and then to be retired. These are ideal loans for bank or savings and loans to make. The loan needs to be structured so that money from the loan is made available over a period of time as the construction proceeds. The loan amount is not fully disbursed at closing, like a permanent loan; rather the proceeds are disbursed in a series of draws based upon a pre-arranged construction schedule. Because of this they are almost always interest only transactions.

The process begins with the raw land. Raw land is either purchased in cash or financed. This has a bearing on the transaction because land equity is considered a part of the down payment for the construction lender. In addition, when converting the construction loan into a permanent loan, the permanent lender may require that the valuation be based upon the acquisition cost, as opposed to the final value of the home. This acquisition cost formula may be a problem for the borrower with permanent financing because of loan-to-value restrictions and issues such as cash out to recapture the initial investment. Often, to escape this dilemma, borrowers elect to do one of two things with a permanent loan: 1.) Arrange the permanent financing (end-loan) at the time of the construction loan closing (referred to as a construction-permanent loan); or 2.) Wait until the property is seasoned to escape the loan to value restrictions imposed by the acquisition cost formula.

The advantage of a construction permanent transaction is that the entire package is wrapped up into one closing, and the buyer/builder doesn't have to worry about the end loan. The disadvantage is that, because the construction loan and permanent loan are tied together, the borrower's end loan terms may not be the most favorable. However, construction lenders are able to force this type of arrangement because they can facilitate a "modification" which is the altering of the final construction loan documents. The modification proceeds like refinances in that new document are executed; however, because the funds transfer is internal, there are no closing costs or taxes.

Construction Permanent Financing

Land Price	$ 50,000.00				
Construction Contract	$ 200,000.00				
Total Costs	$ 250,000.00		Maximum Loan		$ 225,000.00
Down Payment	10%		Construction Loan Rate		8.50%

Draw Schedule	Funds Needed	Cash In	Loan Balance	Number of Days	Interest Carry
Closing	$ 50,000.00	$ 25,000.00	$ 25,000.00	15	$ 88.54
1st Construction Draw (40%)	$ 80,000.00	$ -	$ 105,088.54	30	$ 744.38
2nd ConstructionDraw (15%)	$ 30,000.00	$ -	$ 135,832.92	30	$ 962.15
3rd Construction Draw (15%)	$ 30,000.00	$ -	$ 166,795.07	30	$ 1,181.47
4th Construction Draw (15%)	$ 30,000.00	$ -	$ 197,976.53	30	$ 1,402.33
Final Draw	$ 27,023.47	$ 4,378.87	$ 225,000.00	30	$ 1,593.75
Total	$ 247,023.47	$ 29,378.87	$ 225,000.00	165	$ 4,378.87
Final Interest Payment	$ 1,593.75				

The disadvantage of seeking permanent financing outside of the construction lender is there will have to be a refinance closing, unless an unlikely arrangement can be made with the construction lender to have the construction loan terms modified. The second disadvantage is that the loan to value limitations may impact the borrower, particularly when the borrower wishes to capitalize the very valuable property he has just built.

This can be overcome by seasoning the loan - waiting until the property has been complete for one year - or by financing through a lender who doesn't have a seasoning requirement. As discussed, the construction financing is arranged at a maximum amount, with scheduled disbursements, referred to as draws, as the stages are complete. It works like this.

Investment Property

When an area real estate market becomes dynamic property values fluctuate rapidly.   The purchase of an investment property can provide for both income and equity growth. The major challenges in financing investment property are determining appropriate source of funds for down payment and, at the same time, assuring adequate cash flow.

Initial Equity Source

If you are considering the purchase of an investment property, you more than likely already own a home. If the home was purchased over 2 years ago, this is the likeliest source of initial equity. Refinance or home equity lines are both easy ways to access these funds. The cost of this must be considered to determine that the transaction makes sense. This example shows the derivation of funds:

Step 1 - Home Equity As a Source for Investment Cash

Market Value of Home	$	250,000.00
LTV		80%
Less Existing Mortgage	$	150,000.00
Lendable Equity	$	50,000.00
Transaction Cost	$	7,500.00
Available for Investment	$	42,500.00

Cost of Equity Calculation

The above calculations provide us with the source of equity and the cost of carrying the new mortgage. One hidden benefit is that the new mortgage may be tax deductible. Cash flow is the next challenge.

Step 2 - Calculating the Cost of Home Equity for Investment

	Existing Mortgage	New Mortgage
Rate	6.50%	5.75%
Loan Size	$ 150,000.00	$ 200,000.00
Payment	$ 948.10	$1,167.15
Difference (Equity Cost)		$ 219.04

Cash Flow

How much to pay and whether to buy is a feasibility question. Do market rents support the purchase? One indication of market rent is what the federal government will pay for rental assistance (HAP-Section 8).   This equation determines what the market rent must be to break even:

Step 3 - Determining the Debt Service/Carrying Costs

Sales Price	$	150,000.00	
Transaction Costs	$	4,890.00	
Down Payment	$	30,000.00	20%
Cash Required	$	34,890.00	
Mortgage Amount	$	120,000.00	
Principal & Interest at 9.75%	$	700.29	5.75%
Real Estate Taxes	$	200.00	
Insurance	$	50.00	
Total Debt Service	$	1,096.00	
Expense Factor		75%	
Income Required to Offset Vacancy	$	1,461.33	

What Must the Rent Be?

Alternately, what should the sales price be if the market rent is known? The following calculation determines sales price based upon market rent.

Because these formulas depend on rental income covering the debt service, the lower the interest rate, the better the cash flow.

Step 4 - Determining the Maximum Mortgage When Rental Amount is Known		
Market Rent	$ 900.00	
Real Estate Taxes	$ (100.00)	
Insurance	$ (30.00)	
Available for Debt Service	$ 770.00	
Mortgage Amount @ 9.75%	$89,623.00	9.75%
Downpayment Amount	$ (22,405.75)	20%
Maximum Sales Price	$ 112,028.76	

Investment Property Pre-Qualification

Using the financial calculator, you can determine the maximum sales price an investor can afford. In this case, unlike the housing expense calculation, negative debt service is based upon another property's rent and cash flow. If the property has a positive cash flow using a conservative vacancy factor (like 75%), anyone who qualifies for his or her current rent home can afford an investment property. It is when there is more than a slight negative cash flow that one needs to enhance the calculation.

First, figure out whether the borrower can handle any negative rental. Applying the total debt ratio against the borrower in step 1, and deducting any other obligations in Step 2, reveals the maximum rental negative. Imputing the anticipated rental in-

Investment Property Pre-Qualification

Determines the maximum negative cash flow and sales price for investment property

Step 1: Determine Maximum Debt Ratio

Borrower's Income	$ 4,000.00	monthly
Multiply by Total Debt Ratio	36%	or actual Amount
Maximum Monthly Payments	$ 1,440.00	This is the maximum amount the borrower can afford for all obligations

Step 2: Determine Maximum Negative Cash Flow

Maximum Monthly Payments	$ 1,440.00	from step 1
Less Housing Expense	$ (925.00)	enter amount for current PITI (home)
Monthly Debts (car etc.)	$ (275.00)	all other debts
Maximum Rental Negative	$ 240.00	This is the most the borrower can afford to pay to offset rental income shortfall

Step 3: Determine Maximum PITI for Subject

Anticipated Rental Income	$ 1,100.00	Use actual amount
Less Operating Exenses	$ (275.00)	use 25% vacancy/expense fa
Net Rental Income	$ 825.00	
Plus Maximum Rental Negative	$ 240.00	From Step 2
Maximum Rental Property PITI	$ 1,065.00	

Step 4: Solve for Maximum Sales Price

Maximum Rental PITI	$ 1,065.00	From Step 3
Subtract Tax & Insurance	$ (213.00)	(use actual amount or use 20% of PITI)
Enter as Payment (PMT)	$ 852.00	=PMT
Enter Current Rate	8.25%	=I%
Enter Number of Months	360	=N
Compute Loan Amount	$113,408.48	=PV
Divide by LTV	80%	LTV
Maximum Sales Price	$ 141,760.59	

come for a type of property and applying a vacancy factor gives a net rental income. Add to the net rental income the maximum rental negative a borrower can afford and you have the resultant PITI. Subtracting the taxes, insurance and other fees from this reveals the maximum P&I that can be entered into the calculator for determining the maximum loan amount and sales price.

Rental Properties: Income properties often create problems for potential homebuyers. Aside from the difficulties of managing rental real estate, lenders may have a disparaging view of the impact rental real estate has on the prospective borrower. Restrictions on rental income include:

- Exclusion of 25% of the gross rental income as a vacancy/loss factor. Although a property may carry a positive cash flow, lenders adjust this income significantly to take into account the potential for the property being vacant with no rental income for an extended period of time. This is known as a vacancy/expense factor. While most rental properties experience a 5 - 10% vacancy factor, an additional expense must generally be considered to determine the wear and tear on the property. The exception to this is FHA/VA loans, in which the borrower can demonstrate a lower vacancy factor, or previous experience as a landlord. Then the vacancy expense factor can be as low as 7%. If this is the case, then examine the actual cash flow of the property. Has it been rented for more than two years? If so, can you examine the borrower's Schedule E, Rental and Royalty income, from his or her tax returns? Adding the actual income, less actual expenses (depreciation and depletion added in) may result in a more favorable net rental income than a 25% vacancy factor.

- In many lease situations, properties are rented on a month-to-month basis. If this is the case, the tenant must be contacted to provide a letter attesting to the fact that they intend to continue residing in the property.

- How many properties are financed? If a purchaser owns more than four 1-4 family properties that are financed, and the subject property is an investment property, they are generally ineligible for financing on conforming loans.

- Each property's mortgage must be verified. Also, the taxes and insurance must be obtained separately, either by proving that they are held in escrow, or by providing copies of the paid bills for the obligation.

Requirements for Investment Property Financing

- **Leases:** A current lease showing the monthly rental repayment, lease ending date, and names of landlord and tenant. If the lease is expired, a "tenant letter" will suffice along with the expired lease. The tenant letter is a statement by the tenant giving their occupancy terms and intent to continue occupancy. In certain situations, two years of tax returns may be substituted for leases. A two-year average will be utilized.

- **Insurance:** Rental dwelling coverage is required for all investment property. If the dwelling has more than one unit, rent loss coverage in an amount equal to 6 months PITI is required.

- **Schedule of Rental Comparables** is required to be completed by an appraiser. This is used to substantiate market rents.

- **Operating Income Statement** is required to be completed by an appraiser. This is a line-by-line analysis of the property's expenses. The underwriter will use the net income from the operating income statement to determine income for qualification if the net income number is lower than the net rent shown on the property's lease.

2 to 4 Unit Properties

There exists an anomaly among financing terms when you deal with a hybrid between owner occupied property and 2-4-unit investment property which one owner occupies. In this case the borrower has the disadvantage of owner occupying, particularly if they need the rental income to qualify for the loan. Total debt ratios tend to be very high. Instead of using the rental income to offset the mortgage payment, the rental income is added to income under the Gross Income Method. The Cash Flow Method takes into consideration the fact that the borrower has an effective lower monthly payment.

This is an anomaly that is always encountered when financing owner occupied 2-4 family properties. The fact is that the overall cash flow of the subject is what the borrower's payment should be for qualifying purposes. What we have shown here is that an owner occupant is treated more severely under these guidelines than an investment property. If we categorized this case as an investment property, this borrower would qualify under the cash flow method with ratios of 13/24. The additional irony of this treatment is that it is from underwriting guidelines that are supposed to be more stringent.

The Advantage of Cash Flow Qualifying for 2-4 Family Owner Occupied Property				
		Gross Income Method		Cash Flow Method
PITI	$	3,101.20	$	3,101.20
Net Rental (After 75%)	$	2,175.00	$	2,175.00
Qualifying PITI	$	3,101.20	$	926.20
Qualifying Gross Income	$	8,350.00	$	6,175.00
Monthly Debts	$	527.00	$	527.00
Ratios		35/43		13/24

The only argument against this is that conventional ratios (i.e., 33/38 or 28/36) are based upon gross income and tax consequences of that lease income as if it were straight salary or income taxed at the regular tax rate. The fact is that that income won't be taxed because it will be offset against rental expenses on Schedule E.

Cooperatives

Cooperative ownership, as mentioned earlier, is not actual real estate ownership. It is ownership in shares of a corporation that owns real estate. The owner has a perpetual lease on a specific unit for as long as the shares are owned. FNMA purchases cooperative share loans, and certain banks will loan on the units, however the loans and projects normally have to meet FNMA guidelines.

FNMA Cooperative Classifications

Type 1	Type 2
An established cooperative project in which a lender is providing financing on a spot-loan basis. At least 70% of the total units in the project must have been conveyed to principal residence purchasers. The lender must determine the acceptability of a Type 1 project, unless the project is composed of single-width manufactured housing units.	Any cooperative project that is submitted to Fannie Mae for review--either because it does not meet our eligibility criteria for a Type 1 project (or we have not agreed to waive the criteria it does not meet) or because the lender wants it to appear on our list of accepted projects. The project may be existing, proposed, or under construction. We determine the acceptability of a Type 2 project (including one that

	is composed of single-width manufactured housing units).

More recently, cooperatives have not been apartment buildings but communities that use the corporation business form to manage and control common elements. Since cooperatives are not real estate, closing costs are significantly reduced because there is no title to search and no real estate transfer tax. This can result in the humorous scene where a buyer has to go to the Department of Motor Vehicles, instead of the Land Records, to record the title to the home.

Manufactured /Mobile, Modular and "Kit" Homes

Construction methodology changes as builders seek means to create more affordable housing. Mobile homes are much more sophisticated now than in the past. The quality of interior and exterior finishes makes it difficult to discern a stick-built tract home from a mobile home - until you pull a trailer up, of course. That is the problem - if the house is security for a loan, and you can take the house away, what is going to keep the borrower from taking it away and selling it for cash and defaulting on the mortgage? Most financing restrictions with regard to mobile/manufactured homes have to do with this. For instance, most lenders will only lend on doublewide mobile homes - that is two that are attached - making it more difficult to move. A permanent foundation is another requirement.

A modular home is partially built at the factory, in 2 or more pieces, and then assembled on the foundation at the site. The issues lenders have with these homes have to do with the quality of construction, whether construction will be completed, and the operation of a newly constructed project. The only control that the lender can exercise over these products is builder approval. As long as reputable national builders assemble these, there should be no difference between a stick built home and a manufactured home.

"Pre-fabricated" or "Kit" homes have increased in popularity. The builder assembles all of the pieces for the home in a package, like a toy model kit. The difficulty with a kit is that the kit manufacturer wants to be paid at the time of delivery. Under normal new construction guidelines, the kit wouldn't be fully paid for until the end of assembly.

Commercial Loan Guidelines

In this context, commercial property lending guidelines are nearly non-existent. To a certain extent, this is the only area in which totally subjective common sense plays a role in loan approval. Entire books have been written on the subject of financing commercial properties. From a residential lender's perspective, anything that is not a home or a 2-4 family residential property is a commercial property. However, there are areas in which the two intersect and it is helpful for the loan officer and his customer to understand some basic distinctions.

Commercial Property Types and Basic Guidelines

Type	Description
Multifamily	Any property containing more than 4 units is considered a multifamily property. While FNMA, and FHLMC, as well as FHA , purchase or insure loans in these pro-

Type	Description
	jects, this is normally done through commercial channels. Basically the requirement is for LTV's in the 75-85% range and debts service coverage or 115% (income exceeds debt service by 15%)
Hotel	There aren't many institutional conduits for hotel loans. Generally, the hotel must be an affiliate of a national chain and exhibit occupancy rates of over 70%
Strip Malls	Stand Alone Malls without a major tenant are difficult to finance. Debt service of 125% and near 100% occupancy
Storefront Buildings	Units with Mixed Use commercial and owner occupied may be financed via FHA 203(k) as long as the commercial use does not exceed 49% of total space. SBA financing is available for properties which are 51% or more occupied by the owner at 85% LTV maximum
Office Condos, Single Tenant (Owner Occupied)	SBA financing may be available for single tenant, owner occupied to 85% LTV. May include some build out and facilities acquisition under SBA.
Industrial/ Warehouse	Conduit lending programs do offer some outlets for heavy industrial property. But the environmental due diligence is so intensive as to dissuade most lenders from participating

Warehouse properties, Gas Stations and Small Office Buildings are often SBA candidates. Office buildings, cooperatives, and larger apartments over 25,000 square feet or over $1,000,000 in financing normally find financing through a major life insurer or pension fund.

More than anything you will need knowledge of processing of commercial loans to successfully place this type of transaction. The borrowers are sophisticated, knowledgeable and will place a loan at the best rate, period. To learn more about commercial financing, please order *The Loan Officer's Practical Guide to Commercial Property Financing* available at www.quickstart.net/onlineord.htm.

Appraisals

You will note that not much time is spent discussing appraisals and appraisal technology in this course. The reason for this is that the loan officer's expertise is much more effectively applied towards structuring transactions. Misguided trainers often bring the very complex issues of market value and comparable analysis into the curriculum as a way of adding bulk, not substance, to a curriculum. The issues that arise from appraisals are most often value related from the perspective of the market – something the loan officer has no control over. In fact, the loan officer is legally prohibited from exerting any influence over the value conclusion of the appraiser. Since value judgments are very subjective, having vast knowledge of appraisal technology serves no real use in this argument. The loan officer's best interests are served by developing a close vendor relationship with an appraiser or appraisal department and cultivating a dialogue over which appraised value and property condition issues may be discussed with an eye towards compromise.

Appraisal Basics

An appraisal of the real estate is requested to support the transaction. An appraisal is an estimated value – an opinion - of property by a trained professional to indicate whether the property is adequate to serve as security for a loan.

Loan Officer Knowledge of appraisal technology and underwriting is given an inordinate amount of weight training resources and regulatory authorities. The problem with this is that there is very little, if anything, that a loan officer can do to anticipate or fix problems that arise in this area. Loan officers are expressly prohibited from influencing the value conclusion.

Value Conclusion Methodology

Approach	Description – Weight in Valuation
The Cost Approach	**LEAST WEIGHT** – used for confirmation purposes. The cost to replace or rebuild the existing structure and site improvements based on construction industry estimates is the approach that is given the least emphasis. It is most useful when appraising a property to be built.
The Income Approach	**INDICATIVE WEIGHT** – if an investment property. Used for income-producing (rental) property. In addition to reviewing market rents, the appraiser capitalizes the property (determines if the rental income would recapture the cost of the property). The appraiser must consider future revenue and expenses.
The Market Approach	**MOST WEIGHT** - A comparison of the subject property to similar recent sales using the principle of substitution. Similar properties are called comparable sales or "comps". The appraiser starts with the sales price of a comparable and reduces or increases the relative value of the comparable based upon aspects of the subject that are superior or inferior. In "adjusting" the value of the comparables, the appraiser arrives at a scientific conclusion of the indicated value of a property. This is the approach that is given the most weight in the value conclusion.

States license appraisers, but appraisers may also have designations from industry associations that advance their credentials, such as the SRA (Senior Residential Appraisal) or MAI (Member Appraisal Institute) issued by the Appraisal Institute of America.

Simple Approaches to Resolving Valuation Problems

Concern	Possible Solution
Circumstance – Possible error	Get the appraiser to go back out and re-evaluate the property? Do you have evidence that he or she overlooked something? Did he or she do most of the report at a desk and spend little time at the property? Was it a "rush" order?
Comparable Data	Check the comparable properties listed on the report. Is there someone, like an agent or builder who can provide additional comparables for the appraiser to consider?
New Data	Are there pending or recent sales that might support a different conclusion? Ask an agent or builder in the area of the property if there is any "inside" or soon to be re-leased information that could change the value conclusion. New comparables are very powerful tools, because they don't indicate that the appraiser "missed" something – it's new data.
Desk, Drive by or Limited Appraisal (Short Form Appraisals)	Short form appraisals can be useful if the value conclusion would be better if the basis for the value assessment was tax records – over assessed property. If there is significant equity in the property, or the purchaser is putting a lot of money down, is there even a need for a full appraisal? Did DU/LP require a full appraisal? Will the investor accept a short form appraisal?
Confirm the value independently FIRST	Check the property value independently. One web-site offering this service is domania.com, but there many valuation sites, including tax assessor's offices. A value that appears unobtainable here will be even more difficult to obtain through a full appraisal.

Concern	Possible Solution
Motivated buyer or seller	Even with a low value, the transaction can still work. The purchaser has to make a larger down payment. If the contract is contingent upon loan approval, the buyer may use this as leverage to extract a concession in sales price or costs from the seller. The buyer may cancel a contract that is contingent upon financing, if the financing approved does not meet the terms of the sales agreement.
Excessive Seller contributions	Excessive seller concessions, particularly those that drive the sales price over the list price, can cause value problems. Can the loan be restructured to eliminate these?
New Appraisal	If there were serious flaws in a prior appraisal, the borrower may be willing to pay for a new appraisal. The new appraiser may arrive at the same value conclusion, but you have satisfied the borrowers need for confirmation.
Borrower Provided Appraisals	It is very rare that a customer will be able to use an existing appraisal. Loan officers should be wary of a customer who wants to use an appraisal from a non-approved vendor. What if the borrower were to abandon the loan process or provide a faulty appraisal?

Fraud Alert

Be conscious of strategies outside of normal influences as to valuation. These can be indicative of problems and can cause delays or problems in a transaction.

APPRAISAL
- Ordered by a party to the transaction (seller, buyer, broker, etc.)
- Comps are not verified as recorded or submitted by potentially biased party (seller, real estate broker)
- Tenant shown to be contact on owner-occupied property
- Income approach not used on tenant-occupied SFR
- Appraiser uses FNMA number as sole credential (discontinued program)
- Market approach substantially exceeds replacement cost approach
- "For Sale" sign on the photos of the subject (in refinance loans)
- HUD-1 or grant deed on original purchase is less than two years old (for refinance loans)

Chapter 9
REFINANCING

When you purchase a home you are caught up in the excitement of the moment - the house of your dreams - the mortgage of your nightmares. The reality is that many people do not approach purchasing considering the personal financial planning aspect of the transaction. Often the purchase is made and the consequences of a high mortgage payment or product selection only set in when it's time to make the first payment. However, even with an expensive mistake, there is always an opportunity to correct the circumstance to a more opportune one in the future. Thus, anytime in which it can save money or meet other objectives, it is a good time to change financing terms or "re-finance", that is, finance again.

The refinance transaction is similar to the purchase transaction. The only difference is that no title changes hands. The same costs for settlement services exist. The most important concept in refinancing is to correctly calculate the difference in payments and terms and weight these against the costs of the transaction. This is measured against the time in the home to determine whether there is time to make the transaction feasible.

Where to Start - Determining "Value"

An initial difficulty in refinancing is the determination of the value of the property. Unlike a purchase transaction, there is no sales contract that gives the market indication of what the value of the property is. A Uniform Residential Appraisal Report (URAR) must be performed. The entire scope of the transaction must be considered tentative until a valuation analysis is complete. Loan to value (LTV) limitations can then be accurately determined. For the initial consultation, use a moderate 1-3% rate of appreciation per year of ownership if the borrower does not know what the approximate value of the property is.

"Seasoning"

Another consideration in the value of a home is how long it has been owned. Theoretically, a property could have been purchased at a price well below market. The borrower, knowing this, might try to refinance the property immediately after the purchase in order to more fully leverage it. Even though the property may be appraised at the higher value, lenders will not usually accept this valuation unless the ownership has been "seasoned" – like firewood – for at least one year. Seasoning also applies in "No Cash Out" transactions. If a borrower is refinancing a 1st and 2nd mortgage – any extensions of credit in the last 12 months are considered "Cash Out."

Rate Reduction

The most common reason for refinancing is to reduce a high fixed rate to a lower fixed rate. As with many old wives' tales, there are misleading "rules of thumb" which should be discarded as guiding concepts immediately. For instance, it is commonly understood that there should be a 2% reduction in interest rate in order for the refinance to be feasible. While it is

Basic Rate/Payment Reduction Feasibility Analysis		
	Current Mortgage	**Proposed**
Balance	$ 100,000.00	$ 100,000.00
Closing Costs		$ 2,000.00
Loan Amount		$ 102,000.00
Interest Rate	9.50%	8.50%
Term in Months	360	360
Monthly Payment	$ 840.85	$ 784.29
Monthly Savings		$ 56.56
Number of Months before Closing Costs are Repaid		35.36

certainly more opportune to reduce your interest rate as much as possible, it is not necessary to reduce it by 2%.

The critical concept is to compare the closing costs against the monthly savings to determine the length of time required before there are actual cash savings. This is a method of determining refinance feasibility.

To begin the comparison you should determine the borrower's current interest rate and monthly payments, ***exclusive of taxes and insurance (T&I)*** (take out the TI - these are going to be the same before and after). Then, calculate the costs (closing costs) of the transaction that the borrower absolutely must pay in order to refinance. These costs will vary depending on the jurisdiction. These closing costs may be financed or may be paid in cash. However, they should always be added to the loan amount for comparison purposes because, whether paid in cash or financed, this is the only way of accurately amortizing the cost over time. The actual cost of $2000, in this example, results in savings of $56/mo. Dividing these savings by the cost results in the length of time the borrower will take to break even on a cash flow basis.

This is only one analysis of refinance feasibility, as it does not take into consideration the payment of points in the closing cost scenario. Take the comparison one step further and finance points. A borrower can elect to pay points or not pay points and this has an effect on the cost of the transaction. It is one way of getting a more attractive interest rate. The break-even cost over time must be considered.

Reducing the interest rate further increases the monthly savings but measure the costs. It takes almost 5 years to break even on the cost of refinancing, even though the interest rate is much lower. A question you may ask is "If this is how long it takes to break even, am I going to be in the home less than 3 or 5 years?" This is the reason to include all costs in gauging refinance feasibility.

Time really is money. The cost applied to the savings gives the amount of time it takes to save money. In a rate reduction refinance the costs of the transaction over the existing loan balance must be calculated to accurately determine the length of time it takes to actually save money in refinancing. It should not be construed that the costs of the transaction cannot be paid in cash. They may be paid in cash; however, you should still amortize the costs in this way in order to achieve an objective formula for measuring the costs.

Basic Rate/Payment Reduction Feasibility Analysis Refinance			
	Current Mortgage	Proposed w/o Points	Proposed w/ Points
Current Balance	$ 100,000.00	$ 100,000.00	$ 100,000.00
Closing Costs		$ 2,000.00	$ 2,000.00
			$ 3,000.00
Loan Amount		$ 102,000.00	$ 105,000.00
Interest Rate	9.50%	8.50%	7.75%
Term in Months	360	360	360
Monthly Payment	$ 840.85	$ 784.29	$ 752.23
Monthly Savings		$ 56.56	$ 88.62
Number of Months before Closing Costs are Repaid		35.38	56.42

A disadvantage of points is that, because of amortization, the loan balance declines over time. Points are based on the original loan balance. As the loan balance decreases, the value of those original points paid decreases.

Term Reduction Refinances

If you have ever seen a book or an ad that says "How To Save $100,000" on your home mortgage loan, the term reduction refinance is the principle behind it. In a refinance where you payoff a 30-year mortgage with a new 30-year mortgage, you have increased the total amount of time it will take to own the home free and clear.

The drawback of periodic refinancing is that, without a disciplined approach, the loan never amortizes or achieves a –0- balance. Combining a rate reduction with a reduction in loan term can be one way of saving money over time. Reducing the loan term – a shorter amortization - increases the speed at which the loan must be paid off, thereby increasing the amount of principal to be paid each month - higher payments. A term reduction takes on much more of a personal financial planning facet because higher payments may be involved. Term reductions benefit:

- An individual planning on retirement at the end of the loan term.
- An investment property with significant positive cash flow that could carry higher payments.
- An individual who wishes to force himself or herself to make a higher payment, thereby accumulating more equity.

Since most lenders can offer fixed rate loan terms of 30, 25, 20, 15 and 10 years, why not consider the reduction in term in conjunction with a reduction in rate to enhance the savings of a refinance? Slightly lower interest rates may be available for 20, 15 and 10 year loans.

Term Reduction Analysis

	Current	Proposed 25 Year	Proposed 20 Year	Proposed 15 Year	Proposed 10 Year
Loan Balance	$ 100,000.00	$ 100,000.00	$ 100,000.00	$ 100,000.00	$ 100,000.00
Closing Costs		$ 2,000.00	$ 2,000.00	$ 2,000.00	$ 2,000.00
New Loan		$ 102,000.00	$ 102,000.00	$ 102,000.00	$ 102,000.00
Initial Term	360	300	240	180	120
Interest Rate	6.500%	6.000%	5.875%	5.500%	5.375%
Payment	$ 632.07	$ 657.19	$ 723.42	$ 833.43	$ 1,100.66
Monthly Savings		$ (25.12)	$ (91.36)	$ (201.36)	$ (468.59)
Remaining Months	324	300	240	180	120
Payments Remaining	$ 204,790.04	$ 197,156.23	$ 173,621.58	$ 150,016.52	$ 132,079.32
Life of Loan Savings		$ 7,633.81	$ 31,168.46	$ 54,773.52	$ 72,710.72

This example illustrates that, while a term reduction does not necessarily result in monthly payment savings, there is a definite savings over the life of the loan. The significant savings are realized over time, accomplished through regular monthly payments of principal and interest. Always be prepared to compare these as an alternative to simple payment reduction.

Refinancing to "Cash Out" - Recapture Equity in Your Property

An "Equity Recapture" or "Cash Out" refinance allows the borrower to take money from some of the equity in their home for any legal purpose.

	Current	Proposed		
Loan Amount	$ 100,000.00	$ 125,000.00	Pre-Tax	
Interest Rate	6.500%	6.000%	Payment	Additional Savings
Term	360	360	Increase	due to increased
Principal and Interest	$ 632.07	$ 749.44	$ 117.37	tax deductible
Deductible Interest Portion (Loan				interest
Amount x Interest Rate Divided by 12)	$ 541.67	$ 625.00	After Tax	
Multiply By Tax Rate	28%	28%	Payment	$ 23.33
Tax "Savings"	$ 151.67	$ 175.00	Increase	
After Tax Payment	$ 480.40	$ 574.44	$ 94.04	

When a borrower recaptures equity they are "re-leveraging." Financial leverage is a loan on an asset. The idea is that you purchase a large asset, like a house, with relatively little of your own assets. The financed asset – like the house – appreciates on its own regardless of the financing, at a far greater pace than the relatively small amount of your own assets would have appreciated even at a very high rate of return. It is important that borrowers who are re-leveraging understand the power of their equity. A borrower with a large equity position in their home isn't receiving any more appreciation on the home than a borrower with little or no equity.

Taking cash out becomes a smart idea for a number of other reasons.

- ❑ Mortgage interest is tax deductible.
- ❑ Most loans can be prepaid without penalty.
- ❑ Almost any other investment will outperform real estate equity.

Reasons to Take "Cash Out"

- ❑ To pay off other "high cost" loans which may not be tax deductible
- ❑ To pay for the cost of education
- ❑ To make home improvements
- ❑ To purchase investment property
- ❑ To make other investments
- ❑ To finance retirement

Low Cost of Cash

Because of the fact that mortgage rates are predominantly much lower rate products than any other lines of credit, it should be the first source for cash in a borrowing situation. In addition, there are tax benefits due to mortgage interest deductibility. Borrowers who need tax deductions are essentially volunteering to pay a higher tax when they keep a lot of equity in their homes.

Cash Out for Debt Consolidation

There are few situations where a borrower who is overextended with consumer debt will not be able to take advantage of debt consolidation even if the rate on a new mortgage is substantially higher than the existing rate. As such, for the loan officer it is an easy sale. However, there are certain processes that must be addressed to make the most effective use of the homeowner's equity.

- Payoff the debts with the highest payment proportionate to the balance. Select these by dividing the payment by the balance. The lower percentage payments should remain.
- If there is limited equity and all debts cannot be paid from proceeds, investigate lines of credit that the borrower can make us of to consolidate smaller accounts into one larger payment independent from the refinance.
- If the borrower needs to pay off debts to qualify, those accounts MUST BE CLOSED, not just paid off.

Debt Consolidation Analysis

	Current Loan		Proposed Loan		
Property Value	$ 125,000.00		Max LTV/Loan	80%	$ 100,000.00
			Max Proceeds		$ 25,000.00
			Costs		$ 5,000.00
Loan Mortgage Balance	$ 75,000.00		Net Proceeds Available		$ 20,000.00
Interest Rate	9%		Interest Rate		9%
Term	360		Term		360
Payment	$ 603.47		Payment		$ 804.62
Other Obligations	$ 1,785.00		Other Obligations		$ 1,127.00
Total Cash Flow	$ 2,388.47		Total Cash Flow		$ 1,931.62
			Savings		**$ 456.84**

Debt Concolidation Analysis

Installment Loans	Balance	Payment	Term/Balance	Payoff Amount	Payment After
Ford Motor	$ 16,250.00	$ 361.00	36	$ -	$ 361.00
Chrysler	$ 10,250.00	$ 420.00	25	$ -	$ 420.00
	$ -	$ -	0	$ -	$ -
Credit Cards				$ -	$ -
MBNA	$ 12,250.00	$ 389.00	3.18%	$ 12,250.00	$ -
Sears	$ 1,900.00	$ 168.00	8.84%	$ -	$ 168.00
Discover	$ 2,900.00	$ 79.00	2.72%	$ 2,900.00	$ -
VISA	$ 5,900.00	$ 178.00	3.02%	$ -	$ 178.00
Mastercard	$ 4,650.00	$ 190.00	4.09%	$ 4,650.00	$ -
	$ -	$ -	n/a	$ -	$ -
	$ -	$ -	n/a	$ -	$ -
	$ -	$ -	n/a	$ -	$ -
	$ -	$ -	n/a	$ -	$ -
	$ -	$ -	n/a	$ -	$ -
Totals	$ 54,100.00	$ 1,785.00		$ 19,800.00	$ 1,127.00

In this example, the borrower is saving $456 a month. Most borrowers would be happy with this outcome and leave it at that. However, you should show them the additional savings they could realize if they took a financial planning approach. The borrower has already adjusted their personal cash flow to account for this $456 savings. What if he or she took that savings and, instead of investing in personal expenditures, applied them to principal prepayment on their new mortgage?

Applying Debt Consolidation Savings to Principal Prepayment

Mortgage Amount	$ 100,000.00
Rate	9%
Term	360
Note Payment	$ 804.62
Debt Consolidation Savings	$ 456.87
Loan Term After Prepayment	121
Number of Months Saved	239
Monthly Payment Savings	$ 192,455.14

Advantages of Maximum Financing

Property Value		$200,000.00	Loan Type	30 Year	5.875%
Minimum Equity		20%	CD/Alternative Investment Yield		4.500%
Loan Amount		$160,000.00	Amortization in Years		30

Without Leverage			**With Maximum Leverage**		
Loan Amount	$	109,000.00	Loan Amount	$	160,000.00
Principal & Interest	$	946.46	Principal & Interest	$	1,183.08
Taxes*	$	137.42	Taxes*	$	137.42
Insurance	$	41.67	Insurance	$	41.67
Total	$	1,125.54	Total	$	1,362.16
Tax Savings*	$	(257.81)	Tax Savings*	$	(312.64)
Investment Return	$	-	Investment Return	$	191.25
Net Cash Flow	$	1,125.54	Net Cash Flow	$	1,170.91
			Compare (Savings)/Loss	$	(45.37)
After Tax Cash Flow	$	867.73	After Tax Cash Flow	$	858.27
			Compare (Savings)/Loss	$	9.47

Cash flow is enhanced by	**($45.37)**	*Assumes 28% bracket with interest and
Tax Benefits enhance Cash Flow by	**$9.47**	real estate tax deductions
On a cash flow basis the effective rate is	**6.22%**	
On a tax advantage basis the effective rate is	**5.80%**	

Cash out for Investment

Whether to purchase stocks, invest in a company, purchase investment property, or just put money into a CD or mutual fund, the tax benefits of mortgage interest offset the cash flow cost so that even a marginally positive investment makes sense. In this example, the mortgage rate is higher than the rate of return on a Certificate of Deposit. Still, the investment, combined with tax benefits, created a positive cash flow exceeding the cash flow of the smaller mortgage – simply by unleashing the equity in the property.

Cash Out to Purchase Investment Property

The same theory applies to any investment. The appeal to a borrower in this situation is that they are already going through the home financing process – why not use the same documentation for the refinance transaction to purchase an investment property? In this case the benefits are doubled because the tax advantages continue to flow from the investment property. Instead of the income being taxed, it is offset by depreciation. To the extent that the depreciation exceeds the actual income from the property, it becomes a deduction.

The source of the down payment is the equity in the current residence. The larger the down payment in the new property, the more positive cash flow the investment property will yield.

FINANCING ANALYSIS   Investment Property Cash Flow

Income/Expense Assumptions

Sales Price	$ 150,000.00	30 Year Fixed at		8.750%
Down Payment (%)	25%	Annual Taxes	$	2,500.00
Down Payment ($)	$ 37,500.00	Operating Expenses	$	1,800.00
Loan Amount	$ 112,500.00	Total Monthly Rent	$	1,600.00

CASH FLOW ANALYSIS

Cash Flow Based on Current Rent			Cash Flow after 10% Increase		
Gross Income	$	1,600.00	Rental Income	$	1,760.00
Principal and Interest	$	885.04	Principal and Interest	$	885.04
Real Estate Tax	$	208.33	Real Estate Tax	$	208.33
Hazard Insurance	$	31.25	Hazard Insurance	$	31.25
Total Payment	$	1,124.62	Total Payment	$	1,124.62
Plus Other Operating Exp.	$	150.00	Plus Other Operating Exp.	$	150.00
Plus Vacancy (10%)	$	160.00	Plus Vacancy (10%)	$	160.00
Total Expense	$	1,434.62	Total Expense	$	1,434.62
Net Cash Flow	$	165.38	Net Cash Flow	$	325.38
Yield of Alternate Investment (CD, Mutual Fund)		7.50%	Cash Flow of Alternate Investment	$	234.38

Cash Out for Retirement

The same rationale for maximizing mortgage financing applies when considering the needs of individuals planning for retirement. Mortgage refinance proceeds are not taxable as income, and so can be invested in a non-qualified plan such as an annuity, which can compound without the dividends, interest or capital gains subject to taxation.

Often individuals object to maximum financing on the basis that they want to own their property free and clear and not have a mortgage. This is particularly true for individuals who are planning for retirement – they see their home being paid off as a cornerstone to their retirement. However, if the retirement is a few years away, they still will have income that they need to minimize the tax consequences. The mortgage they may take out will not have a prepayment penalty – if the equity is cashed out for retirement planning purposes is placed in liquid investments. The borrower can pay off the mortgage any time it is beneficial. It is merely a balance sheet transfer.

Self-Employed individuals in particular can benefit from the advantages of being able to recapture equity in their home and fund Simplified Employee Pension Plan Individual Retirement Accounts (SEPP-IRA) in an amount up to 15% of annual income or $30,000 – whichever is less. Within these plans, assets grow without regard to taxation.

The key benefits of cash out for retirement are:

- The residence or property being financed continues to appreciate

- The equity is released to invest and yield a return
- The funds may be invested in qualified or non-qualified plans
- The equity invested continues to compound
- The tax benefits of home mortgage interest are increased
- The loan can be paid off any time the borrower decides they no longer wish to carry the debt service.

Refinance to eliminate Private Mortgage Insurance

One of the best reasons for refinancing is to eliminate Private Mortgage Insurance - the insurance a lender will require protecting against default losses when there is less than 20% equity in the property. A lender *may*

Refinancing to Eliminate PMI						
30 year $100,000 Mortgage						
		Current		Proposed		Savings
		9.00%		8.50%		0.50%
Payment	$	804.62	$	768.91	$	35.70
PMI (@ .34% Renewal)	$	28.33	$	-	$	28.33
Total	$	832.95	$	768.01	$	64.93
Refinance Cost	$	2,000.00				
Feasibility Analysis	$	64.93	= 30.80 Months to Break Even			

allow a borrower to petition to remove PMI as a requirement. This can occur under certain conditions, but generally involves documenting significant improvements or prepayment of the mortgage to a level below what would be required on a new loan application. For instance, if there were 20% equity in a refinance transaction PMI would not be required. However, if you are petitioning to have PMI removed from an existing loan you may have to substantiate 25% equity, depending on the amount of time in a house.

When refinancing to remove PMI the amount that the interest rate must be reduced to save money over time is also reduced. In the example above, if the closing costs were approximately $2,000, the break-even formula would indicate the refinance to be feasible if the loan would be held for more than 31 months. When you take into consideration the fact that PMI is not generally tax deductible, the savings over time are more significant. This demonstrates, again, that a large reduction in interest rate is not necessary to achieve savings.

Reduce the Cost of PMI if it can't be Eliminated

When PMI cannot be avoided because of low equity, another approach would be to compare the premium costs for various PMI plans. The standard plans require an initial premium and then require the lender to collect 1/12th of the renewal premiums with the monthly payment. Because PMI is not tax deductible, there are no benefits to paying this monthly. However, if there is sufficient equity, the borrower may be eligible for a

Loan Amount with PMI Premium Financed		
Existing loan	$	100,000.00
x PMI Premium Factor		1.58%
One Time Premium	$	1,580.00
Existing Loan	$	100,000.00
New Loan Amount	$	101,600.00

Comparing PMI Plans				
		One Time		"Classic"
Loan Amount	$	101,600	$	100,000
Payment	$	781.21	$	768.91
PMI Payment (.34%)	$	-	$	28.33
Total Payment	$	781.21	$	797.24
Monthly Savings	$	16.03		
Cash at Closing			$	-

premium financing plan where one payment is made at closing and is financed into the loan. The first step in comparing this is to determine what the new loan amount would be with the new PMI premium financed, and then compare the costs against the loan with a standard payment plan.

In this example, where PMI is a requirement and the choice is between premium plans, the one time program offers monthly savings as well as cash savings at closing. There are also plans which finance the initial premium only, as under the standard plans, and then take 1/12th of the renewal premium with the monthly payments, but this does not provide the benefit of the entire payment being tax deductible, and does not result in a payment reduction.

Using a 1st and 2nd Mortgage to Solve Equity Problems

In the same way that 80-10-10's are used when purchasing a property, a 2nd mortgage combination, "tandem," "piggy-back," or "blend" can be used to allow more flexibility in the structuring of a refinance. The benefit is that there are no extra costs for a 2nd mortgage and the paperwork for the borrower is no different than what is required for the first mortgage.

Property Value	$	200,000.00			
Equity		10%			
PMI Transaction			**1st & 2nd "Blend"**		
Term in Months		360	1st Trust Balance @ LTV	80% $	160,000.00
Interest Rate		8.75%	1st Trust Payment @ Rate	8.75%	$1,258.72
1st Trust Amount	$	180,000.00	1st Trust PMI	$	-
P & I Payment	$	1,416.06	2nd Trust Balance @ LTV	10% $	20,000.00
Monthly PMI	$	81.67	2nd Trust Payment @ Rate	9.50% $	168.17
Payment w/ PMI	$	1,497.73	Payment w "Blend"	$	1,426.89
			Savings with "Blend"	$	70.84

A more effective way of removing mortgage insurance is to combine a 1st and 2nd mortgage in a refinance transaction. If the current loan has Private Mortgage Insurance and still has a property value too low to allow PMI removal, structure the transaction with a "Blended" 1st and 2nd mortgage.

The same effect applies when a borrower has a fantastic interest rate on a 1st mortgage, but a very high rate on a 2nd mortgage. The borrower will often say "Well, I've got a great rate on my 1st trust, but my 2nd mortgage rate is really high." This indicates that the only potential for refinancing in this case might be to refinance the 2nd mortgage. But this isn't always the case – particularly if the first mortgage is relatively small.

Benefits of "Blended" Financing

The benefits of "blended" financing are:

- The borrower avoids PMI and may receive a lower overall rate
- The borrower is able to more effectively make periodic prepayments and eventually retire

a smaller 2nd mortgage at a higher rate – then is left with only a 1st mortgage
- Can structure a transaction with more favorable terms by putting the higher rate 2nd mortgage on a smaller balance and leaving the larger portion of the transaction on the more favorable 1st mortgage

Using Blended Financing to Achieve Payment Savings							
Property Value		$	200,000.00				
Loan Term (Months)			360				
Current Financing				**Proposed Financing**			
1st Trust Balance @ LTV	40%	$	80,000.00	1st Trust Balance @ LTV	80%	$	160,000.00
1st Trust Payment @ Rate	6.75%	$	518.88	1st Trust Payment @ Rate	8.50%		$1,230.26
2nd Trust Balance @ LTV	50%	$	100,000.00	2nd Trust Balance @ LTV	10%	$	20,000.00
2nd Trust Payment @ Rate	11.00%	$	952.32	2nd Trust Payment @ Rate	9.50%		$168.17
Payment w "blend"		$	1,471.20	Payment w "blend"			$1,398.43

Refinancing a 1st and 2nd Mortgage

Note that there may be situations in which a borrower may want to refinance a first mortgage without paying off the second mortgage. For instance, when the second mortgage has very attractive terms, or because it is a home equity line that will be used again and paid down. There are some things to be remembered in this situation:

- With a home equity line of credit, even if the borrower owes no money, the qualification is performed as if there was a full balance. This is because the borrower can, at any time, increase the balance and take on an additional debt burden.
- A subordination agreement is required in order to leave the second mortgage in place. This requires the approval of the 2nd mortgage lender. The 1st mortgage lender will require a subordination agreement that stipulates that the new 1st mortgage will remain as a prior lien chronologically.
- With certain balloon and ARM loans there are inherent contradictions. A conversion option may be offered as an escape to the balloon feature or as a low cost means of fixing the rate for the remainder of the loan on an ARM. This conversion feature will generally prohibit any second liens at the time of exercising the conditional refinance rendering the option moot. This could expose the borrower to potential risk or loss.

Refinancing an FHA Loan

The underwriting philosophy of the FHA refinance program is simple. Are you reducing your current payment? If so, it stands to reason that, if the borrower can afford a higher payment it will be even easier to afford the lower payments. To facilitate this, FHA has implemented what is known as a "Streamline Refinance." This is a simple reduction of the interest rate. The borrower only needs to provide the following information:

- 12 month payment history - current mortgage
- Uniform Residential Loan Application
- Current appraisal to document that the property value has not declined. This may not be

required if the loan amount is not being increased over the current loan amount.

- Verification of any funds needed to complete the closing and evidence of 1 month's PITI in reserve.

A Streamline Refinance can be used to refinance an investment property or a loan that was assumed under the assumption program. Under an assumption, however, the borrower must have made at least 6 mortgage payments.

As a mortgage insurance plan, FHA insures loans. Under section 203 (b), the fund that insures single-family homes, are subject to the UFMIP (Up Front Mortgage Insurance Premium) AND monthly MIP. Condos [234(c)] and Graduated Payment Mortgages [245(a)] are not subject to the UFMIP, but are subject to MONTHLY Mortgage Insurance Premiums. A new UFMIP is collected at closing. This premium is determined by subtracting the FHA MIP refund on the old loan from the amount of new (MIP) to be financed allowing for the appropriate refund on the old loan.

An owner-occupied property is also eligible for cash out refinance. The amount of cash out allowed on FHA cash out is contingent upon the value of the property. Up to 85% of the acquisition cost may be borrowed. A temporary buydown is not allowed under the cash out guidelines, and qualifying ratios are a strict 29/41.

When paying off a FHA loan, it is important for the borrower to review the original loan documents to determine if there is a prepayment penalty. The current holder of the note may require an additional 1-month of interest on the mortgage if there is not a 30-day notice of prepayment. In addition, it is important to close on an FHA transaction at the end of the month because the note holder has a right to collect interest from the date of the payoff until the end of the month. If you are refinancing an FHA loan, the settlement agent must give payoff notice at least 30 days prior to closing. An ***existing FHA loan should be paid off prior to the end of the month*** to avoid paying an additional 30 days of interest.

Refinancing a VA Loan

Much like the FHA program, VA allows for Streamline Refinancing. The same documentation is required when the interest is being reduced. The key is to reduce the interest rate or the payments.

- 12 month payment history - current mortgage
- Uniform Residential Loan Application
- Current appraisal to document property value has not declined. This may not be required if the loan amount is not being increased over the current loan amount.
- Verification of any funds needed to complete the closing and evidence of 1 month's PITI in reserve.

Unlike the FHA program, the VA program is a guarantee program. The fees paid for the guarantee do not get refunded at any time, unlike FHA insurance where the unused portion of the premium is refunded when the loan is paid off. On refinances, the premium is stiff -1.875% of the loan amount regardless of loan to value. More affordable is the rate and term version of the VA refinance - the premium is only 0.5%. The benefit of the VA Refinance Program is that you can refinance ANY loan, not just an existing VA loan, and be able to utilize the VA program guidelines - higher ratios and loan to values on a refinance.

Important Facts With Regard to Refinancing

The process of settling a refinance loan is much like a purchase. Because title is not changing hands, many documents ordinarily required may be waived:

- Initial Truth-in-Lending Disclosure may not be required by the lender on a no cash out refinance.
- Termite Inspection may not be required depending on whether the appraiser states that there are conditions existing conducive to termite infestation.
- House Location Survey may not be required if the title insurance policy does not take exception to encroachments and the borrower certifies that no changes have been made to the physical structure of the property.
- Well & Septic Certification, as with a termite report, may be waived. There are circumstances where the certification is required – such as when an appraiser notes an issue upon visual inspection. Generally, a well and/or septic system would not have visible signs of problems.
- Title Insurance - There may be reduced rates for title insurance. "Reissuing" an existing policy may save the customer money.
- Title Search - A full abstract may not be necessary if there is an existing title insurance policy in effect - many title companies will simply "bring down" the title, meaning they will review from the time that the last search was made, rather than reinvestigate the entire chain of title.

Escrow Accounts - Costs of Refinancing

When there is an existing loan with an escrow account for the payment of real estate taxes, homeowner's insurance, or PMI, these items will generally (unless there is an escrow waiver) have to be funded by the borrower in a new escrow account at closing. This is an interim

Escrows Financed vs. Paid in Cash

	Financed	Paid Cash
Existing Loan	$ 100,000.00	$ 100,000.00
Escrows Placed	$ 2,000.00	$ -
Financed Amount	$ 102,000.00	$ 100,000.00
Payment @ 8.5%	$ 784.29	$ 768.91
Difference in Payments		$ 15.37
Cost of $2000 @ 18%		$ 28.00

measure because the old lender will refund the escrow balance to the borrower once the existing loan is paid off. The question for the borrower is, can he or she reasonably afford to put the required money into escrow from their own funds or should this be financed?

Since this is the current practice, unless the lender is refinancing a loan held in its own portfolio, the borrower receives the refund of the escrow balance after the old loan is paid off, and after the old lender performs an escrow analysis to determine whether there has been any shortfall. As a result, it normally takes 4-6 weeks for the borrower to receive this refund. While this may be a considerable sum of money, in contemplating a rate and/or rate and term refinance, it is advisable to not finance these costs, but place them into escrow with the new lender. Replenishing the escrow account from existing funds will reduce the cost over the life of the loan. Even at an extreme cost, it makes sense to pay escrows in cash if possible.

It appears on face value that it would be more beneficial to finance the $2000 in the mortgage amount. If you borrowed the money on your credit card, wouldn't it cost about $30 per month? Not necessarily. If you received a check from your current lender for $2000, would you send it in and pay off your credit card debt - probably not. Think of it as a savings account. It is $2000 that will pay you $15.37 per month for the next 30 years! 15.37 x 360 = $5533.20 over the life of the loan.

Problems with Existing Financing

In refinancing it is often encountered that there is a problem with the way the existing financing or titling is in place. Some problems are solved following these suggested solutions.

Title Held In The Name Of A Corporation: When property is owned in the name of any entity other than a "natural person" - an individual - the title must be transferred. This is because a corporation automatically is a commercial enterprise, not residential in nature. The difficulty comes when transfer tax or other municipal charges apply to this transfer. Because no title normally transfers in a refinance, this would technically be called a purchase transaction. There is the potential for a less than arm's length transaction - presenting risks for the lender because the sales price could be artificially inflated in order to obtain maximum financing. However, if it can be demonstrated that the individual wishing to refinance closely holds the entity, the fear of a less than arm's length transaction can be mitigated.

Spousal Buyout: In a divorce situation the parties may wish to dispose of their interest in a property or redistribute the equity. While this is not an ideal personal situation, it can be an excellent opportunity to purchase an estranged spouse's interest. This is not a transfer, because one person is simply assigning his or her interest in a property to someone who already owns the property. However, from a loan to value point of view, this can be treated as a purchase. The separation agreement sets forth the sales price, an appraisal is performed, and normal purchase loan to value limitations apply.

Existing Loans with Conversion Options

With certain 5 and 7-year balloons, and adjustable rate mortgages, an existing loan may have a conversion feature. Prior to pursuing a refinance on an existing balloon or ARM, examine the note for evidence of a conversion option. It may benefit the borrower to exercise the conversion option in lieu of refinancing. See Chapter 2, Loan Programs, for a detailed description of conversion options. Another version of a conversion option is in a situation where a borrower has an existing loan with a specific lender. That lender may offer a "modification" which is a streamlined refinancing process. This is generally only available from lenders who retain the servicing (collection of the monthly payments and payment of taxes and insurance) on a specific loan and that loan exists in their portfolio.

Chapter 10
The Secondary Market

Secondary marketing is how we arrive at pricing for our loans, the guidelines and products. Often in the course of the day we hear that the reason something is being done a certain way is because of secondary marketing. Succinctly, secondary marketing is the process of buying and selling loans after the money has been lent. Mortgage companies making loans to homebuyers represent the primary market. The buyers of these loans create the guidelines for the business. It is therefore important to know what it is and how it works. It is also the way the financial aspect of the mortgage business reconciles itself. Secondary Marketing takes into consideration not only the fees that are earned in the origination of a mortgage, but the hedging value, and the servicing value, financially, to the mortgage industry.

Lock or Float

Secondary marketing is abstract except when a customer calls and asks about interest rates. Most frequently, the request is for a "lock-in" of the interest rate. A lock-in is a rate guarantee and is insurance against rates going up. Alternately, the customer can defer the decision to lock-in. This is referred to as "floating." Floating is insurance against rates going down. Understanding these options can help you guide your customer through the interest rate lock decision process.

Lock Option	Description	Protects Against
Lock-in	A lock in fixes a borrower's interest rate and point options for a specific period of time. If a lock in expires prior to the borrower's closing the borrower receives the market interest rate or the original interest rate, **whichever is HIGHER.** If a borrower decides to guarantee the rate and point option, the loan officer must assure there is sufficient time to process and close the loan under that lock term. The benefit of locking in is that there is certainty in the final interest rate.	Rates rising dramatically
Float	A float is a deferral of the decision to fix the interest rate. Regardless of whether interest rates increase or decrease, the borrower can lock in at those rates in the future. The benefit of floating is that the loan application can be processed and approved prior to locking in – the borrower can then execute an "immediate delivery lock" for 5, 7 or 15	Rates falling or staying the same

Lock Option	Description	Protects Against
	days, which can be substantially better pricing than the 60 day lock-in	
Float Down Lock	The borrower can cap or lock in their interest rate at a current rate. If rates decline within a specific period of time prior to closing, the borrower can "re-lock" at a lower interest rate. The benefit of the Float Down Lock In is that the borrower is protected against dramatic fluctuation in rates.	Rates Rising or Falling Dramatically

The problem with lock-ins is that many people rush to lock in after interest rates have already risen. This is like buying insurance AFTER a car accident. Rates rise and fall – within a generally predictable seasonality pattern. There are periods of time when rates traditionally rise – such as, in the spring or fall home buying seasons as demand for mortgages tends to drive interest rates up - where no one should defer the lock decision.

Seasonality Patterns

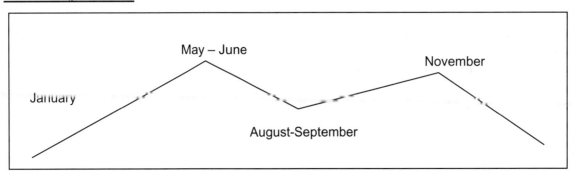

Immediate Delivery

The longer the rate lock, the higher the interest rate. This is because the further away you go into the future, the greater the amount of uncertainty regarding future rates. Conversely, while we are used to looking at 45- or 60-day lock-ins, there are very short-term lock-ins that can offer a lower

Typical Lock Term Pricing Matrix

	7	15	30	45	60	90	180
7.625	-0.25	0.00	0.25	0.50	0.75	1.00	1.25
7.500	0.25	0.50	0.75	1.00	1.25	1.50	1.75
7.375	0.75	1.00	1.25	1.50	1.75	2.00	2.25
7.250	1.25	1.50	1.75	2.00	2.25	2.50	2.75

rate because there is virtually no rate uncertainty. This is an argument for deferring the interest rate lock-in decision in a period where interest rates are anticipated to stay at or near current interest rates, or go lower.

This is illustrated to show that there are rate lock options that can add value to the customer. IN NO CIRCUMSTANCE SHOULD YOU EVER LOCK IN AN INTEREST RATE FOR A CUSTOMER AND NOT LOCK IT IN WITH AN INVESTOR OR SECONDARY MARKETING. This is called "Playing the Market."

The Secondary Market

The secondary mortgage market is simply a network of investors whose common thread is investment interest in one financial instrument -- the mortgage. A mortgage is a loan that is secured against real estate as opposed to personal property or unsecured loans. These mortgages can be first or second liens and can be secured against residential single-family units, multi-family units, or commercial properties.

When a borrower obtains a loan secured against real estate, the process is termed primary origination. Lending directly to the owner of the property makes an "originator" a primary originator and thus is a transaction in the primary market. When an investor purchases a mortgage or many mortgages from a primary originator, the investor is obtaining an asset - the loan. Here this loan becomes a commodity that can be bought or sold the same way sugar, pork bellies or gold are. Like commodities, the future price can be locked in with options on the futures exchanges.

Normally the mortgage enters the market in the form of a security after it has been packaged with numerous other mortgages into pools or packages of loans. However there are also individual buyers and institutional buyers. The mortgage securities market is relatively robust because it is a fixed income market. The same buyers of treasuries, municipal bonds and corporate bonds buy mortgages.

Who's Who in the Secondary Market

Fannie Mae (FNMA - Federal National Mortgage Corporation) was created by Congress in 1938 as a Government Corporation, and became partially private in 1954. In 1968 it was partitioned into GNMA (Government National Mortgage Association) and FNMA and became a private corporation. Initially FNMA purchased only government insured loans, but in 1970 it entered the conventional loan market. Now it purchases 1st & 2nd mortgages, multi-family property loans and programs originated by local agencies and federal subsidy programs.

Ginnie Mae (GNMA- Government National Mortgage Association) was created in 1968 by Congress to stimulate mortgage credit markets for Government Insured or Guaranteed mortgages. Congress created Freddie Mac (FHLMC - Federal Home Loan Mortgage Corporation) in 1970 to enhance the liquidity of mortgage investments. Freddie Mac is a congressionally chartered corporation. The President appoints the members of the board of directors, who also oversee the operation of the 12 Federal Home Loan Banks and all federally chartered savings institutions.

There are also a number of private secondary market entities that purchase loans and use them as collateral for securities (referred to as "securitizing") mortgages and mortgage-backed securities - names like RFC (Residential Funding Corporation), General Electric Credit, Sears Mortgage Securities, Norwest, and Nomura.

The secondary market also includes small banks purchasing mortgages originated by local mortgage bankers, private individuals who buy seconds "taken back" by sellers, life insurance companies investing premiums against future claims, pension plans investing contributions to provide future benefits and individuals who purchase "GNMAs" from a stock or financial broker.

The Development of the Market

As rates in general started to rise in the late '60's and early 1970's, there was a greater demand for mortgage money than local banks and savings and loans could absorb. There were pockets of demand that created shortages in financing. Then there were areas in which there was not enough demand and bankers could not obtain a desired yield. These cyclical swings would create mini real estate booms and depressions throughout the country. The answer to the question of how to make home finance money more readily available was the creation of a place where loans could be bought and sold - a secondary market.

"Standardization" of the Mortgage Investment

By standardizing the loans in accordance with secondary market guidelines, the mortgages became liquid commodities. This market then makes a redistribution of mortgage money possible throughout the U.S.A.

This standardization is one reason that rates on loans that are sold to FHLMC can be lower. Because FNMA, GNMA and FHLMC are quasi-governmental agencies, the credit risk is improved. Standard & Poors, and Moody's are rating agencies that assign various levels of risk to investments. Obviously, treasury securities carry the lowest level of risk. However, FNMA, FHLMC and GNMA are assigned "Agency" ratings by these services. As a result these carry lower risk and lower yield than commercial paper.

Speaking of Risk

Another advantage of the secondary market is the diminution of mortgage lending risk. There are two types of risks associated with any type of mortgage lending: the borrower will not pay the money back and the loan itself will decrease in value.

Standardization ensures that the mortgage carries an acceptably low level of risk of default. The secondary market has required the mortgage industry to develop standard underwriting criteria with regard to credit, income and property risk. It is this rigorous risk aversion strategy that spawned the growth of private companies that developed insurance programs to protect the lender against default. This private mortgage insurance (PMI) has also increased the flow of investor money into the mortgage markets and has proven to be a viable alternative to Government insurance (FHA) and guarantee (VA) programs for high loan to value (LTV) mortgages.

In addition, the risk in mortgage investment is mitigated by the fact that the loans themselves are secured - by real estate. A mortgage is a secured loan against a very durable type of asset. Real property is an asset that keeps its value (they aren't making any more of it). As a matter of fact, it may appreciate rather than depreciate. In addition, real property has a formalized legal ownership system. All ownership is recorded with our government, and mortgages can be recorded and tracked.

Par is not a Golf Score

How two loans of different interest rates are compared illustrates the function of yield over time versus purchase price today. The market is seeking a certain yield among all of the options available. Let's assume, for the purpose of illustration, that yield is 8.5%. A $100,000 instrument bearing an 8.5% yield would be worth $100,000 in the market. However, a yield of 9.0% would be a higher rate of return. The market compensates for this higher value by making the purchase of this yield more expensive. If you were a yield seeking investor you could buy a 8.5% yielding instrument for $100,000, or a 9.00% yield for $103,000. Conversely, an 8.00% yield would be worth less to an investor, but "discounting" the cost of purchasing this instrument could make up this deficit in value. The value of the 8.00% instrument might be $97,000. In this way the market equalizes yield and allows individual loans with different interest rates to be packaged together for a blended yield.

Illustration of Typical Discounts in 1985		
Yield	10%	10.5%
Price for Delivery in		
October	94.14	**97.12**
November	94.06	97.04
December	93.18	96.24
January	93.02	96.16

Example: a 10.5% $100,000 loan for delivery in October would be worth $97,120. The lender would have to charge 3 discount points to make up the difference.

In describing this, keep in mind that this is a vast oversimplification of the pricing mechanism. There are also the concerns of prepayment - where borrowers repay their loans at a much faster rate than anticipated and the general risks of investing in interest rate-based derivatives.

If a bank lent $10 million in mortgages at prevailing rates, their value could decline rapidly in a very short time period, representing a potential huge paper loss. Long-term investors are not subject to intermediate fluctuations and make the most ideal holders. The secondary market enables an institution to make mortgage loans and then sell them to not be subject to the risks of long-term interest rate fluctuations.

How Lenders Make Money

Mortgages are sold in the secondary market in several forms. A simple sale of an individual mortgage is known as a "whole loan" sale. The sale of partial interest in a mortgage is known as a "participation" sale. Third, mortgages or participation in mortgages are collected together in aggregations, known as "pools," which are used to back securities. Principal and interest collected by the securities issuer for the pooled mortgages are passed though to the securities holders. Each of the mortgage-backed securities holders has an individual beneficial interest in the pool's cash flows. Pools of mortgages are also used to secure mortgage-backed bonds - debt securities issued in the secondary market.

As mentioned earlier, though mortgages are usually for 15 or 30 years and are priced in tandem with long-term "non-callable" assets, their average life is much lower due to mobility of our populace or refinancing at times of lower interest rates. Therefore, the eventual "holder" of the mortgage will not own it for 30 years, but closer to 7-10 years.

Mortgage companies' profits are not driven by the "interest" rates they charge. They make the same amount of money regardless of whether rates are 14% or 4%. Principal sources of revenue are:

1. Origination fee income. If the mortgage company charges a 1% origination fee this equates to $1,000 of income on a $100,000 loan. Usually this income is used to cover the overhead of making the loan.
2. Marketing Gain/Loss. Marketing gain occurs if the individual loan appreciates in between the time the loan was made and the time it is sold. It should be noted that these commodities are usually priced in the present and sold in the future. Therefore, if the value of the commodity goes down a marketing loss may result. Since there is equal risk of prices going in either direction, it is understandable that marketing gain can equally be a loss.
3. Servicing income - If the mortgage company "retains the servicing" for a loan it originates and then later sells the loan itself, but maintains the role of passing the principal and interest payments through to the securities holder, the owner of the loan, this is referred to as retained servicing. There is a fee earned for this service, which normally means that the servicer retains a small percentage of the interest each month. Unlike the origination of loans, servicing is a year round source of income for the bank.
4. Sale of Servicing Rights - Because of the fee that can be earned, the rights to collect and pass through monthly payments can be quite valuable. Often the value of these rights will appreciate to the point that there can be a significant gain realized in the sale of the rights. Typical servicing rights sales yield between .75 and 2.5 points, depending on the loan type.
5. Other Fees - Lenders also may charge fees for document preparation, underwriting, tax service, etc. Some of these fees are a pass-through only. Others are an income source.
6. Warehouse Differential - When a lender funds a loan with a "line of credit" or warehouse line at a bank, the lender pays interest on the line until the loan is sold. If the interest charged on the loan exceeds the interest rate paid to the bank, there will be additional income. Likewise, there may be a shortfall.

Following a Loan Through the Secondary Marketing Process Step By Step

1. A $100,000 loan application is taken on October 1, 1987.
2. Loan is "locked" at 11 % with 2 discount points and 1 origination fee for 60 days.
3. Lender buys a commitment to deliver the closed loan on January 15.
4. Loan is processed and approved.
5. Settlement documents are prepared for December 20 closing.
6. Settlement department requests a warehouse line of credit advance from bank.
7. On date of settlement, funds are wired from warehouse bank to closing agent's account.
8. Money is disbursed to applicant and seller for consummation of transaction.
9. Settlement agent sends completed documents back to Mortgage Company.
10. Post closing/delivery sends original mortgage note to warehouse bank and closed loan package to investor that purchased commitment.
11. Loan is purchased by investor - Note is delivered by bank to Investor.
12. Loan is assembled warehoused at investor's bank pending accumulation of enough mortgages to issue a "pool" of mortgages.
13. Pool of 1000 loans assembled yielding 10%-11%, face value $100,000,000 +/- 5%.
14. FNMA purchases pool and investor's warehouse line is replenished.

Into the Tranches

The mortgage now is part of a pool and all of the primary and secondary originators have replenished their lines of credit. Nothing is simple anymore and with a $100,000,000 security, there is little likelihood that any one investor is going to purchase the entire security. Enter the REMIC (Real Estate Mortgage Investment Conduit) which is the pool of loans and their 10.5% yield divided up to suit the needs of a wider array of investors with differing needs. These divisions are called "tranches" (like "launches") which split the interest and principal payments into different components.

A typical REMIC has between 7 and 13 tranches. A portion trades like bonds, yielding various interest rates at various maturities to anticipate the imminent prepayment of the underlying mortgages. Some trade like regularly renewable corporate obligations with a rate floating over short-term rates. Then there is a residual tranche that captures whatever is left. This is a derivative type gamble because, if interest rates stay low, there will be a large amount of interest coming into the residual. However, it may come up short if there is a great deal of prepayment. This impacts how the mortgage is actually made and where the money comes from.

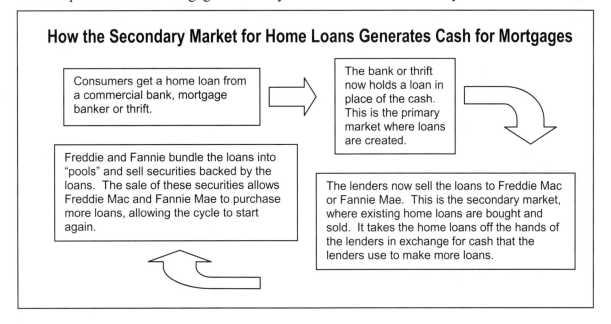

How the Secondary Market for Home Loans Generates Cash for Mortgages

Consumers get a home loan from a commercial bank, mortgage banker or thrift.

The bank or thrift now holds a loan in place of the cash. This is the primary market where loans are created.

Freddie and Fannie bundle the loans into "pools" and sell securities backed by the loans. The sale of these securities allows Freddie Mac and Fannie Mae to purchase more loans, allowing the cycle to start again.

The lenders now sell the loans to Freddie Mac or Fannie Mae. This is the secondary market, where existing home loans are bought and sold. It takes the home loans off the hands of the lenders in exchange for cash that the lenders use to make more loans.

Interest Rate Drivers

At the most basic level interest rates are driven by inflation. This is because a lender's biggest fear is that money lent today will be worth less in the future - a textbook definition of inflation. As a result "real interest rates" are a composite of what money is really yielding from an interest rate perspective less the common belief regarding future inflation. To understand what drives interest rates, you must understand what drives inflation, as well as other economic and market factors. Remember that John Kenneth Gailbraith said, "There are only two kinds of people when it comes to knowing about the future of interest rates - those that don't know, and those that don't know they don't know..."

Energy Prices	Every product or service is in some way affected by how much energy costs, because energy is used in the manufacture or delivery of every good or service. If oil prices rise, inflation will rise and interest rates will follow.
Unemployment	The cost of labor comprises roughly 2/3 of the cost of any good or service. If labor becomes scarce, prices will rise. Conversely, if there is high unemployment, labor costs should be low.
Demand/Supply	Fundamental variations in seasonal demand drive up interest rates. If the government, industry and individuals are all borrowing at the same time, there will be a scarcity of money that will tend to drive rates up. Conversely if the government doesn't borrow money (budget surplus), then demand for credit will be low reducing rates.
Currency Values	If the dollar is strong relative to world currencies, it can take more foreign currency to lend in dollars, diminishing the supply of lending capital. This can be opposed by a higher demand to invest in dollar denominated securities.
Instability	Uncertainty of any kind will generally drive interest rates higher in the interim, regardless of outcome. War, falling markets, political crises all tend to create higher interim rates.

Playing the Market

Loan officers are admonished to never "play the market." Playing the Market is when a loan officer gives the borrower a lock-in, but doesn't actually lock it in with secondary marketing. The loan officer hopes that interest rates will improve, meaning a bigger commission. However, if rates don't improve, the loan officer and, more likely the company, will have to fund the loan. This can be a large loss.

While markets change throughout the day, lenders try to price their commodities to the market once a day. If your lender allows you to lock in a loan (generally only new loans) until a specific time (e.g. 9:30 a.m.), you can take advantage of this anomaly by watching the news for any sign that rates are going to decline. If you meet with a customer in the evening, and there is a probability that rates will be lower in the morning you may offer the current market price. If the morning's data appears to indicate a lower interest rate environment, simply wait until new pricing is available to lock in the rate. If the data is unfavorable, lock the loan in immediately.

ACRONYMS

Many abbreviations are used in the mortgage business. This is technical jargon that many professionals use to abbreviate correspondence and extemporaneous communication.

ACH	Automated Clearing House - Federal Reserve clears automated payments.
ADP	Automatic Data Processing
ALTA	American Land Title Association (Lenders require this type of policy with extended coverage).
APR	Annual Percentage Rate (Cost of credit disclosed in the form of rate, on TIL)
ARM	Adjustable Rate Mortgage - Mortgage instrument; interest rate changes periodically during life of loan
CAIVRS	Credit Alert Interactive Voice Response System
CBA	Controlled Business Arrangement
CHBP	Community Home Buyer's Program
CHUMS	Computerized Home Underwriting System
CMO	Collateralized Mortgage Obligation
COFI	Cost of Funds Index - Most commonly used in description of loans based on 11th Federal Home Loan Bank Board members cost of funds (rate paid on deposits)
CRA	Community Reinvestment Act - requires financial institutions to reinvest in their communities
CRV	Certificate of Reasonable Value - VA appraisal
DE	Direct Endorsement underwriter - FHA approved underwriter
ECOA	Equal Credit Opportunity Act - Regulation B
EMD	Earnest Money Deposit - Deposit on property to indicate serious purchase intent
FCRA	Fair Credit Reporting Act
FDIC	Federal Deposit Insurance Corporation
FHA	Federal Housing Administration - Insures loans against loss through default and foreclosure
FHLBB	Federal Home Loan Bank Board
FHLMC	Federal Home Loan Mortgage Corporation - Secondary market investor
FIRREA	Financial Institutions Reform, Recovery and Enforcement Act of 1989 - Responsible for formation of RTC; regulates financial institutions, restricts appraisal procedure
FNMA	Federal National Mortgage Association - Secondary market entity
FRB	Federal Reserve Board ("Fed")
FTC	Federal Trade Commission
GEM	Growing Equity Mortgage - mortgage instrument; an accelerated payment schedule starts with 30-year P & I, but pays off loan in 15 - 18 years
GFE	Good Faith Estimate - Discloses settlement costs on loan
GNMA	Government National Mortgage Association - Secondary marketing entity; securitizes government loans for bond market
GPM	Graduated Payment Mortgage - Flexible payment mortgage with scheduled negative amortization
HECM	Home Equity Conversion Mortgage
HOA	Home-Owners Association
HOLC	Home-Owners Loan Corporation
HOW	Home Owner Warranty – Builder warranty
HUD	Department of Housing and Urban Development - Federal department under which FHA functions
HMDA	Home Mortgage Disclosure Act - Prohibits "redlining"
IRRRL	Interest Rate Reduction Refinancing Loan
LDP	Limited Denial of Participation
LIBOR	London Inter Bank Offered Rate - Rate at which money center banks in England lend to each other.
LTV	Loan-to-Value Ratio - Ratio of mortgage amount/value of real property
MCAW	Mortgage Credit Analysis Worksheet
MCRV	Master Certificate of Reasonable Value
MAI	Member, Appraisal Institute - Highly respected appraisal designation
MBA	Mortgage Bankers Association
MC	Mortgage Condition - Seen on FHA loan approvals
MIC	Mortgage Insurance Certificate - Issued by HUD as evidence of mortgage insurance

MIP	Mortgage Insurance Premium - Annual premium charged by FHA for insuring loan; collected monthly from borrower, with mortgage payment
MSA	Metropolitan Statistical Area
OCC	Office of the Comptroller of Currency - Regulator of Banks in addition to FDIC and FRB
OTS	Office of Thrift Supervision - Regulates federally chartered savings associations
PITI	Principal, Interest, Taxes and Insurance - Monthly mortgage payment
P & L	Profit and Loss statement
PLC	Personal Line of Credit
PMI	Private Mortgage Insurance - Insures conventional loans, as FHA does for government loans; private industry
PUD	Planned Unit Development
RAM	Reverse Annuity Mortgage - Mortgage instrument; lender makes monthly payments to borrower
RESPA	Real Estate Settlement Procedures Act – Requires the Good Faith Estimate of Closing Costs, HUD-I Settlement Statement, and Transfer of Servicing Disclosure
RTC	Resolution Trust Corporation - Replaced FSLIC in regulation of savings and loans
TIL	Truth-in-Lending disclosure - Discloses APR
URLA	Uniform Residential Loan Application
UFMIP	Up Front Mortgage Insurance Premium – Insurance premium charged by FHA at time of loan closing for insuring loan; paid by borrower; can be financed
URAR	Uniform Residential Appraisal Report - Conventional appraisal report form
VA	Department of Veterans Affairs - Guarantees loans to veterans
VOD	Verification of Deposit - Form used to document cash accounts, through bank
VOE	Verification of Employment - Form used to document earnings through employer
VOM	Verification of Mortgage - Form used to document payment history of housing through Lender
VOR	Verification of Rent - Form used to document payment history of housing through landlord

State and County Transfer and Recordation Tax

2004 Maryland

County	Transfer	Recordation	Total
Allegany	0.70%	0.60%	1.30%
Anne Arundel	1.50%	0.70%	2.20%
Baltimore City	2.00%	0.55%	2.55%
Baltimore	2.00%	0.50%	2.50%
Calvert	0.50%	1.00%	1.50%
Caroline	1.00%	1.00%	2.00%
Carroll	0.50%	1.00%	1.50%
Cecil	0.50%	0.66%	1.16%
Charles	0.50%	1.00%	1.50%
Dorchester	1.25%	1.00%	2.25%
Frederick	0.50%	1.00%	1.50%
Garrett	1.50%	0.70%	2.20%
Harford	1.50%	0.66%	2.16%
Howard	1.50%	0.50%	2.00%
Kent	1.00%	0.66%	1.66%
Montgomery	1.50%	0.69%	2.19%
Prince George's	1.90%	0.44%	2.34%
Queen Anne's	1.00%	0.66%	1.66%
St. Mary's	1.50%	0.80%	2.30%
Somerset	0.50%	0.66%	1.16%
Talbot	1.50%	0.66%	2.16%
Washington	1.00%	0.76%	1.76%
Wicomico	0.50%	0.70%	1.20%
Worcester	1.00%	0.66%	1.66%

Principal and Interest Factor Table

Multiply Loan Amount By Interest Rate Factor and Divide by 1000 for Payment

Rate	5 Year	10 Year	15 Year	20 Year	25 Year	30 Year	40 Year
3.000%	17.968691	9.656074	6.905816	5.545976	4.742113	4.216040	3.579844
3.250%	18.080002	9.771903	7.026688	5.671958	4.873162	4.352063	3.725412
3.500%	18.191745	9.888587	7.148825	5.799597	5.006236	4.490447	3.873910
3.750%	18.303918	10.006124	7.272224	5.928883	5.141312	4.631156	4.025260
4.000%	18.416522	10.124514	7.396879	6.059803	5.278368	4.774153	4.179385
4.125%	18.472985	10.184027	7.459676	6.125872	5.347632	4.846497	4.257462
4.250%	18.529556	10.243753	7.522784	6.192345	5.417381	4.919399	4.336202
4.375%	18.586234	10.303691	7.586203	6.259219	5.487613	4.992853	4.415594
4.500%	18.643019	10.363841	7.649933	6.326494	5.558325	5.066853	4.495628
4.625%	18.699912	10.424202	7.713972	6.394167	5.629513	5.141395	4.576293
4.750%	18.756912	10.484774	7.778319	6.462236	5.701174	5.216473	4.657579
4.875%	18.814019	10.545558	7.842974	6.530700	5.773304	5.292082	4.739473
5.000%	18.871234	10.606552	7.907936	6.599557	5.845900	5.368216	4.821966
5.125%	18.928555	10.667756	7.973204	6.668805	5.918959	5.444870	4.905046
5.250%	18.985984	10.729170	8.038777	6.738442	5.992477	5.522037	4.988703
5.375%	19.043520	10.790794	8.104654	6.808465	6.066450	5.599712	5.072926
5.500%	19.101162	10.852628	8.170835	6.878873	6.140875	5.677890	5.157703
5.625%	19.158912	10.914670	8.237317	6.949664	6.215747	5.756564	5.243023
5.750%	19.216768	10.976922	8.304101	7.020835	6.291064	5.835729	5.328876
5.875%	19.274731	11.039382	8.371185	7.092385	6.366821	5.915378	5.415251
6.000%	19.332802	11.102050	8.438568	7.164311	6.443014	5.995505	5.502136
0.125%	19.390978	11.164926	8.506250	7.236610	6.519640	6.076105	5.589522
6.250%	19.449262	11.228010	8.574229	7.309282	6.596694	6.157172	5.677396
6.375%	19.507652	11.291300	8.642504	7.382323	6.674172	6.238699	5.765748
6.500%	19.566148	11.354798	8.711074	7.455731	6.752072	6.320680	5.854568
6.625%	19.624751	11.418502	8.779938	7.529504	6.830387	6.403110	5.943845
6.750%	19.683461	11.482411	8.849095	7.603640	6.909115	6.485981	6.033568
6.875%	19.742276	11.546527	8.918543	7.678136	6.988252	6.569288	6.123728
7.000%	19.801199	11.610848	8.988283	7.752989	7.067792	6.653025	6.214313
7.125%	19.860227	11.675374	9.058312	7.828198	7.147732	6.737185	6.305313
7.250%	19.919361	11.740104	9.128629	7.903760	7.228069	6.821763	6.396719
7.375%	19.978602	11.805039	9.199233	7.979672	7.308797	6.906751	6.488520
7.500%	20.037949	11.870177	9.270124	8.055932	7.389912	6.992145	6.580707
7.625%	20.097401	11.935519	9.341299	8.132537	7.471410	7.077937	6.673270
7.750%	20.156960	12.001063	9.412758	8.209486	7.553288	7.164122	6.766199
7.875%	20.216624	12.066810	9.484499	8.286774	7.635540	7.250694	6.859484
8.000%	20.276394	12.132759	9.556521	8.364401	7.718162	7.337646	6.953117
8.125%	20.336270	12.198910	9.628823	8.442362	7.801151	7.424972	7.047088
8.250%	20.396252	12.265263	9.701404	8.520657	7.884501	7.512666	7.141388
8.375%	20.456339	12.331816	9.774262	8.599281	7.968209	7.600722	7.236009
8.500%	20.516531	12.398569	9.847396	8.678232	8.052271	7.689135	7.330941
8.625%	20.576829	12.465522	9.920804	8.757509	8.136681	7.777897	7.426176
8.750%	20.637233	12.532675	9.994487	8.837107	8.221436	7.867004	7.521705
8.875%	20.697741	12.600027	10.068441	8.917025	8.306532	7.956449	7.617521
9.000%	20.758355	12.667577	10.142666	8.997260	8.391964	8.046226	7.713615
9.125%	20.819074	12.735326	10.217160	9.077808	8.477727	8.136330	7.809979
9.250%	20.879898	12.803272	10.291923	9.158668	8.563818	8.226754	7.906606
9.375%	20.940827	12.871416	10.366952	9.239837	8.650233	8.317494	8.003487
9.500%	21.001861	12.939756	10.442247	9.321312	8.736967	8.408542	8.100616
9.625%	21.063000	13.008292	10.517805	9.403090	8.824015	8.499894	8.197984
9.750%	21.124244	13.077024	10.593627	9.485169	8.911374	8.591544	8.295586
9.875%	21.185592	13.145952	10.669709	9.567545	8.999040	8.683486	8.393413
10.000%	21.247045	13.215074	10.746051	9.650216	9.087007	8.775716	8.491459
10.125%	21.308602	13.284390	10.822652	9.733180	9.175273	8.868226	8.589718
10.250%	21.370264	13.353900	10.899509	9.816434	9.263833	8.961013	8.688182
10.375%	21.432030	13.423604	10.976622	9.899974	9.352682	9.054070	8.786846

Loan Officer Boot Camp
Fulfillment of Course Requirement

In order to receive a satisfactory completion certificate the loan officer must register to take the on-line certification class at www.lenderbootcamp.com. In addition, the loan officer may complete the marketing plan assignment as outlined in the Loan Officer's Practical Guide to Marketing.

Developing a Loan Officer Marketing Plan

Each loan officer is given a general assignment to prepare this plan:

Marketing Plan Preparation/Inventory

1.) *Prospective Referral Source List* - derive the number of loans per month needed in order to achieve your personal income goals.
   a. That number, times 3, is the number of active prospects needed. Generally you need to have 3 prospects for each one established referral source. (No more than 30)
   b. Develop a list of alternative sources of business to include financial planners, investment advisors, insurance agents, CPA's, attorneys, as well as real estate related sources (home improvement, design, architects, property managers) and financial partners (non-mortgage banks, mortgage brokers). Generally, there should be about 20.

2.) *Weekly Plan* – Learn how time should be allocated and program the schedule on a personal organizer (preferably automated) such as Outlook, ACT!, or PALM Desktop. Once complete provide a printout of weekly schedule.

3.) *Plot the Office Visit Plan* – Plot out – on a map – how to achieve visiting prospect offices.

4.) *Develop an Introductory Package* – Assemble the package to be used on appointments with referral sources. Hopefully this will contain –
   a. Value added services (Open House, Pre-Approval, FSBO, Homebuyer Seminar)
   b. Specialty Niche – a focus on the product guideline/specialty (such as 2nd homes, 100% financing, condos, 203(k), rehab/construction, investment property, self-employed borrowers/no doc, 1st time homebuyers, relocation, immigrant/emerging markets, to name a few)
   c. Referral Network
   d. Biography
   e. Introductory letter or Specific Mission Statement

Upon completion, the project is reviewed with management and used as a tool to measure and adjust the loan officer's progress towards the goal.

About the Author

Thomas Morgan has 24 years of mortgage banking experience, originating, processing and closing $546,382,250 in loans in his career. He has functioned as an originator, processor, manager, underwriter, closer and servicer, in addition to owning his own mortgage banking firm. Since 1996 he has built Quick-Start/lendertraining.com into a national consumer finance training firm and consulting concern. QuickStart has developed training programs for 8 of the top 100 mortgage banking firms in the country.

Thomas lives with his wife, Karen, and their two sons, Taylor and Matthew, in Potomac, MD.

Loan Officer Bootcamp
Initiation and Product Knowledge Training

Course Objective
To teach new and relatively new initiates or recruits the fundamental concepts and information they need to form a foundation for understanding the home mortgage product and process.

Course Methodology
Through classroom instruction teach fundamental math skills, products and programs, asset, debt and income qualification. Teach the physical loan application process through drills, case studies and role-playing. Students receive written tests to verify progress. Upon conclusion of the course and completion of all assignments the student receives a certificate. Management receives a complete written evaluation based on student's aptitude for numbers, product knowledge and marketing.

Mortgage Math & Loan Program Comparisons	FHA/VA and Conventional Loans	Qualifying Income/Asset and Credit	Taking a Complete Application EZ Method	Self Employment Property Types Refinancing
For the new loan officer and processor. Understand ratios, LTVs, qualifying and how to use a financial calculator, taxable equivalency and leverage concepts. Major Loan Types: Fixed, ARM and others	For all loan officers and processors. Understand guidelines and specifications by comparing Government and conventional loans. Includes Maximum Loan Amount Computations, MIP/PMI, Ratios, Guidelines, Closing Costs	SUPERQUAL! All facets of income analysis, asset sufficiency and credit history and scoring are reviewed. Context is that of basic sufficiency and how to maximize various components to anticipate problems or help borrowers qualify for more!	Pre-Application screening, applicant preparation, step-by step completion of required forms and disclosures, loan file set up, status process and emergency processing procedures	Simple and detailed treatment of self employment - forms of ownership and income analysis. Construction-Permanent, 2-4 Families, Condos and PUDs. Refinancing issues, methods and concepts
Day One	Day Two	Day Three	Day Four	Day Five

Materials Provided

Text

Loan Officer's Practical Guide to Residential Finance- Published since 1992, and updated annually, this 160 page textbook was written as an answer to the "sink-or-swim" training methods of many mortgage firms. The format is designed to give the newly initiated loan officer/agent, lender, processor, or other initiates the practical information they need to do the loan officer's job.

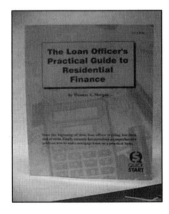

Palm OS Based Financial Calculator

Loan Officers learn to compute all financial calculations on a Palm Based financial calculator

Loan Officer Bootcamp
Developing a Marketing Plan

Objective

To assist experienced and new loan officer/agents in identifying their strengths, packaging them into a polished marketing collateral presentation, and establishing a system supported by software or other mechanism to methodically approach a territory or marketplace. As a an implementation tool, teach Loan Officers to maximize their "in house" software, mortgage pre-qualification and processing software and basic applications for Microsoft Office products to integrate automation into sales and pipeline management efforts.

Course Methodology

Today's loan officer needs to add value. Understanding the needs of the referral source allows the student to understand the value added services they can bring to their prospects and build reciprocal relationships. The course is delivered in Seminar format, designed to coax intuitive approaches. Role playing, preparation of marketing materials, programming of calendars on a properly planned basis, analyzing and categorizing customers in a contact management database, designing and implementing campaigns, selecting a specialty and developing referral networks and alternative sources of business.

An initial assessment is made to Inventory existing experience, programs and marketplace. Once initial target marketplace is determined, the students can design approaches that address specific needs. The class focuses on assembling a portfolio of products that specifically match the target marketplace preparing collateral that accurately reflects needs of target market.

Then students bring those materials to use by delivering mission statements in role-playing environment, so they can carry the lessons to the public immediately when they return to work

Course Environment/Schedule

Students bring their current real databases, customer lists and marketing material learning how to integrate the software into their daily routines.

Materials Provided

Textbook - Developing a Loan Officer Marketing Plan – Contains templates, forms, spreadsheets, letters and programs that are incorporated to the presentation with each student receiving a disk containing hundreds of collateral pieces and tools.

Book Order Form – fax to 1 (877) 729-4033

Name	
Company Name	
Address	
Phone Number	
e-mail address	

Product			
Loan Officer's Practical Guide	$44 + $6	#	$
Loan Officer Marketing Plan	$89 + $6	#	
Practical Guide to Processing	$89 + $6	#	
Commercial Loan Officer Guide	$89 + $6	#	
Total Charge to Card — Card #		exp	Total

Register your copy of the 2007 Copy of the Loan Officer's Practical Guide to Residential Finance to receive free updates for one year by subscribing to the Mortgage Professional.
www.quick-start.net/mortgageprofessional